IN SEARCH OF PEACE

IN SEARCH OF

LOUISIANA
STATE
UNIVERSITY
PRESS

PEACE

THE SENATE MUNITIONS INQUIRY, 1934–36

John E. Wiltz

FOR SUSAN

PREFACE

My DEBTS for assistance in preparation of this manuscript are many. I wish to thank the staff at the Manuscripts Division of the Library of Congress; Harold Hufford, Buford Rowland, and their assistants in the Legislative Branch of the National Archives; E. Taylor Parks of the Historical Division of the Department of State; Herman Kahn and the staff at the Franklin D. Roosevelt Library; and Mrs. Mary O. Katsuki of the Swarthmore College Peace Collection.

The following individuals offered valuable recollections of events of 1934–36: Brooke Alexander, Homer T. Bone, William S. Carpenter, Robert E. Curtin, Jr., Charles W. Deeds, Mrs. Dorothy Detzer Denny, William Flook, Leon Henderson, Russell C. Leffingwell, George Whitney, and Roger Williams. A useful memorandum came from the E. I. du Pont de Nemours and Company.

I must especially thank former Senators Gerald P. Nye and James P. Pope, and Stephen Raushenbush. Senator Nye granted two long and candid interviews and gave access to his personal papers. Senator Pope and Mr. Raushenbush granted interviews and later responded to written inquiries.

The following individuals read and criticized all or part of the manuscript: Maurice G. Baxter, Thomas D. Clark, H. Trevor Colbourn, Wayne S. Cole, Carl B. Cone, Frank Freidel, Enno E.

Kraehe, Robert E. Quirk, Ronald Schaffer, Leo F. Solt, John W. Snyder, Rena L. Vassar, and Piotr S. Wandycz.

There are two individuals to whom I am especially indebted, Bennett H. Wall and Robert H. Ferrell. Bennett Wall stimulated my interest in the munitions inquiry, provided encouragement, and offered direction and criticism. Robert Ferrell contributed in so many ways that it is impossible to enumerate them. He meticulously scrutinized several drafts of the manuscript, offered candid criticism, detected errors and distortions, and made literally hundreds of suggestions regarding interpretation, content, organization, and style.

J. E. W.

Bloomington, Indiana
November, 1962

CONTENTS

ILLUSTRATIONS

IN SEARCH OF PEACE

ORIGINS OF
THE MUNITIONS
INVESTIGATION

In the year 1934 a special committee of the United States Senate undertook a curious investigation. It sought to show that people who profited from war—munitions manufacturers, shipbuilders, financiers—bore responsibility for war. Before its inquiry ended the committee tried to explain American entry into the First World War in 1917 as a result of such special interests.

The munitions investigation "caught on." It had an enthusiastic newspaper press, and even obtained large support from distinguished scholars. The reason? It came precisely at the right historic moment, when people were willing to hear such odd gospel.

Americans had gone to war seventeen years before—in April, 1917—to make the world safe for democracy. Their crusade failed. In the 1920's and early 1930's bolshevism and fascism, arising from the chaos of the Great War (as people continued to call it), challenged democracy anew. The ideals of war then turned, by an altogether understandable chemistry, into desire for peace. Through the 1920's this desire sometimes submerged itself in the frivolities of the decade, but those frivolities were themselves a sort of inverse demonstration of America's dedication to peace. As war clouds gathered in the early 1930's Americans became obsessed with desire to avoid repetition of the quixotic crusade of 1917–18. They were ready to support any nostrum, however impractical, if it offered hope of preserving peace. The nostrums of the 1920's—international law, disarmament, outlawry of war—no longer seemed adequate. The nostrums of the 1930's were nonintercourse with belligerents, removal of war profits, control of the munitions trade.

I

It is impossible to determine when people first began to consider the munitions trade a threat to peace. The first measure providing for munitions control appeared in the Brussels Act of 1890, an international agreement to suppress slavery in Africa. ARTICLE 8 obliged signatories to embargo "firearms, and especially . . . rifles and improved weapons, as well as powder, ball and cartridge" to the region from the Sahara Desert to South Africa.[1]

In subsequent years there were other arms embargo measures. To enable the President of the United States to act if he suspected American munitions were finding their way into Spanish hands, Congress in April, 1898—upon outbreak of the Spanish-American War—adopted a resolution authorizing the President to embargo munitions from any American port. President William McKinley found no cause to use the measure, but each of his successors from Theodore Roosevelt through Herbert Hoover invoked the authority of this and later legislation to prevent arms from going to such countries as the Dominican Republic, Mexico, China, Honduras, Cuba, Brazil, and Nicaragua. These restrictions sought to stop domestic violence in countries where law and order had collapsed. They contained no suggestion that the armament business threatened peace among nations. Nor did they indicate that producers of munitions were promoting war for their own personal profit.

Such novel views regarding the munitions trade were taking form, however. In April, 1915 at The Hague, less than one hundred and fifty miles from the Western Front, the First International Congress of the Women's International League for Peace and Freedom found "in the private profits accruing from the great arms factories a powerful hindrance to the abolition of war." During its Second Congress, at Zurich in 1919, the Women's International League again appealed for abolition of private manufacture of munitions, urging the League of Nations to create an international commission "to inquire into the facts regarding profitmaking due to war and preparation for war." Meanwhile there had been some rumblings in the United States. During debate over entry into war in April, 1917 Senator George W. Norris of Nebraska charged that vast propaganda was forcing America to war to guarantee "the enormous profits of munition manufacturers, stockbrokers, and bond dealers." [2]

The Paris Peace Conference of 1919 revealed this same uneasiness about private manufacture of arms. ARTICLE 8 of the League of Nations Covenant said: "Members of the League agree that the manufacture by private enterprise of munitions and implements of war is open to grave objections. The Council shall advise how the evil effects attendant upon such manufacture can be prevented, due regard being had to the necessities of those Members of the League which are not able to manufacture the munitions and implements of war necessary for their safety." ARTICLE 22 called for control of the munitions trade in some of the mandates, and ARTICLE 23 stated that members would entrust to the League supervision of the arms trade with countries in which control of the trade was necessary to the common interest.

Then there was the Convention of St. Germain, signed in that Paris suburb during the peace conference. On September 10, 1919 representatives of twenty-eight countries signed a Convention for the Control of the Trade in Arms and Ammunition. The convention stirred minor interest, largely because it was a nebulous document which hoped to control the trade in arms through publicity. Americans assisted in drafting it, and Frank L. Polk, Henry White, and General Tasker Bliss headed the list of signatories, but the Senate's failure to consent to the Treaty of Versailles brought the convention the same fate of the other Paris treaties. Between 1921 and 1923 the League urged American ratification of the convention, arguing that as long as a principal manufacturing country remained unbound, other countries would decline restrictions. But at that time few Americans had accepted the idea that the munitions trade threatened peace. There also was the embarrassment that the convention delegated supervisory functions to the League.

Despite American apathy, the League of Nations bravely maintained an interest in sales of arms. A subcommittee issued in 1921 perhaps the strongest indictment of the private munitions industry to that time. According to the subcommittee, armament firms had inspired war scares, bribed officials, exaggerated reports of military and naval programs, organized international munitions combines, and sought to influence public opinion through the press. The report came ten years too soon. It created hardly a ripple in the United States.

Hope continued at Geneva, and in 1923 the Council of the League requested the United States to indicate the manner in which it would co-operate to control the arms trade. The reply was evasive, but early in 1924 the United States sent a delegation to observe League efforts to draft a new convention. Loose enough to secure American support, so the League hoped, the drafted convention sought to control the arms trade through licenses by governments to their nationals dealing in munitions. To provide international co-operation, it proposed a special organization to keep a registry of licenses and make annual reports to the League Council. The United States dashed hopes for this convention when Secretary of State Charles Evans Hughes disclosed that the United States would not consider the arms control question under the roof of the League.

Deferring to the United States, the League in 1925 proposed an International Arms Traffic Conference to consider the 1924 convention. When the conference met at Geneva in May, 1925 an American delegation was present. Headed by Representative Theodore E. Burton of Ohio, the delegation took an active part, and observers credited Burton with saving the conference, although he devoted much energy to preventing provisions to

censure or seriously curtail private manufacture of arms. Burton asked: "What of the private manufacturers, many of whom
have the most pacific intentions? What have they done that
there should be this discrimination against them?" The Americans prevailed, and the conference approved a convention—
the Geneva Arms Traffic Convention of 1925—apparently innocuous enough to arouse no objections. Signatories would
permit exporters and importers to handle munitions only with
government license. Governments could exercise as much control over movement of munitions as they wished, since they
could prevent shipments by withholding licenses. Control
would be national; the convention provided no control by an
international body. The convention bound signatories to record
arms shipments in an out of their own countries, to transmit
such information to the League (which would compile and
publish it), and to prevent export of arms to any nation object-
ing to such shipment.[3]

The 1925 convention continued the St. Germain principle of
dealing with the arms trade through government supervision
and publicity. Some supporters of munitions control thought
such methods inadequate, that only nationalization of the
arms industry in every country would provide proper regulation. They went along with proponents of government control
and publicity, however, because they recognized that their
position had no chance of acceptance.

The 1925 convention received acclaim as a victory for peace,
but unfortunately the United States Senate again was indifferent. Although President Calvin Coolidge transmitted the convention in January, 1926, it slumbered in the Foreign Relations
Committee for eight years. The Senate's failure rendered the
convention ineffective, since most other countries conditioned
their approval upon action by the United States. Some supporters of the convention suspected that a munitions lobby was
responsible for the Senate's lethargy. A more plausible explanation is that in absence of any aroused public opinion the Senate,
busy with other problems, did not feel impelled to act.

The League carried on. The United States sent a delegation

to a League conference in 1927 to secure agreement on publicity of statistics on munitions production. The Americans insisted upon statistics on production in government as well as
private factories, but Italy and Japan balked, and had the
sympathy of most other European powers. The conference
failed. The League sought vainly to organize another arms
trade conference in the late twenties, but many individuals
who favored regulation were concluding that such rules would
hurt their own countries.

II

Apathy toward control of the arms trade hardly
could have been greater when, late in the summer of 1929, a
new name appeared in the headlines of American newspapers.
William Baldwin Shearer, who described himself as an American, Christian, Protestant, and nationalist, was known in naval
circles during the 1920's as an advocate of preparedness. Like
the late Captain Alfred T. Mahan, he believed that a powerful navy and large merchant marine were the key to world
leadership. Despite a range of activities, he had made himself
acquainted with marine and naval affairs, and used this knowledge to promote the view that the United States must be powerful on the seas. He lobbied in Congress for large naval expenditures, and through speeches, articles, and pamphlets he sought
to arouse public opinion to the need for sea power. He wrote
a novel entitled *Pacifico,* published in 1926, concerning discovery by an American naval officer of a Japanese plot to crush the
United States. The novel aimed to demonstrate the need for
strong defenses in the Pacific. Shearer was a foe of the League
of Nations, Great Britain, Judaism, pacifism, internationalism,
and communism. Playfully he described himself as an enemy
of "pink, yellow, and Red." He was quick-tempered, given to
name-calling, inconsistent. He considered his adversaries intellectually incompetent, disloyal, and dishonest.

Shearer came to the public eye when he filed suit in the
New York Supreme Court in August, 1929 against the Beth-

lehem Shipbuilding Company, the Newport News Shipbuilding and Dry Dock Company, and the American Brown Boveri Electric Corporation—the "big three" of the shipbuilding industry—for $257,655. He claimed that these firms had retained him to promote their interests in New York, Washington, and Geneva during the period December, 1926—March, 1929. The companies, he said, had agreed to pay $250,000 plus expenses. His expenses ran to $58,885. The shipbuilders had paid $51,230, leaving a balance of $257,655. The suit showed that Shearer had been in the shipbuilders' employ when he attended the Geneva Naval Conference of 1927. Observers of the unsuccessful conference recalled that he had masqueraded there as a newspaper representative. He had created discord, and received credit in some quarters for the conference's failure.[4]

This piquant suit made Shearer a public figure. The view prevailed that the shipbuilers had used Shearer to sabotage the conference. For what other purpose would builders of war vessels pay a lobbyist and propagandist a large sum to attend a conference called to reduce naval arms? President Hoover, who was making plans for what became the London Naval Conference of 1930, shared the country's dismay, and at a press conference on September 6, 1929 scored Shearer for criticizing naval disarmament and trying "to create international distrust and hate." The President could not believe that directors of shipbuilding companies had been parties to such a transaction, but hinted at vigorous action if the government found them guilty.[5]

The Senate demanded an investigation, and appointed a subcommittee of the Naval Affairs Committee, composed of Samuel M. Shortridge (Rep.) of California, Henry J. Allen (Rep.) of Kansas, and Joseph T. Robinson (Dem.) of Arkansas, to study the case. The senators proved halfhearted students. They made no large effort to discern the truth surrounding Shearer's employment. They sent no investigators to files of shipbuilding companies, subpoenaed no documents; they accepted the evidence proffered by the companies. They deferred to the shipbuilders, seldom challenging their testimony or exploring questions which documents and testimony raised. For Shearer the subcommittee showed only contempt.[6]

The shipbuilders admitted the seriousness of their economic problems in 1927, and said that if successful the Geneva Naval Conference would have brought further troubles. But they denied hiring Shearer to wreck the conference; his job was to observe. They told the subcommittee that they had considered it important to have firsthand reports on the "trend of the conference." Constructing a ship, they explained, was complicated, and information on the outcome of the conference received two or three days in advance of formal announcements or newspaper reports could save thousands of dollars.

Shearer avowed he had been busy at Geneva in 1927. Upon arrival, and in his guise as a correspondent, he had started a campaign against naval disarmament and against the British government. He entertained, conferred with delegates, distributed tracts and broadsides. One of his pamphlets, *The Marine Follies,* asserted that "a fanatical set of pygmies" had "since 1922 consistently driven British nails of steel into America's commercial coffin." British delegates made no secret of their distaste for Shearer, but the Americans present had declined to silence him. Indeed, he had enjoyed approval of the naval contingent of the American delegation.[7]

The shipbuilders acknowledged receipt of copies of material that Shearer distributed at Geneva, but said they ignored him when it became clear that newspapers were giving the conference adequate coverage. Although they had taken no steps to curb him, several witnesses testified that they had disapproved of his activity.

Shearer claimed that he had acted with knowledge and consent of his employers, yet refused to admit that his mission was to wreck the conference. His purpose, he claimed, was to demonstrate that naval disarmament would weaken America's defense, and reduce its influence as a world power. During the Senate munitions hearings in 1935 he said "of course they used the term 'observer.' And observer does not mean a thing in the world. All the newspaper men there and correspondents are

Darling in the New York *Herald Tribune*

MAYBE THEY DIDN'T DIE SUCH A NATURAL DEATH

excellent observers. They can read all of it in the daily papers. What they wanted was me to get out the facts." [8]

When the conference of 1927 collapsed, a few people had blamed Shearer. A Geneva newspaper discussed him in an article which carried the banner, "The Man Who Wrecked the Geneva Conference." Drew Pearson, then a correspondent, had written that "Anglo-American harmony was seriously impeded at Geneva by the presence of a paid American big-navy propagandist who disseminated the most violent anti-British propaganda among newspaper men, and who appeared to be encouraged by some of the American naval experts." But Shearer's reputation did not rise until 1929, when he entered his lawsuit.[9]

The Shortridge subcommittee issued no report, and in June, 1930 Shortridge declared the matter closed. The subcommittee, he said, had discovered no evidence that shipbuilders had dispatched Shearer to Geneva to defeat plans of the government. Of Shearer, Shortridge said that "he may have been extravagant and assertive, but so far as I see it there is no reason for criticizing him." [10]

Having momentarily obtained some notoriety, Shearer's reputation went back under a cloud, and stayed there until later events—a growing public concern over the private international arms trade—brought him again to prominence. His importance for American history in the twentieth century probably was not that he did so much, but that people thought he did so much. In the 1930's he became a sort of symbol of evil, a criminal arms-traffic hireling par excellence. His supposed activities passed into historical myth. One suspects that his *cause célèbre* became for a time a staple of classroom comment in courses in recent American history.

The Shearer literature grew easily. A pamphlet published in London in 1932 said that "but for the greed of Mr. Shearer, the fact that such methods were being used by armament firms to promote the sale of armaments would never have been known to the mass of persons likely to suffer violent deaths through the world's failure to disarm." In *Iron, Blood and Profits,* published in 1934, the writer George Seldes devoted a chapter to the Shearer case under the interesting title of "Saboteurs of Peace." Seldes believed that "all the great scandals of the prewar era, the Krupp-Brandt case in Germany, the Thompson case in England, the Vickers-Mitsui affair were eclipsed" by the Shearer disclosures. Philip Noel-Baker, in 1959 a winner of the

Nobel Peace Prize, wrote in *The Private Manufacture of Armaments* (1937) that "most people who read the literature of Private Manufacture have heard so much of Mr. Shearer that they are more than weary of his name. But it is none the less impossible to leave out Mr. Shearer from this chapter, for he it is who gives us absolute proof that Private Manufacturers of Arms have indulged in direct forms of propaganda against Disarmament and the other policies of peace." [11]

III

Beginning in the year 1929, the world moved into the Great Depression. Many Americans considered the depression a reaction to World War inflation, and this view quickened their determination to avoid war.

Then, beginning in 1931, international relations began to deteriorate. War broke out in Manchuria. Then—in 1932, in the Gran Chaco, and—in 1935, in Ethiopia. Hitler meanwhile had come to power in Germany, and begun to upset the Paris peace settlement. The prestige of the League of Nations declined, and Americans awoke to realize that the Kellogg-Briand Pact had been little more than an international kiss. How to stop this procession of disasters? How, at least, to avoid American involvement in war? A growing number of Americans concluded that a good course would be to curb those individuals who profited from war.

People who reached this conclusion did not confine attention to companies and individuals who profited from war through manufacture and sale of munitions. They realized that every industrial leader, financier, laborer, and farmer took profits from war. Many Americans feared that some of these people, if given the power, would plunge the United States into a new war, perhaps as a means of getting out of the depression. Patrick J. Hurley, Secretary of War in the Cabinet of President Hoover, acknowledged in 1935 that he had heard that what the country needed to recover from the depression was a little war. Few Americans proposed such a remedy for the country's ills, but some citizens suspected that should opportunity for war appear, many people would not try to avoid it.[12]

Various groups and individuals therefore began to urge legislation against abnormal profits in the hypothetical case of the United States's becoming a belligerent in a future war. The American Legion had advocated similar measures since 1920, in belief that they would promote industrial efficiency and improve battlefront morale. Groups of Americans interested in world peace, founded into small private organizations dedicated to that purpose (notably the American Peace Society, but also many others), previously had ridiculed arms-control proposals as fascist, but under stress of the depression and the ensuing international tension they joined such groups as the Legion to advocate taking the profits out of war. These people came to believe that if individuals in business, labor, and agriculture knew the government would not permit high returns in war, they would have larger interest in peace.

Congress in 1930 responded to this new pressure by creating the War Policies Commission, composed of four Cabinet members, four senators, and four members of the House of Representatives, to study proposals for removing profit from war and make recommendations for new laws. In sixteen days of hearings, from March 5 to May 22, 1931, the commission listened to spokesmen for peace organizations, patriotic organizations, veterans groups, organized labor, industry, the armed forces, the Federal Council of Churches, and Congress, as well as individuals who by experience or study or assertion were authorities on the subject.

The commission and most witnesses were cautious. Everyone opposed inflation and profiteering in wartime, but a view prevailed that maximum production demanded "normal" profits. According to General Douglas A. MacArthur, chief of staff of the Army, efficiency in war was desirable, but effectiveness in war was mandatory. Few witnesses concurred with Richard Bartholdt, a former congressman from Missouri, who wanted to remove all profit from war. Bartholdt told the commission that "war profits constitute a greater menace to peace than any other factor, and . . . the human family will never enjoy the boon of enduring peace until that danger is removed." He concluded that "with the profits taken out of war, those who heretofore hugged war as their benefactor and friend, probably would not recognize it if they met it in the street." The commission and most witnesses agreed with Bernard M. Baruch, who found it unthinkable "that any human could be persuaded by the prospect of personal gain, however magnificent, to invoke the horrors of modern war." In its report the commission recommended legislation for price-fixing and excess-profits taxes in wartime. This proposal was not restrictive. Corporations could keep earnings equal to their three-year prewar average plus 5 per cent. Despite a considerable interest in the commission's work, Congress failed to act on its recommendations.[13]

Many Americans did not share congressional apathy, and in the early 1930's found support in their First World War experiences for the view that war profits threatened peace. History, they argued, now proposed that the submarine alone had not brought the United States to war in 1917. Allied propaganda and economic ties were equally responsible. Some individuals went a step further and concluded that the financial-industrial-commercial community had dragged the United States to war to perpetuate the prosperity which war had brought to America in 1914–17, and insure victory to the Allies, whose obligations to American financiers might go unrequited if the Allies lost the war. The news analyst Raymond Swing wrote that "it is almost a truism that the United States went into the World War in part to save from ruin the bankers who had strained themselves to the utmost to supply Great Britain and France with munitions and credits."[14]

In a special category among people who profited from war was the munitions maker. In the view of most people who pondered war profits he was the real merchant of death. He was taking profits from tension and war the world over—from the steaming jungles of the Chaco to the valleys of Manchuria. He was, moreover, the most dangerous type of war profiteer. The great majority of persons who would profit from wartime mobilization ordinarily dealt in articles of peace. War was not a requisite for their prosperity; it merely opened new vistas of opportunity. But the munitions maker, so people thought, could not survive in a peaceful world. Thus he constituted a perpetual threat to peace. The result of such views was a veritable campaign to eliminate the munitions maker.

Peace organizations and religious groups assumed leadership in this campaign. At its annual meeting in October, 1931 the National Council for Prevention of War—an organization managed by the former Congregational minister Frederick J. Libby —declared that disarmament depended upon control of the munitions trade. The Federal Council of Churches in 1932 said that "the world cannot be effectively organized for peace until this private traffic in arms, credits, and sinews of war has been brought under strict control." Similar views came from the United States Section of the Women's International League for Peace and Freedom, the General Assembly of the Presbyterian Church, the Central Conference of American Rabbis, the Rabbinical Assembly of America, the Methodist Commission on World Peace, the National Council of Jewish Women, the World Alliance for International Friendship Through the Churches, and a peace organization cleverly entitled S.O.S.— Stop Organized Slaughter.[15]

The campaign did not end with protest. The Nofrontier News Service, a pacifist agency, distributed Alexander Hamilton's "Report on Manufactures" of December 5, 1791. Hamilton, still a hero of American business, had said it seemed improvident to leave national defense to private speculation. As a general rule Hamilton in 1791 had found government factories undesirable, but considered munitions works an exception. Pacifists picketed such armament plants as Winchester, Remington, and Smith and Wesson. A superintendent at Winchester told pickets he could not give an opinion on the Kellogg-Briand Pact of 1928, the well-known treaty against war as an instrument of national policy, because his view might run counter to that of company executives. Meanwhile a poet had added his thoughts to the discussion:

Munitions men, bowed down with care,
And worries here and everywhere,
Each nite must breathe this little prayer—

Now I lay me down to snore,
I hope tomorrow there'll be war—
Before another day shall pass
I hope we sell some mustard gas;
Bless the Germans, bless the Japs,
Bless the Russians, too, perhaps—
Bless the French! let their suspicions
Show the need for more munitions!
Now I lay me down to snooze;
Let the morrow bring bad news! [16]

Respected national leaders of opinion supported this attack upon the private munitions trade. In a letter to President Hoover in January, 1933 Secretary of State Henry L. Stimson wrote that "it is becoming more and more evident that the international traffic in arms must be supervised and controlled by national and international action" if efforts to further peace "are not to be frustrated." Former Secretary of State Frank B. Kellogg wrote in 1934 that "while it is hard to put your finger on the particular offenders, in my opinion there is no question whatever that the world munition manufacturers are adding their influence and in every way trying to prevent disarmament." Professor William E. Dodd, at this time American ambassador to Germany, wrote in his diary that "the arms manufacturers over the world are the cause of most of this trouble in Europe." In Great Britain a reporter quoted Sir William White, "one of the grand old men of armament salesmanship," as saying that armament firms had no national or political prejudices, were unconcerned about the ulterior objects of war, and had left to the discussion of idle and metaphysical minds the value of such abstract ideas as liberty and justice, or employed those terms as convenient euphemisms.[17]

The campaign against the munitions trade achieved a modest success in 1932 when the General Commission of the General Disarmament Conference meeting at Geneva appointed a Commission for the Regulation of Arms and Implements of War. The committee quickly went into deadlock, however, largely because of differences between supporters of nationalization and advocates of supervision and control. The latter contended that nationalization would compel nonproducing countries to erect arms factories, and maintain large stocks of munitions to meet legitimate needs of national defense. They believed that nationalization would strengthen the strong and weaken the weak—would place most countries at the mercy of a dozen nations favored by raw materials and industrial organization with adequate arms producing potential. Advocates of nationalization countered that as long as the munitions industry remained in private hands no amount of supervision and control would suffice to eliminate the danger which the industry posed to peace. Nationalization, they thought, was the only solution.

The only hopeful development at this point was American abandonment of the principle that the Federal Constitution prevented the United States from supporting a convention involving supervision and control of munitions manufacture in the several states. The United States had always insisted that it could agree only to regulation of the trade in arms, not manufacture of arms. But the American delegation at Geneva in November, 1932 told the Bureau of the Disarmament Conference that the United States would accept supervision of private manufacture provided there was supervision of state manufacture. Secretary of State Stimson had prepared the way for this change a few days earlier by citing the decision in *Missouri vs. Holland* (1920) as a precedent for action with other countries to cope with an international problem. *Missouri vs. Holland* had resulted from a treaty between the United States and Canada on migratory birds. The Supreme Court had ruled that it was necessary to consider the national interest, which in this instance required action with another country.[18]

IV

Although diplomats at Geneva failed to agree on control of the munitions industry, large numbers of people

St. Louis *Post-Dispatch*

WORKING BOTH SIDES OF THE WORLD

throughout the world were accepting the pacifist dictum that
control was mandatory. In the spring of 1934 this sentiment
found expression in the United States in a magazine article and
two books which attracted wide attention.

The article, entitled "Arms and Men," appeared in *Fortune*
Magazine. Unsigned because several staff members assisted in

its preparation, the article presented a sordid tale of international intrigue in connection with the munitions trade. In shockingly crude language its authors sought to prove the culpability of munitions makers:

> According to the best accountancy figures, it cost about $25,000 to kill a soldier during the World War. There is one class of Big Business Men in Europe that never rose up to denounce the extravagance of its governments in this regard—to point out that when death is left unhampered as an enterprise for the individual initiative of gangsters the cost of a single killing seldom exceeds $100. The reason for the silence of these Big Business Men is quite simple: the killing is their business. Armaments are their stock in trade; governments are their customers; the ultimate consumers of their products are, historically, almost as often their compatriots as their enemies. That does not matter. The important point is that every time a burst shell fragment finds its way into the brain, the heart, or the intestines of a man in the front line, a great part of the $25,000, much of it profit, finds its way into the pocket of the armament maker.

This article claimed that the Armorer's Philosophy was: "Publish periodical war scares. Impress governmental officials with the vital necessity of maintaining armaments against the 'aggressions' of neighbor states. Bribe as necessary. In every practical way create suspicion that security is threatened." It declared that "the armament leopards have never changed their spots. Detail upon detail, incident upon incident, illustrate how well the armament makers apply the two axioms of their business: when there are wars, prolong them; when there is peace, disturb it."

An obscure British sea captain, and hearsay, were sources of the article's most moving example of merchants of death perfidy. This was a claim that during the First World War businessmen of opposing countries had traded in war materials through such neutral countries as Sweden, Norway, Denmark, Switzerland, Spain, and Holland. Germany allegedly had shipped, month after month, an average of 150,000 tons of scrap iron,

steel, and barbed wire to Switzerland, where it was transhipped
to France. France in return sent chemicals to Gemany via
Switzerland.[19]

The article offered no proof of its assertions. Still, sponsorship
by *Fortune* carried an aura of authority; *Fortune* was a respectable journal which reflected a conservative business position.
Senator Gerald P. Nye of North Dakota entered it in the *Congressional Record* with the remark that "I think there has not
been published in ages anything quite so enlightening as is this
article appearing in Fortune." Probably few people read the
article in the *Record,* but in May, 1934 it reached a wide
audience when *Reader's Digest* published a condensed version.[20]

About the same time there appeared two books, *Iron, Blood
and Profits; An Exposure of the World-Wide Munitions Racket*
by George Seldes, and *Merchants of Death, A Study of the International Armament Industry* by Helmuth C. Engelbrecht
and Frank C. Hanighen. *Merchants of Death* was the more in-
fluential, and became a best seller. It was a Book-of-the-Month
Club selection in April, 1934. Similar to the *Fortune* article, it
claimed that international munitions makers were risking peace
to sell armament. These munitions makers, the authors thought,
had organized an international combine or ring. The ring included Vickers-Armstrong of Great Britain, S. A. Bofors of
Sweden, Schneider-Creusot of France, Skoda of Czechoslovakia,
Krupp of Germany, and E. I. du Pont de Nemours and Company of the United States. According to the authors, "the arms
maker has risen and grown powerful, until today he is one of
the most dangerous factors in world affairs—a hindrance to
peace, a promoter of war." They drew upon the Shearer episode,
concluding that "the activities of individuals like Mr. Shearer
illustrate the lengths to which armament companies will go in
trying to further their business." [21]

Merchants of Death and *Iron, Blood and Profits,* like "Arms
and Men," purported to be scholarly analyses of the munitions
trade, and received the accolade of "excellent" from R. L. Duffus
when reviewed in the New York *Times.* Yet most of the docu-

mentation came from secondhand sources, and none of it established the premises from which conclusions derived.[22]

In the climate of opinion prevailing in 1934 few defenders of munitions makers ventured forth. *Army Ordnance* stated mildly that "whether or not we are descended from monkeys, certainly many things happening today might tempt a cynical or pessimistic man to believe that large sections of the human race are intellectually degenerating toward the monkey stage. A striking example is the current controversy over munition makers." The same journal claimed that to say munitions makers caused wars was akin to saying that policemen caused crime or fire engines fire. But who read *Army Ordnance* in the year 1934? [23]

By the spring of that year many Americans had become convinced that munitions makers were the root of many of the world's ills. Curb these merchants of death and peace would follow. These sentiments had the support of all manner of Americans in 1934. Today, of course, everyone admits that at best the merchants-of-death thesis expressed a limited truth. Senator Nye told the present writer in 1958 that he never believed munitions makers created tension and war to promote sales. This remark did not square with many of his pronouncements in 1934–36. Nye is not alone. The author has never heard any of Nye's contemporaries admit that they were taken in.[24]

When one reads the literature of the mid-thirties he can understand why millions of people looked critically at the munitions trade. The mere quantity of writing purporting to prove the evils of munitions makers was almost overwhelming. Then some of the evidence seemed impressive, such as the story that during the World War the Allies had refrained from bombing the Briey Basin, where there was a German munitions works, because businessmen in Allied countries had invested in the works. Pierre-Étienne Flandin, Premier of France in 1934–35, indeed had said of Briey shortly after the war: "There was a means of shortening the war, but this means was neglected for more than two years. The prolongation of the war for those who made the weapons of death was a good business." There were other stories of Germans storming Fort Douamont and withering on barbed wire supplied by German factories, and of Germany and France exchanging carbides and cyanamides for magnetos through Switzerland. There was President Franklin D. Roosevelt's statement that "the private and uncontrolled manufacture of arms and munitions and the traffic therein has become a serious source of international discord and strife." If such allegations had been country store or main street gossip that would have been one thing. They were something else when echoed by the President of the United States, the Premier of France, two former Secretaries of State, the League of Nations, *Fortune* Magazine, the *Christian Science Monitor,* members of Congress, the peace movement, leaders of religion, and even the *Wall Street Journal* and the Chicago *Journal of Commerce.* Who could blame people in the mid-thirties for taking seriously this heady business about merchants of death? [25]

It seemed so reasonable. Businesses always wished a climate favorable to their merchandise, and if markets did not exist they tried to create them. Why would people selling munitions act differently? This explanation of private skulduggery on an international scale fitted prejudices inherited from the World War and from a century of American isolation in international affairs.

The next step for Americans was to secure proper congressional sanction. Just as the Pecora Committee in 1933–34 had exposed the money changers to a disgusted American people, so a munitions committee might expose the merchants of death. By the spring of 1934 sentiment for a congressional investigation had reached the point of action.

THE MUNITIONS
COMMITTEE ORGANIZED

N o o n e knows who first thought of a munitions investigation, but a movement for an inquiry began in earnest in 1932 when the annual convention of the United States Section of the Women's International League for Peace and Freedom adopted a resolution urging the Senate to investigate the private munitions trade.

Leading this campaign was Miss Dorothy Detzer, executive secretary of the WIL. Her first problem was to find a senator who would sponsor a resolution embodying her organization's ideas, and this task proved difficult. She selected twenty senators who she thought might take the initiative, but most of them equivocated or (so she later wrote) replied: "Do you want me to commit political suicide?" Only Senators George W. Norris of Nebraska and Robert M. La Follette, Jr., of Wisconsin showed genuine interest, but Norris was too ill and La Follette was too busy to assume responsibility for such an investigation.

At its annual convention in May, 1933 the WIL reiterated its appeal for a munitions investigation. The organization cited reports (and rumors) that munitions makers had provoked war scares, opposed peace measures, and corrupted public officials. The resolution's brevity did not prevent mention of the Shearer case as proof of the bad faith of armament producers. Meanwhile other peace societies—including the National Council for

24

Prevention of War, the Fellowship of Reconciliation, and World Peaceways—were demanding government action. In the summer of 1933 the WIL asked the Senate Committee on Banking and Currency, at that time investigating American banking interests, to obtain information on relations between munitions companies and such financial houses as J. P. Morgan and Company. The committee considered such information irrelevant to its inquiry, whereupon the WIL turned to the National Recovery Administration. The WIL hoped that the NRA, through its code authority, might keep watch on munitions makers. President Roosevelt showed interest, but General Hugh S. Johnson, chief of the NRA, issued such strong objection that the White House abandoned the plan.

In the autumn of 1933 Miss Detzer resumed her search for a senator to sponsor a munitions investigation. She later reported that the senators showed greater resistance than ever to her appeal. Discouraged, she again turned to Norris. Norris invited her to his office, and in the late afternoon calm of a snowy day just before Christmas of 1933, they scrutinized a list of the members of the Senate. When they had finished they had crossed off all names except one—Gerald P. Nye. Leaning back in his chair, Norris said: "Nye's our man. He must be persuaded to do it." He cited Nye's energy, courage, and enthusiasm, and said that "Nye doesn't come up for election again for another four years; by that time the investigation would be over. If it reveals what I am certain it will, such an investigation would help him politically, not harm him."

Armed with Norris's endorsement, Miss Detzer approached Nye. When told that Norris had called him "our man," Nye, deeply moved, asked: "Did Norris say that?" Miss Detzer replied affirmatively. Then, as she recalled more than a decade later, "Nye sat silent for a little while, tapping his fingers together; then he got up and walked to the window. Beyond, in the soft winter evening, were the snowy trees and the wide spaces of the sloping Hill." At length he turned and said: "I'm afraid my conscience won't let me refuse you again. I'll do it." [1]

At that moment Nye began a new phase of his career. He

would become the champion of the movement to curb the merchants of death. He would earn a reputation as the country's most eloquent isolationist. He would become a leader in the campaign to preserve peace for the United States at almost any cost—to put America first. He would become anathema to all individuals in the armament business, to all advocates of American co-operation with other countries to "wage peace" even at risk of war.

I

Gerald Prentice Nye in 1934 was a handsome, almost boyish-looking man of forty-two. Of average height, he had a strong, muscular physique, but his most striking features were pale blue eyes, widely set, and an angular jaw and chin. These combined with a brisk, erect gait to convey an appearance of determination and integrity. His largest asset as a public figure, aside from good looks, was a bell-like voice which he used with skill either from a speaker's rostrum or before a radio microphone. He spoke with the modulated accent of the upper Middle West, an accent always pleasant and persuasive. Although genial, he was not a glad-handing first-namer, and sometimes gave impression of a reserved and angry man. Such an impression missed the mark. In truth, despite the exuberance he displayed in public addresses, he was somewhat diffident.

Nye was not a man of intellectual depth. His mind was illtrained. He had little sense of history, was poorly read, was averse to hard logical thinking. He was not imaginative, not a man of ideas. No important legislation bearing his name resulted from nineteen years in the Senate. He was a gifted speaker who could take the ideas of other people and translate them into oratory with a fire reminiscent of William Jennings Bryan. One might, indeed, carry to some length an analogy between Bryan and Nye. Like Bryan, he symbolized a movement which he did not originate, and like Bryan he was uncomplicated and narrow, but confident he could resolve a difficult problem of his time. He was honest and sincere, as was

Bryan. He was not cynical. He possessed few qualities of leadership. Like Bryan, he could inspire masses of ordinary people, but was ineffective at leading politicians.

Nye was not a pretentious person. He was, one might say, a rather typical midwesterner. Comparing him with his Munitions Committee colleagues, one observer wrote in 1935 that "he looks less like a senator than any of them. . . . He has no flowing mane, but a recent haircut. He has no senatorial bay window, but the lean build of a second baseman." The same reporter continued: "He is, I should say, pretty much the average man in his tastes, abilities, beliefs, and suspicions, with a little more drive and energy than most of us have." Nye lived with his wife and three children in a modest home in a Washington suburb. He found relaxation in western fiction and major league baseball games.[2]

Nye's personal characteristics made for political success in North Dakota in the interwar years. His integrity, zeal, energy, and courage won admiration from midwesterners only a generation away from the frontier. That he was not a sophisticated intellectual helped rather than hindered him. Despite his modest talents, the citizens of North Dakota elected him to the Senate three times. Only when a new generation of voters appeared did North Dakota turn away from Nye.

When Nye consented to sponsor a resolution to investigate the munitions industry, the country knew him as a Progressive Republican. His reputation did not rest upon antimilitarism or isolationism, but denunciation of business monopoly and defense of the farmer. He was a member of that band of Progressives whom Senator George H. Moses in 1929 had called "sons of the wild jackass"—to which Nye retorted: "I'll frankly confess that in a sense we Westerners have been jackasses. Year after year we have gone on paying high tariff rates for the benefit of New England and her industries." One could best describe Nye in 1934 as an apostle of the senior Robert La Follette. And no description would have brought him greater pleasure. (In the years since the 1930's Nye's progressivism has worn thin, and he can speak reverently of the principles of

Robert A. Taft, but his eyes sparkle and his voice rasps with emotion when he discourses on "Fighting Bob.") [3]

Born in Hortonville, Wisconsin, in 1892, Nye, a relative of the humorist Bill Nye, was of English and Danish descent. He lived his formative years in Wisconsin, during that era when La Follette was earning a national reputation for his crusade against plutocracy and privilege. Nye's father edited country weekly newspapers and supported La Follette; it was natural that the son became imbued with La Follette liberalism. Only during the First World War did he waver in his faith—for interesting reasons, considering his subsequent career. He protested La Follette's opposition to American entry into the war, and wrote in 1917 that La Follette had "made himself the most thorough anti-American on American shores and the most thorough ass of his time, Kaiser Wilhelm excluded perhaps." This estrangement was short-lived, and in 1924, Nye helped La Follette and the Progressive party carry North Dakota. [4]

In his early years Nye revealed no political ambitions. His formal education had ended with graduation from Wittenberg (Wisconsin) High School in 1911, and by 1916 he had settled in the western regions of North Dakota. While most of his future Senate colleagues were studying law or toiling in local and state politics, he was learning the trade of newspaper editor. He devoted attention to politics, of course, and his editorials reflected Progressive convictions. When the Non-Partisan League began in North Dakota he was a fervent supporter. He won recognition from agrarian liberals, and in 1919 a group of farmers invited him to edit their newspaper, the Griggs County *Sentinel Courier*. Here in the eastern part of North Dakota he drew attention by asking justice for agriculture and attacking the "interests" for exploiting the farmer. He directed much of his fire toward Washington, and almost from the day of Warren G. Harding's inauguration in 1921 he showed the Non-Partisan League's contempt for Republican administrations. Such expressions alienated regular Republicans, but endeared him to Progressives.

Perhaps it was inevitable that a man of Nye's convictions,

eloquence, and energy should find his way into politics. Nye
made his first important step in that direction in 1924 when,
campaigning for La Follette and the Progressives, he sought a
seat in the House of Representatives. He lost, but in the summer
of 1925 Senator Edwin P. Ladd died, and the following autumn
Governor Arthur G. Sorlie in a surprise move appointed Nye.
Nye later said: "When the governor handed me my credentials,
if there had been the slightest breeze, I would have blown out
the window." Why Sorlie appointed Nye remains a mystery.
Thirty-three years old, the new senator had never traveled east
of Chicago.[5]

The "village Greeley," as one observer called him, arrived in
Washington in December, 1925, but did not take his seat immediately. The Senate Committee on Privileges and Elections
scrutinized his credentials for twelve days, presumably because
of doubt that his appointment was constitutional but in truth
because regular Republicans did not welcome admission of
another maverick. Progressives, led by Norris and William E.
Borah, took the initiative in the move to seat Nye, and they
received support from Democrats who hoped to embarrass the
Republican majority. Nye entered the Senate when Norris and
Borah took advantage of the absence of a couple of regular
Republicans and brought the matter to a vote. The tally was
41–39. Nye retained his seat in the election of 1926 by defeating
L. B. Hanna, a relative of Mark Hanna, by a large plurality. He
ran for re-election in 1932, a bad year for Republicans, and
braved the Democratic trend to win by 107,000 votes, although
Franklin Roosevelt carried North Dakota by a plurality of
105,000.

As expected, Nye from the outset allied himself with Progressive-Republicans. Like other Progressives, he distrusted
Wall Street and supported the shopkeeper, farmer, and con-
sumer. An observer wrote that "in Nye, whose appearance at
that time was distinguished chiefly for a high-water haircut and
yellow shoes, American small-town life had a representative who
would fight monopoly and privilege with indomitable courage
and religious zeal." He joined Progressives in assailing the Re-

publican administrations of the twenties. He denounced the deflationary policy of the Federal Reserve (blaming bankers), criticized the protective tariff (which, he conceded, might help farmers "if it could be made to work"), assailed the Mellon-Coolidge tax policies, and attacked all GOP administrations for failure to deal effectively with the farm problem. He demanded reduction of farmers' debts, supported the McNary-Haugen Bill for disposing of surplus farm products, and shared Progressive resentment over White House failure to approve the bill. His running debate with the Republican leadership led to conflict with Coolidge over North Dakota patronage, and when he emerged the victor the Baltimore *Sun* dubbed him "Gerald the Giant Killer." [6]

Nye opposed Herbert Hoover's quest for the Republican presidential nomination in 1928. His candidate was Norris. Before the Republican convention Nye wrote that "this man Hoover, whom some are trying to drive down our throats, believes that agriculture is improving. If agriculture is improving, it is dying of improvement." In the subsequent campaign, however, he gave lukewarm support to Hoover. According to one observer, for Nye to have done otherwise "would have distressed good Republican friends, and Nye dislikes disappointing friends." But when Hoover as President failed to improve the lot of farmers, Nye quickly became his outspoken critic.[7]

The Great Depression, increasing farm distress, sharpened Nye's hostility toward big business. He stepped up his attacks on monopoly and concentrated wealth, supported higher inheritance and income taxes, assailed chain stores and branch banking. The inauguration of Franklin Roosevelt in 1933 had slight effect upon Nye's crusade. While there was much in the New Deal program which he could accept, especially the Agricultural Adjustment Act, he became an archenemy of one of its principal measures, the National Industrial Recovery Act. With his friend Borah he denounced the NRA in a series of impressive if exaggerated speeches. Calling the Blue Eagle "a bird of prey on the masses," he charged that the NRA had produced monopoly, that large corporations were using the codes to suffocate small competitors. Roosevelt attempted to mollify Nye by inviting him to membership on the NRA board to "guard the interests of small businessmen," but he declined. After April, 1934 he devoted major attention to the munitions inquiry, yet remained a critic of NRA until the Supreme Court eliminated it in May, 1935.[8]

As a senator, Nye gradually came into public prominence. He first attracted attention in the late 1920's when as chairman of the Committee on Public Lands and Survey he presided over the Continental Trading Company phase of the Teapot Dome investigation. His supporters claimed that this inquiry resulted in recovery of between seven and eleven million dollars in taxes and penalties, more money—so Nye liked to remind critics of congressional investigations—than all such inquiries had cost since the government began. Nye received credit, moreover, for forming the questions which sent Harry F. Sinclair to jail. Later he secured chairmanship of the special committee to scrutinize senatorial campaign expenditures in the 1930 elections. He was especially proud of his part in this inquiry. According to his authorized biographical summary he exposed the campaign methods of Ruth Hanna McCormick in Illinois, the attempt to defeat Norris in Nebraska by placing on the same ballot the name of a grocery clerk named George W. Norris, the large expenditures and corrupt methods in Pennsylvania, and the source of campaign funds in Colorado and other states. These revelations "gave a picture of the use of massed wealth in the election of representatives to Congress." During the Ruth McCormick episode private detectives shadowed Nye, searched his past, and according to Nye supporters hired women to lure him into hotel rooms. The attempt to "get something" on Nye failed. Thanks to publicity accompanying these inquiries, Americans became aware of the investigating skill of North Dakota's junior senator. Even organized baseball took note, and in 1931 considered him a possible successor to Judge Kenesaw Mountain Landis, baseball's high commissioner. But it remained for the controversies over munitions makers and neutrality to make Nye a national figure.[9]

Nye's views on foreign affairs were those of most Progressives. He opposed membership in the League of Nations, opposed imperialism, voted against bills for naval expansion (although he favored adequate national defense), and opposed use of the Army and Navy to protect private investments overseas. Like other Progressives, he felt disillusion over failure of the World War to strengthen democracy, and now believed that La Follette, Norris, and other members of that "little group of wilful men" had analyzed correctly the causes of American entry into the war. And failure to achieve President Woodrow Wilson's exalted war aims was not the only source of Nye's dismay over American foreign relations. There was the farm depression of the twenties, which he considered the result of wartime inflation. Farmers had responded patriotically to meet the needs of war, expanding production, enjoying brief prosperity, but they found that the depression was their final reward.* Although he had endorsed American entry into the war and headed two Liberty Loan drives in his home county, Nye came to sympathize with those Americans who believed war futile—who would go to great length to keep the United States out of any war.[10]

II

Nye did not act immediately after his promise to Miss Detzer. He feared senatorial friends of the munitions industry. His delay brought consternation to Miss Detzer, but on February 8, 1934 he noticed that few senators who might object were on the floor. He snapped his fingers for a page, and dispatched to the desk a resolution to investigate those individuals and corporations engaged in manufacture, sale, distribu-

* Since organized religion provided much impetus for the peace movement, it is worth noting that Nye was not active in church affairs at this time. He said in 1954 that at age eighteen he had moved into the world and felt no need for religious activity, and "for many years that followed, including the 19 in which I was a member of the Senate, I found within me no urge for church affiliation." Eventually he became an active Lutheran.

tion, import, and export of munitions. Miss Detzer, sitting in the galleries, expected an angry reaction. She later wrote: "Across the floor, Senator Ham Lewis rose in his place. His frock coat, putty-colored spats and waistcoat, the famous pink whiskers, all gave him something of the over-stuffed, elegant solemnity of a plumed hearse horse. He started to protest, then with a flourish of coattails reconsidered, and sat down." Without protest, and with the press gallery looking on indifferently, the chair accepted Nye's resolution and referred it to the Foreign Relations Committee.[11]

Other obstacles remained in the way of Nye's measure. Chairman Key Pittman of the Foreign Relations Committee refused to consider the resolution, and early in March, taking advantage of Nye's absence from the floor, secured consent to transfer it to the Military Affairs Committee. Nye, Miss Detzer, and other interested persons were apprehensive, since most members of the Military Affairs Committee sympathized with the military and presumably would not favor inquiry into the private munitions industry. They suspected that the committee might eliminate the resolution or, by assuming responsibility for the investigation, might whitewash the munitions industry.[12]

Miss Detzer and the other pacifists who were assisting her sought a solution to this problem. They noted that earlier in the session Arthur H. Vandenberg of Michigan had introduced a resolution for review of the findings of the War Policies Commission of 1930–31. The Vandenberg Resolution had received support from the American Legion, which saw in it a hope for a wartime industrial mobilization law, a Legion goal since 1920. Why not combine the Nye and Vandenberg resolutions? "By combining the . . . resolutions, the measure would gain a double-barreled support from two diametrically opposed wings of public opinion—the peace movement and the Legion." Nye and Vandenberg agreed to this stratagem, and on March 12 submitted a combined resolution, S. Res. 206, for investigation of the munitions industry and review of the War Policies Commission's findings. Whereupon Miss Detzer and her colleagues persuaded the Military Affairs Committee to recommend a select committee to carry out the provisions of the resolution.[13]

Combining the measures of Nye and Vandenberg did not insure Senate acceptance. According to Miss Detzer's tabulation
only twenty senators favored S. Res. 206, with forty-five opposed and twenty-nine uncommitted. Concentrating upon the
uncommitted twenty-nine, the doughty secretary of the WIL
and her associates learned that twenty-two would follow the
wishes of the administration.[14]

Their attention turned to the White House. Miss Detzer approached Secretary of State Cordell Hull who, although sympa-
thizing with her campaign, said that only the President could
give administration endorsement to a munitions inquiry. Fortunately Roosevelt shared Hull's sympathy, and consented to
the inquiry.[15]

This still left the measure in doubt. The nation's numerous
peace societies then mounted a campaign to arouse support for
the inquiry. Miss Detzer has recorded that "the peace movement, the churches, labor, all rallied to the struggle and began
a barrage of telegrams, letters, and deputations to the Senate.
This was supplemented everywhere with meetings and conferences. In Washington the WIL organized a mass meeting at
the Belasco Theatre, while organizations in New York and
Chicago held simultaneous ones." [16]

The campaign received an important boost from the article
in *Fortune*, "Arms and Men," published that same month—
March, 1934. Nye said later that the article, appearing in a
periodical noted for generous treatment of business, did more
than anything else to arouse sentiment for an arms investigation.
He doubted that the Nye-Vandenberg Resolution could have
won passage without it. Miss Detzer in 1960 seconded Nye's
view: "It was certainly a major help primarily because it made
the Investigation a much more 'respectable' undertaking." For
S. Res. 206 "Arms and Men" was a lucky accident. *Fortune* had
not planned the article to stimulate the movement for an arms
inquiry. Representatives of peace societies had nothing to do
with it, and according to *Fortune*, the article's "appearance dur-

ing the time that the Nye investigation was pending was merely coincidental." [17]

There were other developments. The book by Engelbrecht and Hanighen, *Merchants of Death,* appeared at this moment, but had slight influence until after adoption of the resolution. Such was not the case, however, regarding a speech by Senator Borah on March 5, 1934 during debate over a naval construction bill. Borah charged that the world's munitions manufacturers (he called them international racketeers), particularly those in America, were spreading propaganda on the possibility of war between the United States and Japan. Their aim was to spur sales of armament. Borah's remarks received wide publicity, and helped arouse support for the Nye-Vandenberg Resolution.[18]

Meanwhile Nye was trying to bring the resolution to a vote. He saw his chance on April 12. For several days Pat Harrison of Mississippi had sought passage of a tax bill, only to have his efforts frustrated by amendments, and by April 12 had grown impatient. When the tax debate resumed in the afternoon, and following disposal of a complicated amendment by Robert La Follette, Jr., Senator Nye secured the floor and introduced another amendment, this one calling for a 98 per cent tax on individual incomes which, during any year when the United States was at war, exceeded $10,000. Nye then spoke for a half-hour on the evil of war profits. "We show no hesitation at all in time of war in going out and destroying and damaging not only lives but property as well," he said. "Why, then, we should hesitate when it comes to what might amount to be confiscation of income, confiscation of wealth, is beyond me to understand." He asked passage of the Nye-Vandenberg Resolution, and concluded: "Profits! Profits! Mr. President, profit plays more of a part in preparing for war, in occasioning war, than any other thing."

Vandenberg quickly claimed the floor, and endorsed the Nye amendment.

From the galleries Miss Detzer saw that "Pat Harrison

watched the clock with increasing exasperation. Finally, he rose
and strode angrily across the floor to Nye's desk. The pantomime
which followed was extremely diverting. Harrison scolded; Nye
shook his head, and Vandenberg talked on. Harrison, throwing
his eyes and hands to the heavens, resumed his seat. He had
discovered that Nye had secured eleven senators to speak on his
amendment, and had figured that the time to be consumed
would cover five days."

After Huey P. Long interrupted the tax debate with a discourse on how racketeers were robbing Louisianians of their
home-loan funds, the Senate returned to the Nye amendment.
Harrison, foreseeing a long debate, suggested that the Senate
interrupt the tax bill proceedings to consider the Nye-Vandenberg Resolution, and if it adopted S. Res. 206 refer the Nye
amendment to the munitions investigating committee. Nye and
Vandenberg accepted this proposal, and upon Harrison's suggestion Nye asked unanimous consent for the Nye-Vandenberg
Resolution. The presiding officer, James P. Pope of Idaho, asked
if there were any objections. He raised his gavel. Miss Detzer
later recalled: "I held my breath. On the floor below, Huey
Long was strutting about the chamber cracking his knuckles,
and gazing at the galleries with the furtive look of a bad boy
who has just pulled the wings off a fly. Freddy 'Rowboat' Hale,
chairman of the Naval Affairs Committee, was engrossed in a
copy of the Washington News. Senator Copeland, the inevitable red carnation in his buttonhole, was sleeping peacefully.
[Alben W.] Barkley appeared to be writing a letter. Norris put
his hands flat on the desk in front of him. Bob La Follette moved
back from the cloakroom door. Nye and Vandenberg leaned
forward tensely like runners at the start of a race. Every man in
the press gallery stood up and waited."

The gavel fell. Without objection the Senate adopted S.
Res. 206.[19]

The resolution directed the Vice-President to appoint a seven-
member committee "to investigate the activities of individuals,
firms, associations and of corporations and all other agencies in
the United States engaged in the manufacture, sale, distribu-

tion, import or export of arms, munitions or other implements of war; the methods used in promoting or effecting the sale of arms, munitions or other implements of war imported into the United States and the countries of origin thereof, and the quantities exported from the United States and countries of destination thereof." It directed the committee to investigate existing legislation and treaties pertaining to the munitions trade, review the findings of the War Policies Commission, and inquire into the desirability of nationalizing the munitions industry. The committee could subpoena witnesses and documents. The resolution authorized $15,000 for the investigation, $35,000 less than Nye and Vandenberg had requested. It was clear that senators who were lukewarm toward the inquiry hoped that $15,000 would restrict the committee while satisfying popular demand for an inquiry.[20]

III

Interest in the munitions trade and profits from war thus had increased dramatically. An outpouring of articles and editorials now discussed the awful dealings of peddlers of death. The *New Republic* stated on April 25, 1934 that the special munitions investigating committee would have the task of moving along "the tortuous track of blood money." The editors wrote that "the track is there, the blood-dripping profits are there, a vast, worldwide network of incorporated murder is there." An article in the *Railroad Telegrapher* said that "the American people are showing signs of awakening to the system which encourages wars, slays and tortures millions to build a few swollen fortunes, and leaves the common man and woman staggering under crushing debts. . . . Labor's millions are called on to fight all wars, to suffer the mud, lice and blood of the trenches while the bosses gather their dollars and the bosses' sons become officers. And, after the war is over, labor pays and pays and pays." John Gunther reported in *Harper's* that more than two hundred firms in the world were earning "cold cash profits on smashed brains or smothered lungs." Writing in the

Nation, Johannes Steel said that the "world's greatest racket is the armament racket," and concluded that there were enough facts available "to show conclusively that there would be fewer wars if there were fewer armament makers." [21]

Senator Nye found it impossible to await the verdict of the investigating committee. He announced that munitions makers were guilty as charged. Two days before approval of the Nye-Vandenberg Resolution he told a national radio audience of a parade of 5,000 soldiers past the Capitol the previous week during Army Day ceremonies. "Yet, even in that inspiring moment, I could not fully restrain myself and be blind to the fact that those glistening steel helmets, for example, were the profit-returning products of American manufacturers, a product intended to protect those fine heads under the helmets against the shrapnel and shells which the same manufacturers had sold to the military departments of other nations which might some day be our foe in war! What madness! What rotten commercialism! Name a more inhumane trade! Was ever a more insane racket conceived in depraved minds or tolerated by an enlightened people?" At New Haven on April 29 he said: "I confidently predict that when the Senate investigation is over, we shall see that war and preparation for war is not a matter of national honor and national defense, but a matter of profit for few." Next day at a luncheon of World Peaceways in New York he saw futility in trying to get out of the depression when "we are preparing for new wars which will be and ought to be the end of our whole civilization." He dismissed rumors of war between the United States and Japan with assertion that there was "not a chance in the world" for such a conflict. After castigating armament expenditures as insane, he declared the time coming when there would be understanding "of what monkeys the munitions makers can make of the otherwise intelligent people of America." [22]

Nye sought to keep opinion aroused in other ways. He sent a letter to Walt Disney on April 11, 1934 asking the cartoonist to consider making "one of your delightful pictures on the subject of the insane course which the world is pursuing with respect to preparation for war, national and 'adequate' defense, and what you may call it." He enclosed a cartoon containing an idea "which might be expressed in such a picture." [23]

The munitions industry found few defenders at this point. Thus it must have taken satisfaction when the New York *Times* expressed reservation about the central article of the merchants-of-death credo—that munitions makers caused war. Said the *Times:*

> Excitement reigns in the books and magazines about the international armament manufacturers. It is one more attempt to find a personal devil as the explanation for things gone wrong. The odd thing is that munition makers should be pilloried as war makers just when the world situation teems with evidence pointing elsewhere. Japanese militarism in the Far East is not the militarism of capitalist steelmasters eager to create a market for guns and shells and gas containers. The aggressive drive in Japan which began with the seizure of Mukden two and a half years ago has a distinct anti-capitalist cast. The Fascist elements at Tokyo have been saying the same bitter things about capitalist-parliamentary corruption that the royalists in Paris are saying.[24]

Such attempts to deflect the attack upon munitions makers (Nye called them "soulless madmen") proved ineffective. Not only were the attackers in the United States moving forward inexorably, but news arrived from the Gran Chaco that fighting had broken out again between Bolivia and Paraguay. This tedious war, which had blown hot and cold, seemed to lend substance to the merchants-of-death argument. Here were two small countries almost without industry; surely neither had an industrial establishment capable of sustaining a war machine of any consequence. Yet both had accumulated stores of arms from abroad and were fighting over a seemingly useless expanse of jungle. To millions of Americans it seemed logical that international munitions makers had goaded the two countries to war to promote the sale of weapons. Even those people who refused to accept this extreme conclusion were appalled at the blood-letting in the Chaco, where a small Paraguayan army was defeating the larger, better equipped, European-trained army of Bolivia. Most Americans, therefore, seconded the demand for an arms embargo to both Latin belligerents. Embargo sentiment grew in the spring of 1934 as casualty figures from the Chaco appeared concurrently with statistics on sales of guns, airplanes, and ammunition by American firms to Bolivia and Paraguay.

President Roosevelt responded by asking Congress for authority to embargo arms shipments to the Chaco. He did not stop there. In his message of May 18, 1934 he also called for ratification of the Geneva Arms Traffic Convention of 1925, and lent prestige to the merchants-of-death thesis by stating that "the peoples of many countries are being taxed to the point of poverty and starvation in order to enable governments to engage in a mad race in armaments which, if permitted to continue, may well result in war. This grave menace to the peace of the world is due in no small measure to the uncontrolled activities of the manufacturers and merchants of engines of destruction, and it must be met by the concerted action of the people of all nations." The President delighted Nye and Vandenberg by expressing gratification that the Senate had resolved to investigate the munitions trade. F.D.R. urged the Senate and the executive departments to co-operate with the munitions investigating committee.[25]

Within an hour of receiving the presidential message Senator Key Pittman introduced a joint resolution, drafted by the State Department, prohibiting shipments of arms from the United States to Paraguay or Bolivia. Five days later Congress unanimously adopted the resolution.

The Chaco embargo had several objectives. The United States hoped that by depriving the belligerents of an important source of munitions the embargo would help bring peace in South America. Then the embargo had a moral purpose. It would end profiteering by citizens of the United States in blood and death in the Gran Chaco. Americans also wanted to assist the League of Nations. For some time the League had sought an international arms embargo against Paraguay and Bolivia, and recent history had shown that few arms-producing countries would take action without assurances that the United States would do likewise. Now, for a change, the United States had assumed the initiative, even to the extent of taking action without co-opera-

tion of other nations, despite the time-honored belief that unilateral embargoes discriminated against American business. The
League unfortunately could not secure a general embargo. Ten
countries, including France, Italy, Belgium, and Czechoslovakia, made approval contingent upon acceptance by Japan and
Germany. Germany ignored League queries. Japan, having
withdrawn from the Geneva organization, replied that it had
adopted a policy of abstaining from League activities of a political character. The League abandoned hope of an embargo
in June, 1934, although twenty countries eventually imposed
unilateral embargoes on arms shipments to Bolivia and Paraguay.

The Senate on June 15, 1934 ratified the Geneva Arms Traffic
Convention of 1925, with reservation that the treaty would not
bind the United States until ratified by Belgium, the British
Empire, Czechoslovakia, France, Germany, Italy, Japan, Sweden, and the Soviet Union. France, Great Britain, and Sweden
previously had given conditional ratification, and there was
hope that American action would encourage the others. Nobody
suggested that the convention, if ratified by all arms-producing
countries, would curb the arms trade. The language of the
treaty assured as much. It stated that each country would supervise arms trade of its own nationals according to its own laws.
There would be no uniform policy, and no international agency
to control the movement of arms. American strategy was to
secure support for the 1925 convention, and move from that
base to a more inclusive agreement. President Roosevelt said in
his May 18 message that he hoped delegates to the Geneva
Disarmament Conference would agree upon regulations "more
far-reaching than those which were embodied in the convention of 1925." The hope was vain.* The ambitions of Japan,

* The Geneva Arms Traffic Convention of 1925 did not receive Roosevelt's signature until June, 1935. Because of a reservation sponsored by
Senator William H. King of Utah that the convention's terms should not
apply to the region of the Persian Gulf (it might infringe upon Persian
sovereignty, King said), the President rejected the convention as ratified
in 1934. In the summer of 1935 the Senate again ratified the convention,
this time without the King reservation. The convention then received
Roosevelt's signature.

Germany, and Italy nullified any chance of agreement on restricting the munitions trade.[26]

IV

Nye and Vandenberg meanwhile were taking steps to implement S. Res. 206 by organizing a special committee to investigate the munitions industry and study industrial mobilization in wartime. Soon after passage of the resolution Vice-President John N. Garner conferred with the two senators, and asked that they submit names of four Democrats and three Republicans. After talking over the matter with colleagues Nye and Vandenberg submitted seven names, which Garner approved: Bennett Champ Clark of Missouri, James P. Pope of Idaho, Homer T. Bone of Washington, and Morris Sheppard of Texas (Democrats); W. Warren Barbour of New Jersey, Nye, and Vandenberg (Republicans). Before the inquiry began Walter F. George of Georgia replaced Sheppard.[27]

Who were these men who together formed the committee? Clark, like Nye a youthful man, was forty-four years old, and he quickly became the Number Two committee member. The son of the well-known former Speaker of the House of Representatives, Champ Clark, he bore marked physical resemblance to his father. A large man, more than six feet tall and weighing over two hundred pounds, he had his father's barrel chest, broad shoulders, rectangular jaw, and thin mouth. He was amiable toward colleagues, but often was tactless. One observer said he had "a genius for public rudeness." Another reporter called him a "deceptively jovial" man "who asks smiling questions dangerously."[28]

The young Senator Clark shared many of his father's views. Like his father, he was a reluctant liberal who looked upon economic changes with misgiving. Although he went to the Senate in 1933, a year when most Democrats followed Roosevelt with hardly a murmur, he was not a New Dealer. He supported the New Deal's monetary policy, but fought such measures as the Agricultural Adjustment Act and National Industrial Recovery

Act. Like his father, Clark was an isolationist and opposed America's declaration of war in 1917, although he later entered the Army as a captain. After the war he became active in the American Legion and endorsed the Legion's program for removing the profit from war.

Clark venerated the memory of his father, and could not forgive the Democratic National Convention of 1912 for passing over his father to nominate Woodrow Wilson for the Presidency. The elder Clark had won a majority of the convention delegates, but lost the nomination because of the Democratic Party's two-thirds rule. Still smarting from this disappointment, the son would lead a fight in the 1936 Democratic convention for abolition of the two-thirds rule. During his political career the memory of his father's experience in 1912 influenced Clark's attitude toward Wilson. Most Democrats of the 1930's revered Wilson. Clark did not. When the Munitions Committee in 1936 examined Wilsonian neutrality policy, observers detected evidence of Clark's antipathy for Wilson.

From the outset Clark was a wheelhorse of the munitions investigation, and demonstrated his abiding interest by attending more hearings than any member except Nye. Nye attended eight-five of the ninety-three hearings. Clark attended eighty-four. The Missourian had a good mind. He proved adept at interrogating witnesses, and made a larger impression in the hearing room than Nye. Unlike Nye, he delighted in cross-examination. His hearing room demeanor usually was courteous, but occasionally he became impatient and caustic. Clark was active behind the scenes. He helped plan the investigation, and was involved in committee dealings with the White House. He developed close personal relations with Nye, and especially in the inquiry's latter stages the names of Nye and Clark often were linked in dispatches concerning the investigation.

Vandenberg, fifty years old, had entered the Senate in 1928. Although other responsibilities prevented him from taking such an active part as Nye or Clark, he provided much force to the munitions investigation. Other committee members respected his judgment, and he played a large role in planning the inquiry. He attended seventy-eight hearings, was active in interrogation, and distinguished himself by perceptive questions and observations. While never failing to explore evidence of malpractice, he was courteous and drew conclusions only when evidence warranted. The committee's secretary called Vandenberg the committee's outstanding intellect.[29]

Vandenberg cast a fine image at the hearings. He personified the popular ideal of a senator, and an observer wrote that "a Hollywood director would cast Arthur Vandenberg . . . for a United States Senator on sight. He not only looks the part, he acts it." A large man, he had dark brown eyes under heavy black brows and graying hair parted far to one side to conceal baldness. A reporter wrote that "during Senate inquiries, his rimless spectacles, his quizzical glance, his trick of shrouding the lower half of his face with his hand and his extreme patience in questioning witnesses often creates the feeling of an extraordinarily kindly professor." An isolationist in 1934–36, Vandenberg was a conservative but not a reactionary. In the New Deal period he voted for the Securities and Exchange Commission, sponsored an antichild labor bill, and helped write the Social Security Act, but defended holding companies and opposed NRA, AAA, the Tennessee Valley Authority, the Wagner Act, and the Wage and Hour Act.[30]

Senator Homer Bone received invitation to serve on the Munitions Committee because Nye and Vandenberg wanted a core of senators inalterably dedicated to the objectives of the inquiry. They believed that Clark and Bone, with themselves, would provide this core.[31]

Bone, fifty-one years old, was a product of West Coast radicalism. His election to the Senate in 1932 had come largely from support of the Continental Committee on Technocracy— the production-for-use people—and from the Unemployed Citizens' League. In foreign affairs he was an isolationist. His family background influenced him in that direction. His father had served with the Seventh Indiana Volunteer Infantry during the Civil War, been captured, and spent six months in Libby Prison. His mother's first husband had died in the Battle of the

Wilderness, and two of her younger brothers also had died in the war. Referring to his mother, Bone wrote in 1959: "She thought that war was man's chiefest insanity and I agree." [32]

One reporter described Bone as "small, stooped, and caustic." Certainly he was the Munitions Committee's most quotable member; during hearings he often gave blunt expression to his liberal and pacifist views. His eloquence sometimes led to reckless statements, yet outbursts were infrequent and he served the inquiry well. While his attendance at hearings was sporadic, he made a considerable impression when he did attend. [33]

Idaho's junior senator, fifty-year-old James P. Pope, had entered the Senate in 1933, and he was the committee's only bonafide New Dealer. He also was an outspoken advocate of collective security and supporter of the League of Nations. His invitation to serve on the investigation came because Nye and Vandenberg wanted a balanced committee, and believed it necessary to include a man of Pope's persuasion. Many years later Pope, a friendly man, denied that the White House had influenced his attitude toward the munitions inquiry, but his enthusiasm in 1934–36 seemed to run parallel with that of President Roosevelt. In the early stages, when the committee probed the munitions trade and studied industrial mobilization, he took an active part, but when the committee considered American neutrality in the First World War, Pope, an admirer of Wilson, disapproved. While never a dominant member, Pope was an asset to the committee. [34]

W. Warren Barbour, a millionaire best known for boxing prowess, had come to the Senate in 1931. He was forty-six years old when he joined the Munitions Committee. A man of six feet two inches, he had been an outstanding heavyweight boxer, winner of the national amateur championship by a knockout in 1910. Barbour, so Nye and Vandenberg hoped, also would give balance to the committee. He was the committee's closest approximation to a regular Republican. During the New Deal years he voted for the Railroad Retirement Act, Social Security, and legislation creating the Home Owners Loan

Corporation, but opposed AAA and stoutly defended New Jersey industrial interests. Barbour did not completely sympathize with the investigation, and seemed to threaten to become a self-appointed defender of the arms industry. But the possibility failed to materialize, and he made no large effort to impede the investigation. After the early stages of the inquiry Barbour, a man of modest talent, made little impression.[35]

Then there was fifty-six-year-old Walter George, the senior member of the committee both in age and service in the Senate. Nye and Vandenberg had two things in mind when they invited George to membership after the resignation of Morris Sheppard. They wanted him to help balance the committee (they considered him a conservative internationalist), and they also wanted his dignity and respectability. Nye later acknowledged that acceptance by no other senator had elated him so much, but it developed that George took an inconsequential part in the inquiry. He attended a third of the hearings, mostly in the earliest stages, and seldom spoke. Pope later surmised that George came to fear the investigation's effect on national defense, since the American Army and Navy depended on the private munitions industry.[36]

Who would serve as chairman of the Munitions Committee?

Since the Democrats controlled Congress and had a majority on the committee, it seemed that a Democrat would preside. But on April 23, 1934 the committee in executive session elected Nye, a Republican.* Nye had not expected the chairmanship. He thought the committee would choose Clark, but Clark nominated Nye, and the committee unanimously accepted the proposal. Nye had investigating experience, did not face reelection until 1938, could devote much time to the chairmanship, and had enthusiasm for the inquiry. Moreover, according to Pope, the senators believed selection of a Republican would demonstrate their intention to conduct a nonpartisan investigation.[37]

As chairman, Gerald Nye gave his name to the Senate Com-

* Unfortunately the minutes of this committee meeting are missing from the committee records in the National Archives.

mittee Investigating the Munitions Industry. It quickly became known as the Nye Committee, and as such ranks with the Pujo, Pecora, Kefauver, and McCarthy committees among the best-known congressional investigating groups. According to Nye, constant reference to "the Nye Committee" was embarrassing, since it implied one-man control over the investigation. But the senator probably was not too embarrassed. He enjoyed the limelight and made no effort to dispel the notion that he was the committee's tactician and moving force—that he *was* the committee. In truth, he did not wield, nor did he try to wield, absolute authority. As Pope later pointed out, and as committee records demonstrate, the chairman took no important step without full discussion and consent of the committee of the whole. In the inner councils of the committee, moreover, the voices of Clark, Vandenberg, and the committee's secretary carried as much force as that of Nye. Nye made routine administrative decisions, but these aroused little friction. Except for a protest by Pope and George during study of World War neutrality, and criticism of Nye's release of some documents several months after completion of the inquiry, harmony prevailed.[38]

The Munitions Committee was organized and had a chairman. One move remained before the investigation could begin: employment of a man to supervise the battery of investigators which the committee would dispatch to the files of companies and government departments to gather evidence for interrogating witnesses; who would supervise the committee's administrative affairs; who would assist committee members in organizing evidence. First choice for this job was the writer-economist John T. Flynn, but Flynn declined with the lament that "nothing in my life have I ever regretted so much as the circumstances which made it impossible for me to undertake that job." Upon suggestion of Dorothy Detzer and other people in the peace movement, the committee offered the position to the shy, quiet, heavy-browed Stephen Raushenbush, a man of large energy and intelligence. Raushenbush accepted.[39]

THE EVIDENCE

T HE Munitions Committee's case rested upon documents assembled by investigators. The committee acted on the hypothesis that manufacturers and salesmen of armaments had committed crimes against humanity, but it could not prove this notion merely by summoning the accused to Washington to answer questions. And it could not, as Senator Shortridge's subcommittee had done in 1929 when studying the Shearer case, rely upon witnesses to provide embarrassing documents. The committee, therefore, did what congressional investigating committees usually do: it subpoenaed records of companies and individuals under investigation. It removed interesting documents, then ordered persons involved to appear in Washington. In the hearing room the usual procedure was to produce a letter or memorandum or report, and then interrogate witnesses.

Gathering evidence from files of perhaps fifty companies and individuals involved in the arms trade was a large task, and required a large staff. Usually the committee staff numbered about twenty persons, although during the twenty months of the inquiry the committee employed about seventy different people. Several of these individuals came from the Federal Emergency Relief Administration and later the Works Progress Administration, enabling the committee to conduct a broader

48

investigation within the limits of its budget. The supervisor of this staff was Stephen Raushenbush, sometimes referred to as chief counsel of the Munitions Committee. He was in truth the chief investigator, although his title was secretary to the committee. The committee had no chief counsel, and in this respect was unique. As Raushenbush later explained, the committee did not wish a repetition of the Pecora investigation a year earlier, when the Committee on Banking and Currency's chief counsel, Ferdinand Pecora, not the senators, received the headlines.[1]

Although the committee granted him, publicly at least, second-class status, Raushenbush became a key figure in the investigation. Nye presided over the committee and, with general acquiescence, established policy and defined the broad outline of the inquiry, but from the field work directed by Raushenbush emerged the briefs (prepared by the staff, not the senators) which determined the course of the investigation. Prior to hearings the senators studied the briefs, and on the appointed day asked witnesses questions which the briefs indicated—in many cases specified. So important was the secretary's role that one might contend the name Nye Committee was a misnomer.* Nye was absent from Washington when much of the committee's work took place. He was on a two-month junket to the Far East in the autumn of 1935 when Raushenbush and the investigators gathered data and prepared briefs for presentation when the committee aired America's World War neutrality policy and interrogated J. P. Morgan—in the view of isolationist members, the investigation's most important phase. Nor was any other committee member active in the investigation at that point, complicating Raushenbush's job since there was no senator available to sign subpoenas.[2]

* Raushenbush insists that the senators "took such an active part in preparing themselves for questioning of witnesses and in discussing the meaning of all the material that it was unusually a Senate committee rather than a researcher's committee." Nevertheless, in the words of Dorothy Detzer, "as Nye and each member of his committee were so often to testify, it was Steve—quiet and self-effacing—who was the genius of this undertaking."

In relying heavily on its staff the Munitions Committee was not unusual. Staff members can give full time to an investigation, but a senator has other responsibilities. It would be unwise, even if possible, for him to devote most of his energy to an inquiry of this type.

I

Stephen Raushenbush was the son of Walter Rauschenbusch (the son dropped the two Germanic "c's" from his name), the famous advocate of social Christianity, and from his father he inherited the belief that war was one of the largest obstacles to social justice. Like most Americans in 1917, however, he considered the World War a democratic crusade, unfortunate but necessary. Upon graduation from Amherst College he enlisted in the United States ambulance corps attached to the French armies, and was among the first 10,000 Americans to reach France. Assigned to front line duty, he became acquainted with modern war before the bulk of American troops landed. His experiences in the trenches of the Western Front stimulated his dedication to peace. In later years the apparent futility of war had similar effect—for he had expected the war to make the world safe for democracy.[3]

Politically Raushenbush was a liberal. After the war he followed a varied career, but most of his activities aimed to promote progressive causes. He studied the coal and power industries, and wrote *The Anthracite Question* (1923), *Power Control* (1928), and *The Power Fight* (1932), liberal analyses of conditions in coal and power. For a time he was assistant professor of economics at Dartmouth College, but resigned in 1930 to become economics adviser to Governor Gifford Pinchot of Pennsylvania. He served on state commissions which investigated the utilities industry, child labor, and sweatshops. He was secretary of the Pennsylvania Security League, an organization of 50,000 members which sought old-age pensions, minimum wages, and unemployment insurance. Some of his critics concluded from such activities that Raushenbush was a social-

Opening day of the Munitions investigation. The first witnesses, officials of the Electric Boat Company, listen as Senator Nye (at left) reads opening statements.

Stephen Raushenbush

Dorothy Detzer

Raushenbush (second from right) and Investigator Alger Hiss (standing) meet with Senate Committee members (left to right) Vandenberg, Barbour, Nye, Clark, and Pope.

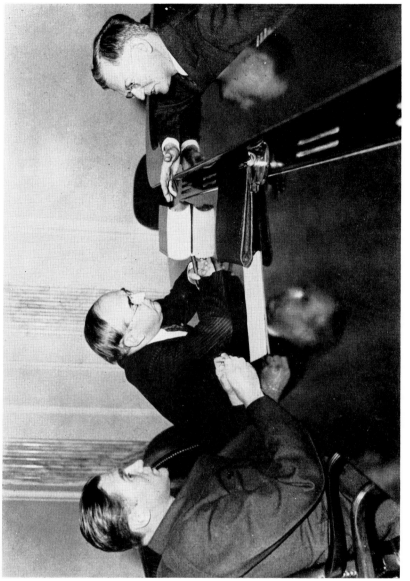

John Flynn (right), New York author and attorney, presents plan for eliminating war profits to Nye (left) and Vandenberg.

Leaving the White House after conferring with President Roosevelt are (left to right, front row) Senators George, Nye, and Bone; (back row) Senators Pope, Barbour, Clark, and Vandenberg.

J. P. Morgan (left) in conversation with Barbour and Nye as the banker prepared to testify.

William G. Shearer

ist. It was true that he had friends in the socialist movement and had written articles for socialist journals criticizing capitalism. But he told a reporter in 1934, "I am registered as a Republican, although I feel that most orthodox Republicans consider me a free independent." [4]

When chosen to direct the munitions investigation in 1934, Raushenbush was thirty-eight years old. He was a handsome, lanky six-footer who spoke slowly and with a drawl. With his heavy crop of hair, moustache, quiet voice, deliberate movements, and briar pipe, he did not convey the appearance of a relentless chief investigator. He brought to his position with the Munitions Committee a well-trained and resourceful mind, as well as investigating experience. These assets appeared in his direction of the staff and during the seventy-five hearings he attended. In the hearing room he joined Clark and Vandenberg in carrying the burden of interrogation. During cross-examination he was undramatic, but always was prepared and competent. He was, moreover, a dedicated man, whose energy seemed limitless. He suffered because he was not a lawyer, but he had excellent legal assistants on his staff, and his researches had taught him the rules of evidence. A more serious handicap was his belief in the culpability of the munitions makers. Yet like Nye he determined to conduct an impartial study, and the result was, later criticism notwithstanding, a surprisingly restrained and judicious performance.

Below Raushenbush in the hierarchy of the investigative staff stood Calvin J. Nichols, Ben T. Moore, Donald Y. Wemple, Floyd La Rouche, Robert Wohlforth, Lawrence Brown, and Josephine Joan Burns. These people had varying backgrounds, but were united in affinity for peace and adherence to liberal principles (using liberal here to mean support of government restrictions on business, and economic security for society's victims). All were talented, energetic, loyal, and convinced of the need to expose the "merchants of death." Raushenbush gave well-defined responsibilities to each of these people. Nichols and Moore, usually working with Raushenbush in Washington, performed a range of tasks, including assembling data brought in by investigators and helping in preparation of briefs. Wemple had charge of the committee's branch office in New York City, an important position since most committee investigators operated from the New York office, nearer than Washington to many of the companies under scrutiny. Wemple acted as Raushenbush's intermediary with field investigators, conveying directives and channeling data to Washington. (Raushenbush, however, often bypassed Wemple, and communicated directly with field investigators.) Robert Wohlforth, the most quotable member of the staff, headed study of the munitions trade. He provided a periodic lift to Raushenbush through humorous letters, and also brought in many of the documents which furnished the hearings with drama. Floyd La Rouche, a writer and economist, directed investigation of the shipbuilding industry. Lawrence Brown directed study of Wall Street financiers, and Miss Burns of Mount Holyoke College, who joined the staff in February, 1935, worked in the State Department files relating to United States neutrality during the World War.

Another member of the staff was Alger Hiss. Most people who can recall the Munitions Committee have forgotten the roles of Vandenberg, Clark, and Raushenbush, but remember the participation of Nye and Hiss. This was not the case at the time of the investigation. Hiss was not well known, and received little notice. But more than a decade later—in 1949—Whittaker Chambers testified that Hiss had used his committee position to gain access to classified State Department documents, copies of which he handed over to Soviet spies. Chambers offered no proof for his assertion, and in December, 1949 Joseph C. Green, the State Department's liaison man with the Munitions Committee in 1934–36, gave a deposition refuting Chambers's testimony. Green said that the committee had assigned a lady expert in international law to work with the State Department. She examined the department's files and selected documents pertinent to the inquiry, whereupon the department studied, cleared, and made copies of the documents. According to Green, the department at no time gave original or secret documents to the committee. Senator Nye, on the other hand, with every reason to defend his own committee, later said he believed Hiss had used his committee position for espionage in the way Chambers had described.[5]

Hiss's title was legal assistant, and like Nichols and Moore he performed a range of tasks. The committee engaged him because it wanted a keen legal mind. Hiss had served as Oliver Wendell Holmes's secretary and seemed an excellent choice. Later publicity to the contrary, his part in the inquiry was secondary. He had no voice in mapping the investigation, nor was he a major figure in the hearings. He attended 16 hearings out of 93, and during only a few did he cross-examine. His infrequent interrogations were courteous and proper, despite Senator Carter Glass's alleged complaint about the "'dad-bum questions' of the young prosecuting attorney, Alger Hiss." (The record shows that on the day to which Glass referred, Hiss had said nothing.) Senator Bone wrote many years later that "the part Hiss played in this investigation was so minor . . . that I have practically forgotten the part he played." Hiss's largest effort was the preparation of the final report, a cautious document.[6]

In addition to Raushenbush and his staff, the Munitions Committee appointed an advisory council consisting of John T. Flynn, Manley O. Hudson of Harvard, and Dr. Harold Moulton of the Brookings Institution. The committee showed its good intentions when Nye wrote Hudson that "we are going to greatly appreciate that very splendid help which we know you can afford." When the investigation was getting underway the advisory council met with the committee several times, but after the early weeks it did not function, although Hudson did some testifying and Flynn drew up the committee's plan for removing excessive profits from war.[7]

II

It took some time for the committee to gather steam. In a broadcast of June 18, 1934 the "world observer," sponsored by World Peaceways, acknowledged receipt of many letters asking what was delaying the munitions inquiry; the Senate had authorized the investigation two months before. The world observer explained that "the munitions industry, as you will realize once the investigation gets under way publicly, is one of the most intricately ramified in the country. Many of its dealings are, by their very nature, dark, obscure and subversive. It isn't an easy matter to probe them overnight." [8]

To be sure, the munitions industry did not present an easy task for Senator Nye. Investigators could not gather evidence in a moment. As Robert Wohlforth wrote in July, 1934, "everyone is working hard, only they can't butter all the bread in one day." The staff began by making a list of companies and individuals engaged in manufacture and sale of munitions. Investigators next studied all printed information on the business of such firms and people, while other committee agents conferred with directors and managers. After these steps investigators examined files.[9]

The magnitude of the research was one reason for delay. Another was the inexperience of much of Raushenbush's staff. Wohlforth conceded that he and his subordinates were "awfully green about this investigative technique, and some of us pretty dumb," but "under Wemple's direction they are weeding out the unimportant material, concentrating on the juicy fruit." Even after experience investigators found their work required patience. While investigating the Remington Arms Company, Wohlforth reported: "No rape or skulduggery discovered to date. . . . I'm just writing this to keep you informed and to worry the distinguished counsel who is observing us closely." [10]

Sometimes company officials obstructed the inquiry. J. P. Morgan and Company in particular gave grudging cooperation. Lawrence Brown, in charge of the Morgan study, reported in the summer of 1935 that "Morgans and I go through an elaborate pretense of cordiality." Writing to Nichols, Brown said he was sorry his relations with Morgan were strained, "though I can understand why. We have them on the run without any question." Several months later Brown wrote that "relations with Morgan have been growing more and more tense on the problem of prying stuff out of them making an increasing amount of delicate negotiation necessary." At one point Morgan lawyers demanded certificates of good character to cover Munitions Committee investigators. Brown refused to comply. Raushenbush told Brown—so he said in a letter to William T. Stone—"that if the Committee's investigators were to have certificates of good character we would, of course, request them in turn from the Morgan partners. And will that be fun—especially if we refused to accept some of their certificates." On a more serious note, Raushenbush later wrote Bone: "Confidentially, we think that they have cleaned out their files and have lied to us at length." [11]

Some problems were personal. While directing the Remington study Wohlforth announced: "If I meet that Remington lawyer again I'll go crazy, as he gives me a lecture on the ethics of Military business every time I see him." A few weeks later he asked Raushenbush for some time off: "I'm breaking out in boils and my doctor says I'm pretty shot. . . . If I look the way I feel, I ought to be a museum piece." [12]

At the Winchester Repeating Arms Company, Wohlforth encountered a new difficulty. "In Winchester yesterday as per schedule. It is even more dismal a plant than Remington—a cross between an old ladies' home and a prison factory. This bunch are surely down in the mouth since the Olins took over; every department has been cut to the bone and the whole place seems to be wheezing along on one cylinder. . . . As far as I can make out, they use the Ix-nay system of filing. The old crone in the central filing room takes a bunch of papers marked 'U.S. government,' turns around three times with her eyes shut, says 'Ix-nay' and files the papers under 'Venezuela—commercial business.' . . . Needless to say I camped in Mr. Beebe's department [H. F. Beebe, director of the foreign department]. . . . We fell to talking about the 1925 business [a meeting between government and arms company officials]. With another stroke of luck we discover he has all the papers on that little business in a folder, unbeknownst to Apple Annie of the filing room." [13]

Meanwhile Raushenbush had problems of his own. For a time he had difficulty getting reports from Donald Wemple of the New York office. Raushenbush wrote him that "I have realized for some time that you find it difficult to bring yourself to the matter of writing reports and I have been, it seems to me, very appreciative of that attitude. . . . However . . . I [must] have a complete weekly report in my hands from you every Saturday." Wemple replied: "I do not find it difficult to write reports when there is something of importance to report, but I do find it difficult to bring myself to the point of writing numerous letters about daily routine and local gossip. . . . If I were to write you all the details of the daily troubles we have . . . you would undoubtedly be constantly getting excited and worried over matters, which when finally worked out, mean nothing." From then on Wemple submitted reports regularly.[14]

Then there was the matter of funds. This was the most persistent of Raushenbush's (and the committee's) difficulties. The committee never had assurance of enough money to complete long-range projects, and budgetary considerations invariably limited hearings. The Nye-Vandenberg Resolution as amended appropriated $15,000 for the inquiry, and in early June, 1934 Raushenbush reported that this sum would not sustain the committee beyond the end of the year. Nye pointed out that the committee then would have months of work ahead. He hoped, therefore, to build such a strong case before January, 1935 that public opinion would compel the Senate to vote more funds. Fortunately the Senate on June 13, 1934 approved an additional $35,000.[15]

By early autumn it became clear that even $50,000 would not carry the committee through 1934 unless it abbreviated the investigation. Raushenbush tried to persuade Nye to cut the autumn hearings from six weeks to four. Nye deferred to the secretary, and fortunately for the committee the investigation aroused enough enthusiasm to compel more money in January, 1935.[16]

Late in 1935 the investigation again entered financial shoals. While putting together briefs on J. P. Morgan and World War neutrality, Raushenbush reported funds nearly exhausted. He advised that the committee hasten hearings. He told Brown that "the financial situation is such that we will go into January first with a possible $500 on hand, which I want to reserve for the clerical staff for the month of January and even that will probably not quite cover them. That means that all the rest of us must take a gamble on our pay for the month of January and any amount of February that is necessary." Investigators labored through January, 1936 without assurance of pay.[17]

The inquiry ended in February, 1936, with the committee's projects far from complete. Committee critics terminated the inquiry by prevailing upon the Senate to appropriate no more funds then necessary to complete the phase of investigation then in progress. Thus the financial problem, threatening from the beginning, eventually stopped the investigation.

Another problem was security. Raushenbush took precaution against leaks by devising a code which the staff used in conversation, telegrams, and general discussion. The staff referred to du Pont as eleven, Curtiss-Wright as four, and Bethlehem Shipbuilding as twenty-eight. Raushenbush also took care that employees remained loyal to the investigation. He did not always succeed. A minor clerk, Frances Wogisch, who assisted investigator Joel Earnest in study of Navy League files, became friendly with a League official named Mahan. According to Wohlforth, the two became so amicable "that we had to let her go and the laugh is that when Ernest [sic] went over there the other day, whom did he see as Mahan's secretary but the well known Mrs. Wogish [sic]. I don't think this will be a leak as she had no intimates around the office and she doesn't know much. This is a sample of what can happen even with the greatest care in engaging a staff." [18]

Of some concern to Raushenbush and the committee were employees whom the FERA and WPA assigned the investigation. One question was their competence. Wohlforth took a tolerant view that "in the final analysis, the FERA men are just men—many of them are keen for the work and on the job. The others are equivalent in competency, but they need constant prodding and someone to get their eyes off the clock." In another letter Wohlforth expressed a different aspect of the committee's anxiety: "What bothers me is whether we won't lay the committee—if not the whole Senate open to various poor-mouth charges. . . . As an ex-Hearst man, I could figure out a pretty way to smear us—you know, State funds used by U.S. Senate—Is the Greatest Deliberative Body in the World On a Relief Basis? etc etc etc. Of course, many other government departments have utilized Relief projects to implement their work—but the Senate is not another gov't department." Wohlforth's apprehensions came true. When the committee came under attack in January, 1936 hostile senators referred to use of WPA employees. Joseph T. Robinson of Arkansas declared that "it is a most astonishing statement . . . that funds which have been appropriated for the relief of persons in distress should be sought by a committee created by the Senate of the United States, and the Senate should be put in the attitude of going on relief. [Laughter.] In the name of conscience, has this country and has the Senate come to a condition when committees representing the Senate will disgrace it in such a manner?" Raushenbush and the committee, of course, would have preferred to act without FERA and WPA assistance, but the budget problem left them no alternative.[19]

III

A delicate matter confronting the Munitions Committee throughout the inquiry was handling of government and private records pertaining to business between American companies and foreign governments. Much of this material, if used indiscreetly, could have ill effect upon American diplomatic relations.

Aware of the hazards as well as mechanical difficulties in scrutinizing State Department documents, the committee solicited the department's advice and co-operation. Two weeks after passage of the Nye-Vandenberg Resolution, Nye conceded to Secretary Hull that the committee was "more or less in the dark as to just how we might proceed and are especially desirous of knowing what help and information might be available to us through your offices and department to expedite the investigation." Hull pledged full and cordial co-operation, and instructed Joseph C. Green, the department's Director of Western European Affairs, "to hold himself at the disposition of the Committee." With Green as intermediary, the department and committee reached accord on handling diplomatic documents. The department agreed to place files at the disposal of committee investigators, but extracted an understanding that investigators should make no exact copies of communications in diplomatic codes and that the committee would publish no document without State Department authorization. The path thus was cleared, and in the second week of June, 1934 Green reported that committee investigators had descended upon the department and were taking copious notes.[20] *

Not until September, 1934, during the first weeks of hearings, did a threat arise to Munitions Committee–State Department amity. The committee published documents from files of American corporations indicating that Latin American officials had accepted bribes from munitions salesmen, and these disclosures aroused a storm from several Latin American governments and embarrassed the State Department, then laboring for closer relations with the American republics. Similar trouble resulted when the committee exhibited a document implicating the King of England. But in such instances there was no misuse of State Department documents, and while Secretary Hull would have preferred more restraint (the committee might have refrained from publishing names) he seemed to agree that the committee was revealing an aspect of the arms trade in need of exposure. No break occurred, therefore, between the department and the committee. But a few months later, in February, 1935, the committee drew a rebuke from Hull after Senator

* The reader will note a possible discrepancy between Green's deposition of 1949 and the documents regarding the Munitions Committee's use of State Department records. The author has tried to resolve the question, but the documents do not give a complete account and the memories of the participants are hazy.

Clark, in a moment of vexation, exhibited an unauthorized State Department document. Green went to the Senate Office Building to advise Nye, visibly distressed, that Clark's action had angered Hull and that the department would find cooperation difficult if the committee published more documents without authorization. Vandenberg, in Nye's office at the time, agreed that Hull's displeasure was justified, and Nye tried to repair the damage by dispatching an apology. "I want now to assure you," he wrote, "that the use of the documents in question was quite due to inadvertence and everyone concerned is exceedingly sorry in what may appear to have been gross betrayal of the splendid confidence which we have enjoyed with and through your office." Nye's apology satisfied Hull.[21]

More important was a controversy which began in March, 1935 between the State Department and the governments of Britain, France, and Italy over the committee's determination to subpoena documents, including those from foreign governments, pertaining to transactions between American bankers and belligerent governments during the World War. The British ambassador, Sir Ronald Lindsay, initiated the controversy upon learning that the committee had subpoenaed the Guaranty National Bank for records and papers concerning wartime loans. Impressed by the firmness of Sir Ronald's protest, the State Department took up the matter with the Munitions Committee. Declining to abandon plans to study the documents, the committee agreed to postpone return of the subpoena.[22]

Sir Ronald pressed the matter, and on March 20, 1935 wrote Hull that "I feel bound to suggest to you that to proceed with the investigation of this correspondence of my Government without warning or without attempting to obtain its consent can only be characterized as an act of grave discourtesy." Hull, expressing surprise at this communication, replied that he did not believe either international usage or courtesy required the United States to communicate to the British government the intention of any judicial or quasi-judicial body in the United States to subpoena documents from an American corporation which might relate to dealings between the British government

and private American citizens. He said he could not carry out such an obligation if it were incumbent upon him to do so, since ordinarily he would have no knowledge of an intention to issue such a subpoena until it had been served. But Hull had greater sympathy for the British position than this letter indicated. Several days before he had suggested that the President call the committee to the White House and dissuade it from investigating events of the World War. Roosevelt accepted the suggestion, and on March 19 conferred with committee leaders, but failed to move them. (The following day Nye denied that Roosevelt had tried to dissuade them from what Nye called perhaps the most important part of the inquiry.) On March 22, the day after his note to Lindsay, Hull met with the committee and extracted a promise that the committee would not publish British government material until after discussion with the State Department. Then, according to Raushenbush's report, Hull "spoke of his happiness that team work with the Administration on certain important points was being effected." [23]

Such assurances failed to mollify the former Allied governments. Sir Ronald Lindsay advised Hull that Sir John Simon, British Foreign Secretary, believed the delicacy of the international situation made revival of obsolete controversies inopportune. The French ambassador also presented objections. He told Undersecretary of State William Phillips that the moment the documents came into the committee's possession the press, he had no doubt, would get hold of them or their substance.[24]

Considering Anglo- and Franco-American harmony more important than Senator Nye's investigation, Hull continued to hope the committee would forget plans to scrutinize events surrounding American entry into the World War. By mid-April he had brought the President unreservedly to his position. Roosevelt, with Hull present this time, on April 18 again conferred with committee spokesmen—Nye, Clark, and Pope. The President and Secretary argued against examining wartime correspondence betwen Allied governments and American financiers. They argued vainly. Nye reiterated determination to proceed, but affirmed that documents involving foreign governments would receive no publicity until the State Department had opportunity to confer with governments concerned. Emerging from the conference, Nye told reporters that "we agreed to avoid any action raising complications with foreign governments. We are a committee to promote peace, not war." [25]

The former Allied governments remained fearful. Lindsay told Joseph Green in April, 1935 that the Munitions Committee had advised the press it intended to interrogate Morgan partners. He feared lest the committee, questioning the titans of finance, treat the British government as a circus animal which would be made to perform for spectators. Such goings on, he added, would have deplorable effect on relations between Great Britain and the United States.[26]

The Italian government was less disturbed, since its wartime dealings with American financial institutions had been relatively small. The first secretary of the Italian Embassy told Green in June, 1935 that his government attached no large importance to documents from the Italian government during the World War, adding that he doubted publication of the documents would embarrass Italy. Still, perhaps in deference to the British, the Italian Embassy advised the State Department in July that letters by the Italian government during the war period were confidential and should not be published.[27]

Undeterred, the Munitions Committee moved on with its plans, and in August, 1935 agreed with the State Department on procedure for handling wartime correspondence. The committee promised not to insert into the record any document which the State Department had not released, and unless documents were in the record they would be unavailable to persons, including the committee staff, wishing to write on subjects under study. But that same day the British and French ambassadors protested the committee's resolve to examine the wartime accounts of J. P. Morgan and Company, the firm which had handled most transactions between American and Allied governments in the years 1914–18. Fortunately a solution appeared. The State Department assumed custody of Morgan files containing accounts of the Allies. The committee would have access to the documents, but would publish no document without a State Department stamp and release. The way thus was cleared, and on the morning of August 19 a truck with file cases and ledgers of World War correspondence and records of the Morgan firm arrived in Washington. Workmen deposited the material in Room 201 of the State Department.[28]

This arrangement for handling the documents proved satisfactory. The State Department avoided offending the governments of Great Britain, France, and Italy, and the three governments could feel reasonably certain that they would suffer no embarrassment because of publication of indiscreet correspondence. At the same time the Munitions Committee secured access to material which it considered important to its study. That the State Department could restrict use of documents did not disturb the committee. It was clear that the department did not seek to hamstring the committee; it wanted only to preserve harmony with foreign governments. Memories of the reaction to publication of embarrassing documents in September, 1934, moreover, sharpened the committee's anxiety to avoid offending the Europeans. True, if the committee had discovered correspondence which established the culpability of Wall Street in bringing America to war, only to have the State Department rule such evidence off limits, the committee would have complained. But no documents of this nature appeared.

In one instance the committee violated the State Department's trust, although in this case embarrassment fell upon the Democratic party, not the British government. During the hearing of January 15, 1936 Nye and Clark referred to but did not exhibit, quote, or paraphrase a memorandum which Lord Balfour as British Foreign Secretary had transmitted to Secretary of State Robert Lansing on May 18, 1917. Balfour had described how the Allies secretly had pledged to remake the map of Europe if they won the war. The secret treaties no longer were secret in 1936; thus the British suffered no serious discomfort from the committee's indiscretion. But Lansing and President Wilson had told the Senate Foreign Relations Committee in 1919 that they had not learned of the secret treaties until after the war. The Balfour memorandum, to the chagrin of Democrats, contradicted that testimony. The Munitions Committee had asked permission to publish the memorandum, but after consulting the British Foreign Office the State Department had denied the request.[29]

The committee's reference to this document infuriated Hull. Green told Raushenbush that the Secretary had characterized the committee action in language so severe he hesitated to repeat it. The department feared a copy of the document might fall into the hands of someone who would give it to the press or otherwise make it public. It was not necessary, he said, to dwell on the consequences of unauthorized publication of the memorandum. He was too late. The Washington *Times,* a Hearst paper, came forth on January 20, 1936 with the headline: "Hull 'Muzzles' Nye Quiz." There followed a summary of the Balfour memorandum. Green advised Raushenbush that this breach of confidence had hurt Hull deeply. Raushenbush sympathized, but insisted he had no idea how a newspaperman had secured the contents of the memorandum. He said he was trying to collect copies of all confidential documents for return to the department.[30]

Return of all known copies of confidential documents restored harmony, although by this time, January, 1936, the investigation was nearly over. Twenty-one months after the inquiry, in November, 1937, the Balfour memorandum reappeared when the Washington *Herald* carried a banner: "Great Britain's Secret War Aims Exposed." The article quoted the memorandum at length. The British were unperturbed—by 1937 the treaties and memorandum were well known. But Hull formally apologized to the British government. He explained that some unauthorized person must have obtained a copy of the document while in custody of the Munitions Committee. Next day Green conferred with Raushenbush, who discussed the matter with Nye. Both men denied communicating the memorandum to the press, but they were distressed, especially Nye, who was persuaded by Green of his ultimate responsibility for this breach of trust. Neither Nye nor the State Department ever discovered how the newspaper came by the memorandum, and with this exchange in 1937 relations between the committee and the department ended.[31]

Generally the Munitions Committee observed its arrangement with the State Department, as illustrated by Nye's letter to Hull in January, 1936 following committee discovery of important wartime correspondence between the National City Bank and the French ambassador. The committee had no agreement regarding National City Bank's files, but Nye thought it appropriate to secure department approval before using the material. Following a similar action (after the controversy over the Balfour memorandum, incidentally) Hull expressed appreciation to Nye for "the courtesy of the Special Committee of the Senate Investigating the Munitions Industry in submitting, for my examination, a collection of documents in regard to transactions of the Colt Patent Fire Arms Manufacturing Company." [32]

In conclusion, one may say that despite the impression conveyed by Hull's memoirs, relations between the committee and the State Department were surprisingly cordial. The committee caused the department considerable anxiety, and sometimes seemed oblivious to, even unconcerned by, the sensitivity of material under scrutiny. Still, through most of the inquiry the committee tried to avoid damaging America's foreign relations. For its part the State Department seemed to appreciate the committee's popular mandate to conduct a careful investigation. It seemed to appreciate the committee's accommodating spirit, especially since the committee could have ignored department problems and proceeded pell-mell without regard for the exigencies of diplomacy.

IV

In regard to use of documentary material, there were two other interesting cases, one involving a document questioning the integrity of President Roosevelt's son Elliott, and the other concerning the diaries of former Secretary of State Lansing.

Lansing's widow had deposited the diaries in the Library of Congress in 1929 with the stipulation that they should remain unavailable for study for twenty years. In 1935 the Munitions Committee set out to scrutinize all available material pertinent to America's entry into the World War, and naturally wished to examine the intimate writings of a man who had helped make America's neutrality policy in 1914–17—a policy with deficiencies which, the committee majority thought, had taken the United States to war. The committee, armed with the power of subpoena, determined to read the Lansing diaries.

Opposition to this plan appeared immediately. The foremost objectors were Lansing's nephews, Allen W. and John Foster Dulles (Lawrence Brown described the latter as a "rather stiff and smug sort of man, full of moral unction about preserving the secrets of the great and the strict terms of bequests etc. etc."). Supporting the Dulles brothers' objections was Acting Librarian Fred W. Ashley of the Library of Congress, who implored the committee to change its mind. He said the library had received other collections under similar conditions and such stipulations remained unbroken. If the Munitions Committee violated terms of the Lansing bequest other executors might withdraw their deposits. The committee was adamant. Nye replied to Ashley: "While the Committee appreciates the importance of the Library's policy with respect to deposits of this nature, it considers its own obligations to the public under Senate Resolution 206 so great as to warrant a departure from the regular procedure with respect to such deposits." The committee subpoenaed the diaries, although it promised to use only portions bearing upon its study.[33]

The Dulles brothers continued to object, and on August 22 and again on October 3, 1935 Nye reassured Allen Dulles that the committee would make no use of personal items in the diaries. Allen Dulles charged in January, 1936 that Nye had shown an extract to some senators and therefore had made the diaries public, but Nye denied violating his pledge. Nye received some consolation when Raushenbush in January, 1936 advised him that the Dulles brothers had quoted from the diaries in their recently published *War Memoirs of Robert Lansing*.[34]

The dispute proved a teapot affair. The diaries had nothing of value to the Munitions Committee, the Lansing family suffered no embarrassment, the Library of Congress had no apparent loss.

Still, the question remains: was the committee justified in subpoenaing the diaries. Did it set a precedent? Despite absence of ill effects, the committee did call into question the sanctity of other material deposited in the library, and opened the way for assorted mischief. Yet millions of people in the mid-thirties shared the committee's belief that the investigation might mean the difference between peace and war. Surely —if one may invoke the rhetoric of the peace movement—if the national interest could justify conscription of young men into military service for the cause of war, it justified breaking a bequest by Mrs. Lansing for the cause of peace.

Another committee document, involving Elliott Roosevelt, became the source of brief but heated controversy many months after the hearings. This was an affidavit by the Dutch airplane designer Anthony H. G. Fokker alleging that he had contracted with Elliott to sell military aircraft to the Soviet Union. Sale of such planes to the Soviets at that time violated no statute, but contravened American policy. According to Fokker, Roosevelt as middle man in the transaction had received $5,000 in cash, although the deal did not go through. During hearings the Munitions Committee had declined to exhibit Fokker's affidavit. But in October, 1936 the magazine *Aero Digest* published an article which accused the committee of suppressing evidence concerning Elliott Roosevelt while "smearing mud on such dead Democrats as Woodrow Wilson and Robert Lansing and on such live Republicans as the du Ponts." Moved by this criticism Nye released the Fokker affidavit.[35]

Nye's action drew rebukes from Democratic colleagues, inspired perhaps by realization that the national election was one month away. Senator George dispatched a telegram to Nye charging that the *Aero Digest* article would have attracted no attention but for Nye's release of the affidavit. Senator Clark wired amazement at Nye's release of a statement which the committee had not placed in evidence. Upon the motion of Vandenberg the committee by unanimous vote, he said, had decided there was nothing in the Fokker affidavit within jurisdiction of the committee or warranting investigation. He contended that the committee's decision had not come from desire to protect anyone or conceal information ("but solely because committee had neither time money nor inclination to go off on wild goose chases having nothing to do with legitimate scope of our investigation"). Clark said he knew of no member of the committee ("except yourself who has changed his mind as to propriety of that decision"), and insisted that Nye take no further action in the name of the committee without its authorization. In answer Nye wrote that "it is not necessary for me to say to you that your telegram of yesterday carried a personal sting." He said he had hoped Clark would understand his action "and even dared to imagine that you would have done the same thing if your contact with the matter had been as was mine." The man most affected by the Fokker affidavit took a tolerant view of Nye. At Fort Worth, Elliott Roosevelt told reporters that "if I were in Mr. Nye's position and some one accused me of withholding facts from the public I would certainly release whatever sworn matter was in my hands." [36]

Within a few days everybody forgot the Fokker affidavit. Only one more scene remained in the Munitions Committee drama— that stemming from the aforementioned publication by a newspaper of excerpts from the Balfour memorandum in 1937. Following the latter incident no further questions arose from committee evidence, and there were no further discussions among the senators in their capacities as members of the committee. Thus the munitions investigation faded out as it had begun, with the committee concerning itself with problems of handling the essential ingredients of the inquiry—the documents.

Since the documents provided the meat of the munitions inquiry, was the committee successful in its attempt to exhaust the sources of information pertinent to its study?

There was one obvious deficiency. The Munitions Committee was restricted to documentary material in the United States. It had no access to records of munitions companies or chanceries in Europe, Asia, and Latin America. A search of such records would have revealed many documents bearing upon its investigation. The United States, after all, was only the Number Three munitions producer in the world—far behind Great Britain and France. In the files of Vickers, Schneider-Creusot, Hotchkiss, Krupp, Bofors, and Skoda investigators probably would have found stronger support for the merchants-of-death thesis than at du Pont and Winchester. The foreign offices in London, Paris, and Rome, moreover, would have revealed documents regarding America's World War neutrality policy and Allied dealings with American financiers. But the Munitions Committee had to view the arms trade, international in scope, and World War dealings, involving several countries, from an American perspective. Such limitations, though apparent, were impossible to correct.

The committee's study of materials in the United States was methodical and thorough. Almost every private and government depository which promised pertinent information received careful attention of committee investigators. The investigators were competent, energetic, and well directed. One may assume that they overlooked little of consequence. Funds, to be sure, limited the inquiry and forced premature termination, but by February, 1936 the committee had completed investigation of files of the government and the largest companies. Further study would have altered committee conclusions slightly.

Did investigators examine untampered files?

Some companies, such as J. P. Morgan, gave investigators grudging co-operation, and Raushenbush believed Morgan had

removed incriminating material from its files. But the committee never made this charge publicly, and many years later
Nye told the author that the committee did not suspect firms
under investigation of any large effort to cull their records.
Only when the directors of United Aircraft Export appeared
did the committee suggest that it thought a company might
have tampered with its files. Unlike other firms selling armament in Latin America, United's files disclosed no evidence of
bribery. That investigators found many documents revealing
a seamy side of the munitions trade seemed to testify that most
files had gone unculled. Perhaps the companies failed to remove incriminating material because they did not understand
in advance how the committee would proceed. Perhaps the
task of culling was too large, considering the thin personnel
budgets of most companies during the depression. Perhaps the
swiftness with which investigators swooped down on the companies in the summer of 1934 caught them off guard. Whatever the reasons, the committee in most instances apparently
had access to complete records.[37]

Aside from the records of private corporations, the committee
was most interested in files of government agencies, especially
the Departments of State, War, Navy, and Commerce. Only
the State Department placed restrictions, and these did not impair the inquiry. The department was liberal in granting the
committee access to current documents. Current documents
of interest to the committee mostly were reports on the overseas munitions trade and were not particularly sensitive or
confidential. Nor were they very revealing; government de-
positories disclosed little about the inner workings of the munitions business. Only with regard to World War documents—
the committee's main interest at the State Department—did
the department exercise censorship, but this was minimal and
largely was to mollify the former Allied governments. The
Department did not prevent the committee from publishing anything having considerable bearing on the investigation.

Reverting to the question: did the committee exhaust the
sources? One can answer yes, insofar as was practicable. But

the limitation upon the investigation imposed by inaccessibility of foreign documents was important. Thus one cannot accept the Munitions Committee's findings on the arms trade or World War neutrality as final and definitive.*

* The committee, it will be noted, also studied war profits, but this was not much in the nature of an investigation. Rather, it was mostly a hearing of and evaluation of various opinions and plans on how to mobilize the economy and limit profits in wartime.

THE MUNITIONS
TRADE

T HROUGH the summer of 1934 Munitions Committee investigators gathered material, and the senators mapped plans for the first hearings. Senator Nye on July 24 circulated among committee members a confidential memorandum proposing that the committee begin by examining the munitions trade (instead of war profits or the shipbuilding industry). Hearings on that subject, he thought, would show "the extent to which private competition for these sales increases the armament burden of other countries and foments war." He also believed the arms trade would provide sensational disclosures. These, he hoped, would arouse popular interest to a pitch that would assure the committee of appropriations to complete its inquiry.[1]

As hearings approached, interest in the munitions trade and war profits continued at a high level. Millions of people felt certain that the committee was about to expose the rottenness of the munitions industry. There was occasional dissent. Irénée du Pont said the Third International was behind the attack on the private munitions industry. He thought the Communists hoped to weaken capitalist countries by undermining their capacity to produce war material. Nye hooted at du Pont's argument, and told a Chicago World's Fair audience on August 27, 1934 that profits from manufacture of munitions and the "greediness of the dominant industrialists and financiers in this field" were the main cause of war. "During four years of peacetime the du Ponts made only $4,000,000. During the four years of war they made $24,000,000 in profits. Naturally, du Pont sees red when he sees these profits attacked by international peace." [2]

While Nye was refuting du Pont, the committee staff was making final preparations for interrogating the merchants of death. And on September 4, 1934, in the white marble caucus room of the Senate Office Building, the committee conducted the first of ninety-three hearings.

September 4 in Washington was a typical late summer day, hot and humid. As proceedings began at 2:00 P.M. attention focused on the youthful Nye, sitting erect in the place reserved for the chairman, flanked by five older colleagues (Vandenberg was absent), Stephen Raushenbush, and Robert Wohlforth. Nye, immaculately groomed and slightly awed by his responsibility, spoke in deliberate, modulated tones as he opened the inquiry not with a harangue but a brief statement outlining procedure for the early hearings. Still, the atmosphere was charged as senatorial inquisitors peered across paper-littered tables at the titans of industry—in this instance President Henry R. Carse and Vice-Presidents Lawrence Y. Spear and Henry R. Sutphen of the Electric Boat Company, America's leading builder of submarines. Fifty journalists looked on. [3]

I

Did Messrs. Carse, Spear, and Sutphen represent an international ring of merchants of death?

When people pondered the munitions industry in the mid-thirties they often saw the image of an efficient, callous international combine. While appearing dignified and respectable, its members in their inner nature—so many Americans believed—had no moral scruple. Patriotic or humanitarian impulse did not fetter the ring. The ring compromised the integrity of public servants, undermined disarmament, ignored embargoes, lobbied for ever-increasing armament expenditures, plotted war scares, in wartime dealt with all belligerents regardless of moral or legal position. Greed inspired the combine. Its only interest was profit from sale of armament. George Seldes wrote in *Iron, Blood and Profits* that "the armament-makers . . . are organized into the greatest and most profitable secret international of our times—the international of bloodshed for profits." Engelbrecht and Hanighen in *Merchants of Death* described the growth of "international trusts" through "internationalization" of boards of control: "Thus the Great International, which political idealists and labor strategists have sought for so long, was actually taking shape in the armament industry." [4]

For many people, belief in the existence of a munitions ring was a first principle of the merchants-of-death credo. It was the article upon which their faith rested. Remove the idea of the ring and the munitions industry did not seem so formidable. Instead of a ubiquitous monster spreading tentacles over the world (as cartoonists of the 1930's sometimes portrayed it), the industry became a disorganized mass of large and small operators competing furiously for such markets as existed. In the latter form the industry's capacity for evil seemed less imposing.

Engelbrecht, Hanighen, Seldes, and others had written of the ring. They were the experts, and seemed so certain of its existence that few people dared to doubt it. The Munitions Committee accepted the popular verdict, and set out to find proof. It did not consider this task difficult.

Throughout the investigation the committee searched for correspondence and reports and memoranda linking American munitions producers with those of Europe and Asia. The search yielded little evidence. Several American and British firms had made agreements, but this did not prove existence of a munitions ring. Since 1913 Vickers-Armstrong had paid royalties on submarine patents of the Electric Boat Company. The committee might have had something here if the agreement had affected military secrets or national security, but it did not. Vickers and Electric Boat also had agreed not to compete in some parts of the world, while engaging elsewhere in "friendly competition"

A LARGE MOUTHFUL

with compensation for the loser. Then, after 1928, E. I. du Pont de Nemours and Imperial Chemical Industries had apportioned annual sales of products which both manufactured. The two corporations, moreover, agreed to share profits earned by their joint organization in some areas. In America, as Senator Clark pointed out, such arrangements were known in common parlance as agreements in restraint of trade, but they did not project an image of international merchants of death working in concert to stir up conflicts to sell munitions.[5]

Exploring these agreements, the committee had one moment when it thought it was on to something sinister. It suspected that the du Pont–ICI alliance had considered action counter to American efforts to bring peace to the Chaco by embargoing arms to Bolivia and Paraguay. Munitions makers—so the merchants-of-death thesis went—would ignore laws of their own governments should they interfere with profits. Evidence in this case was a letter from a du Pont–ICI agent in South America to Imperial Chemical, dated June 11, 1934, stating that since the American embargo prevented du Pont from quoting prices to the Chaco belligerents, ICI should solicit the business. Du Pont would share profits. Senator Vandenberg asked du Pont witnesses: "Does not that put your company in a very equivocal position, to be faithfully observing the embargo so far as its own shipments are concerned and yet immediately communicating with ICI so that it can achieve the same net results?" Lammot du Pont retorted that the agent had acted in his capacity as agent for ICI in making his suggestion to the British firm. He might have noted that the committee had no evidence that du Pont officials had made or approved such a suggestion or that du Pont had shared profits from ICI sales to the Chaco belligerents after imposition of the American embargo.[6]

A flurry of excitement resulted when the Munitions Committee disclosed early in the inquiry that the world's best-known salesman of armament had used his talents over a period of years in Spain in behalf of the Electric Boat Company and had received $2,000,000 for his services. The man was Sir Basil

Zaharoff, "the mystery man of Europe." Pacifists knew him as the premier salesman of the international munitions ring (Engelbrecht and Hanighen had discussed him in a chapter entitled "Supersalesman of Death"). Other people knew him as the richest man in Europe, a king-maker, the power behind several European and Middle-Eastern thrones. All one could say for certain was that Sir Basil made a striking appearance. He was then eighty-five years old, but photographs revealed a lean, erect frame, angular face, white hair, moustache and goatee. Apparently he had made a fortune dealing in armament, but the nature of his dealings was obscure, as were his parentage and citizenship. One pamphleteer had branded him the wickedest man alive. The author so designated Sir Basil because he "has given his life to an industry so vile and cruel, so fatal to the happiness and welfare of humankind, as to surpass the iniquity of the inquisition, the slave trade, and the pogroms of the Jews." [7]

In Sir Basil's arrangement with Electric Boat the committee thought it had evidence of the munitions ring. Many newspapers and magazines featured the old man's photograph and biographical sketches. But Sir Basil proved another *ignis fatuus*. The committee failed to establish that he had used devious or illegal tactics to further the interests of his American client. There was no evidence linking him with an international arms organization. Interest in Sir Basil subsided as quickly as it had risen.

The committee did not give up easily, and exhibited one other set of documents purporting to show a munitions ring. The documents amounted to little. Prior to the Geneva Arms Traffic Conference of 1925 an International Congress of Gun Makers had met at Paris and announced opposition to an arms trade agreement. It urged reliance upon existing laws and treaties to restrict munitions makers. After the delegates communicated their views to their governments they did nothing more. They did not dispatch lobbyists or propagandists to the Geneva conference. They did not, in brief, act as people in a munitions ring ought to act. [8]

The international munitions ring proved a myth. To people conscious of business organizations, labor organizations, and government organizations the idea of no munitions organization may have seemed illogical. Yet Senator Nye's committee, despite expectations, failed to find evidence that the world's munitions makers had combined to promote sale of armament by fair means or foul. Investigators had no access to European files, but according to the merchants-of-death thesis American firms, especially du Pont, were parts of the ring. Had the ring existed they would have found traces of it.

Peace leaders accepted the committee's failure with equanimity, continuing to believe in the ring, expecting the committee to find the evidence. The *Nation* hopefully pointed out in December, 1934 that exposure of the ring might require "many more months of effort and considerable additional expense." Pacifist expectations never materialized.[9]

Indictment of the munitions makers in the 1930's included criticism of their sales techniques. Their worst tactic, pacifists thought, was the war scare. Surely all salesmen tried to convince customers of the need for their merchandise. How better to "sell" munitions than to demonstrate war as imminent?

The Munitions Committee again set out to find the evidence, but again uncovered nothing of consequence. In only one instance did it find anything vaguely resembling a war scare. In 1932 William Stark Newell, president of the Bath Iron Works, a Maine shipbuilding firm specializing in destroyers, had sent a package of clippings and editorials regarding the possibility of war between the United States and Japan to Guy P. Gannett of the Portland (Maine) Publishing Company. Newell asked Gannett to dispatch the information in the clippings to each member of the Maine congressional delegation, adding: "I think it would be much more effective if you did it than if I did." Gannett honored Newell's request, and also instructed his editors to urge a stronger Navy. "You may be sure," Gannett wrote Newell, "that I will do everything possible to arouse our people to the necessity of building more destroyers." Perhaps this was a plot to promote a war scare, but it was hardly in the grand manner envisioned by peace leaders. The important point was that this was the extent of the committee's war scare findings.[10]

The committee was slightly more successful in demonstrating that a favorite technique of arms merchants was playing off one enemy or rival against another. According to the merchants-of-death thesis, munitions salesmen would sell in one country, and then stimulate sales by discreetly informing the country's adversary that it had better add to its munitions stocks. It all seemed plausible, and the committee expected to find proof. But after surveying the files of scores of corporations investigators discovered only one instance when a firm had employed this tactic. Evidence in this case was quotable, and must have brought some satisfaction to Nye and his supporters, but it was a single piece of evidence, hardly enough to build a case. The document was a letter of February 9, 1933, from Clarence W. Webster, at that time president of the Curtiss-Wright Export Corporation, to a company agent in Peru. The committee exhibited the letter after the company's current president, John S. Allard, denied that Curtiss-Wright Export had used this method to further sales. Webster had written: "For your confidential information you might diplomatically inform interested parties that your neighbor to the extreme north [Colombia] is still purchasing large quantities. Do not overlook such items as bombs, ammunition, machine guns equipment, etc." [11]

Another document disclosed a modification of the tactic of exploiting international rivalries, but added little to the pacifist argument. During the Chaco War, in December, 1933, an agent of Colt's Patent Fire Arms Company reported upon a conference with the Bolivian consul in which the agent quoted the price of one hundred Colt machine guns. "I also explained to him," he wrote, "that it would be advisable for his government to act quickly if they wanted to get these guns, intimating that a certain other government might get them if Bolivia did not act quickly." The other government was Bolivia's enemy, Paraguay.[12]

More fruitful were the committee's efforts to prove that munitions salesmen relied upon commissions to government functionaries and military officers to promote overseas sales. The committee showed that nearly every firm selling armament in foreign countries had employed this technique. When confronted with evidence witnesses usually retorted that in Latin America, the Balkans, the Middle East, and China they had found it impossible to transact business without first "greasing the palms" of key officials. The committee asked Clarence Webster, formerly of Curtiss-Wright Export, if it were not true that such payment was called a commission. Webster replied: "That would be a very polite word for it, Mr. Chairman."

"In fact," Nye asked, "it would be bribery would it not?"

"It would," answered Webster. "It is a rather harsh word, but it would be, strictly speaking." [13]

That their firm had secured business through bribery embarrassed officials of E. I. du Pont de Nemours and Company. Du Pont had given commissions in the Orient, particularly in China, to advance sale of smokeless powder. Du Pont officials insisted that this was not company policy, that the firm avoided bribery in other parts of the world. Felix du Pont told the committee that while bribery was "frowned upon in this country," it was "used in most of the countries of the Orient in all walks of commercial life." He said that "it is no different in the munitions business. . . . It is accepted; not talked about very much; but people in competition in those countries simply could not possibly carry on their trade if the customs of the country were not adhered to." [14]

Other witnesses whose firms had corrupted foreign officials offered the excuse that Europeans had initiated this method of securing business. Americans had to use similar means if they wished to compete. Some witnesses indicated that Americans were amateurs in comparison with Europeans in the art of palm greasing. Thus Europeans were doing a livelier trade in munitions.

The Munitions Committee missed no opportunity to show evidence of bribery, and evidence was abundant. Repeated disclosures, appearing in newspapers day after day, conveyed the impression that the committee was having no difficulty proving the case against munitions makers. They obscured its failure to provide adequate documentation for other parts of the merchants-of-death thesis.

Another sales tactic which vexed peace leaders was that of enlisting government support. The committee exhibited considerable evidence that the Departments of War, Navy, State, and Commerce had assisted armament firms in foreign sales. These disclosures inspired Nye to comment that "it makes one begin to wonder whether the Army and Navy are just organizations of salesmen for private industry, paid by the American Government." Still, such activity was improper only if the arms trade were immoral, if government and industry employed illegal or devious methods, or if the activity violated the interests of the United States. The committee majority, like most Americans at the time, considered the armament trade immoral and contrary to interests of the country, because it prompted tension and war. Government assistance to the arms trade, therefore, was improper. But the Federal government, in the absence of a statute or resolution defining the munitions trade as dangerous, illegal, and immoral, viewed the arms business as legitimate enterprise deserving the same protection and support accorded other types of commerce.[15]

Of different stripe were the activities of Commander James H. Strong, USN, whom the Navy had "lent" to the Colombian embassy in 1932 to advise on war equipment which arms companies were offering to Colombia, then on the verge of war with Peru. Strong became more than an adviser. Unknown to the Navy, and in violation of naval regulations, he pushed the merchandise of at least two American armament firms, and received commissions from them. Yet one instance did not establish a rule. Although it escaped the Munitions Committee, the important point again was that here was the only case of its kind discovered by investigators.[16]

The Munitions Committee looked closely at sales policy as

well as technique. Attention focused on the question: was it industry policy to sell to any belligerent, regardless of moral position?

Evidence showed that munitions companies seldom considered the morality of customers. They sold to anyone with cash or credit. Near the conclusion of the armistice between Peru and Colombia, President Alfred J. Miranda, Jr., of the American Armament Corporation had written that the truce would end in about sixty days and "a big time is expected by all." He went on to say that it was impossible to sell to both sides, since Colombia would refuse to buy from American Armament if it sold to Peru, and vice versa. Because of this unfortunate situation American Armament intended to sell to the Colombians "first and foremost, because they have money (which Peru has very little of) and, then, because of the fact that our connections in official circles in Colombia are just made to order." Most firms lacked American Armament's caution and sold to all belligerents, although they sometimes sought to prevent customers from learning that they were dealing with both sides. Clarence Webster wrote on February 10, 1933 that "if we are able to sell them [the Paraguayans] anything, we will have to work very carefully and quietly . . . as the Bolivian Government would naturally raise 'merry hell' if they believed that we were dealing with their enemies." [17]

Whenever the committee questioned the propriety of selling arms to opposing belligerents, witnesses retored that they had maintained honest neutrality; they had accorded equal treatment to all. They might have pointed out that their conduct had been consistent with traditional ideas of neutrality. In each conflict mentioned during hearings, moreover, the United States government had maintained strict neutrality. Should the munitions industry have gone farther than the government? Should it have designated one side the aggressor and halted shipments to it? Such a discriminatory policy might have embarrassed the United States. Munitions makers, on the other hand, defended the arms trade on the ground that countries which did not manufacture arms had a right to protect them-

selves against aggression; they had a right to purchase armament in foreign countries. But in real situations American
manufacturers, according to their testimony, felt obliged to
sell to aggressors and victims alike for the sake of neutrality
(and profits too, no doubt). This inspired Stephen Raushenbush to write: "It would seem . . . that the [munitions] business is one in which the absence of moral judgment is a primary
essential to success." [18]

Of larger importance was the nature of the munitions trade.
Was it ordinary business and therefore subject to ordinary
ethical and moral standards? Or was it in a different category
—like the narcotics trade? Did the nature of munitions impose
upon the industry more exacting standards of conduct?

Evidence showed that arms manufacturers and salesmen did
not consider their business extraordinary. Raushenbush expressed interest in the "evidencing by the witnesses of the
attitude that their business was like any other business, and
their tendency to forget that in the end some living men are
always on the receiving end of their bombs or cartridges or
powder." They seemed to consider trade in arms as innocuous
as trade in fountain pens or teddy bears. The mechanical director of American Armament described a forty-seven-milli-
meter mortar much as one might discuss the latest model car:
"The 47 mm gun carries just one size of shell weighing about 4.3
pounds. It contains about a third of a pound of high explosives,
a fairly deadly little item. . . . They are cheap to manufacture
and are very popular in the small countries in South America."
Committee members indicated that trade in these items, popular
though they were, should fall into the same category as trade
in narcotics or rattlesnakes.[19]

Surprisingly, in view of the comprehensiveness of its study,
the committee failed to pursue this point, a major tactical error.
The committee sought stringent control of the arms trade, and
the distinctive character of munitions was the strongest argument for such restriction. Concentrating on this point the committee might have built a formidable case. Instead it banked
its hopes upon proving all the particulars of the pacifist indict-

ment of the munitions trade. It diffused its energy. Failure to prove most of the particulars, moreover, weakened the committee's appeal for restriction. When control came (by a provision of the Neutrality Act of 1935) it fell far short of committee wishes.

I I

The munitions industry quaked at the thought of peace. It opposed disarmament and arms embargoes. It disregarded the law when it obstructed profits. These were other particulars in the indictment of the industry in the mid-thirties.

The William B. Shearer case continued to nourish the idea that armament producers opposed peace. It also sustained the view that whenever possible they undermined efforts to promote peace. To the American mind of the 1930's, burdened with problems of the depression and much taken by notions of economic determinism, it seemed natural that men would oppose programs that threatened their economic existence.[20]

The Munitions Committee found scattered evidence to bolster such views. The Peru agent of the Electric Boat Company in 1925 had sought appointment as a delegate to the Geneva Arms Traffic Conference, to do something "for the cause of submarines." A fortnight later President Carse of Electric Boat wrote that he saw no objection to the company's agent serving as a delegate to the conference. This seemed suspiciously similar to the Shearer business. But the committee got little mileage from the episode. There was no evidence that the agent had attended the conference. The affair, moreover, did not fit the merchants-of-death formula. Initiative to do something for submarines had come from a miserable Latin American arms agent, not a board of directors plotting behind closed mahogany doors. Electric Boat did not even pursue the matter. It only saw no objection.[21]

More damaging were some later documents from the files of Electric Boat. Vice-President Spear had lamented in 1928: "It is too bad that the pernicious activities of our State Department have put the brake on armament orders from Peru by forcing the resumption of formal diplomatic relations with Chile." Senator Clark asked Spear if he really had regarded department efforts to improve relations in South America as pernicious. Spear replied: "That is the word I used." Another document found Sir Charles Cravan of Vickers-Armstrong referring to the Geneva Disarmament Conference as a "fancy convention." Later, in January, 1933, Sir Charles wrote that a submarine order might be withdrawn "if Geneva or any other troublesome organization upsets the large submarine." President Carse of Electric Boat explained to the Munitions Committee that nobody wanted international action which would hurt his business.[22]

Disarmament presented a difficult problem for the munitions industry. The industry could criticize partial disarmament agreements, but there seemed little to say against the principle of disarmament. Reduction of arms would lower taxes and, people thought, make war less likely.

An arms embargo was another matter. On that question munitions makers had respectable arguments. The arguments were not new; the industry had stated them many times in periodicals and speeches and testimony before congressional committees. The argument had several parts: (1) Unless all arms-producing countries co-operated, embargoes to bring peace by denying belligerents the tools of war would not achieve their purpose. Such co-operation was impossible. In absence of universal agreement embargoes were unfair to American business and labor, since they would throw munitions orders to foreign competitors. (2) American defense depended upon the private munitions industry. Embargoes would weaken that defense by depriving munitions makers of the best means of practicing their art. (3) Countries which did not manufacture arms would not purchase American weapons in time of peace if they knew they could not purchase them in time of war. All foreign business would fall to Europeans.

The Munitions Committee showed that the industry had used these arguments to discredit arms embargo legislation on several occasions. In the case of the Burton Resolution of 1928 the industry was not alarmed, for it was confident the resolution could not pass in view of opposition from the Departments of War, Navy, State, and Commerce, as well as the American Legion and a host of congressmen. Still, du Pont communicated its opposition to the War Department, and as usually happened during these years, the department endorsed the industry's position in hearings before the House Military Affairs Committee. The industry was less confident when Congress considered embargo legislation in 1932 and 1933, although Aiken Simons of du Pont wrote in December, 1932: "Regarding the attempts of Mr. Hoover and the 'cooky pushers' in the State Department to effect embargoes on munitions sent out of the country, I do not believe there is the least occasion for alarm at the present." This time the industry worked directly with Congress, while again soliciting the support of the War, Navy, and Commerce departments. It helped plan opposition strategy with such men as Senator Hiram Bingham and Representative Edward W. Goss, Republicans of Connecticut, long-time friends of armament manufacturers. The Congress narrowly failed to adopt embargo measures in 1933. It seemed possible that the industry's influence was decisive.[23]

Lobbying against embargoes stirred the anger of peace leaders in the mid-thirties, but lobbying per se held a place in the indictment of the munitions industry. One could almost see the armament lobbyist clad in a $200 pin-striped suit, with jeweled stick-pin, bulging wallet, moving about the halls of Congress in daytime, entertaining lavishly at night.

The Munitions Committee knew better than to accept the pacifist description of the lobbyist, but endorsed the view that munitions lobbying was improper. The committee recognized that an individual had a right to present his views to Congress, but put munitions lobbying in a different category. It believed the aim of industry lobbying was increase of the world's armament stocks. Thus it lobbied against disarmament and arms embargoes and for increased military and naval appropriations. In the committee view, increased munitions stocks threatened peace in geometric ratio. Since peace hung in the balance, no one could justify munitions lobbying. The committee rejected the industry view, endorsed by the Hoover and Roosevelt administrations (and widely held in the 1960's), that only a powerful military establishment provided a deterrent to war. The committee believed that when considering such legislation congressmen should remain free from distractions of lobbyists.

Disregard for law also characterized munitions makers—so went the merchants-of-death thesis. Neither patriotism nor scruple could force them to observe law when it obstructed profits. They would export munitions to rebels, falsify shipping papers, sell arms to intermediaries for transhipment to countries where sale was illegal.

The Munitions Committee found some support for these views. Documents revealed that du Pont had violated Federal statutes by dealing indirectly with the so-called Moukden government in China. The arms embargo act of 1922 had prohibited American exporters from shipping munitions to any regime or individual in China, although the Secretary of State could make exceptions. After 1929 the Secretary sanctioned shipment to the Nanking government of Chiang Kai-shek upon receipt of a permit from the Secretary and approval of the Chinese legation. Shipment to other Chinese regimes, including the Moukden government, remained illegal. But evidence disclosed that a shipment of du Pont smokeless powder had gone to the Moukden regime via the Netherlands. K. K. V. Casey, director of sales for du Pont's smokeless powder department, admitted (after documents had proved it) that the company had known the shipment's destination. Du Pont, moreover, had not consulted the State Department, although the previous day Casey testified that the company would never sanction shipment of munitions to one country for transhipment to another without State Department approval.[24]

In only one instance did the committee find evidence that an arms exporter had disguised munitions by falsifying shipping papers and mislabeling containers. In a letter of September 18, 1933 the Lake Erie Chemical Company had instructed the Barr

Shipping Corporation to make out shipping papers for a tear gas shipment as "various merchandise." Lake Erie added that "the boxes are stenciled for 'Klein & Company, Ltd., Santiago, Chile,' but you should remove the tear gas labels which appear on the shipment before reshipping." Commenting on this and related documents, F. V. Huber, agent for Lake Erie, said of the munitions trade: "This is a shady business all the way through." [25]

Little evidence appeared to indicate that Americans had smuggled arms to rebels. Known in the pacifist lexicon as "gun running," such activity violated the law of the United States as well as that of countries which received shipments. Federal statutes forbade American nationals to aid any person or group endeavoring to make trouble in any country considered friendly to the United States. Committee investigators found only one bona fide case of gun running, but it was the most bizarre incident disclosed during the inquiry. It involved sale of war materials, most of them surplus and obsolete, to revolutionaries during Brazil's Sao Paulo revolt in 1932. The case had minor import, but it had elements of suspense, intrigue, and corruption which would delight or appall any believer in the merchants-of-death thesis.

A. S. Byington and Company of New York, a firm of engineers, contractors, and exporters, had done extensive business in Brazil, dealing in electrical apparatus, radios, refrigeration, and office supplies. After eruption of the Sao Paulo revolt in 1932 the company's Brazilian business came to a standstill, whereupon A. S. Byington, Jr., began to help the Sao Paulo rebels purchase arms in the United States. He hoped the rebels would gain control of the country and restore order, which would enable the Byington company to resume normal operations.

Byington remained in Brazil, but deposited money in the New York bank account of William P. Brown, a modestly paid purchasing agent for the Byington firm. A mysterious Brazilian, known as Dr. Ferreira, and Leigh Wade, a former U.S. Army Air Corps flier of some renown, moved about the United States, ordered munitions, and presented the bills to Brown. Each day Byington, using the name Jackson, discussed purchasing activities with Brown via transoceanic telephone. Brown told the Munitions Committee that he had no idea of the source of the money. He said he ordinarily had carried cash for payments on his person, and on one occasion had gone to lunch with $40,000 in his pockets. Of this experience he said, piquantly, that "if somebody had said 'Boo' to me around those times I would have dropped dead."

Naturally the Byington group did not disclose the destination of its purchases. The group bought aircraft equipment from Curtiss-Wright, allegedly for the government of Chile. Brown told the committee he was sure Curtiss-Wright officials had known the destination, but declined to interfere. In another instance Ferreira and Wade posed as representatives of the federal government of Brazil (which the rebels were trying to overthrow), and negotiated purchase of ten planes from the Consolidated Aircraft Corporation. The alert Brazilian ambassador protested that his government had authorized no such purchase, whereupon Consolidated canceled the order.

The Byington–Sao Paulo case involved graft as well as "gun running." The ten planes from Consolidated had cost altogether $53,000, yet Brown told the committee he had received a bill from Ferreira and Wade for $137,000 and had given them that amount. Somebody apparently would have netted about $84,000 if Consolidated had not canceled the contract. Documents indicated that Brazilian revolutionaries had paid the Byington group $50,000 for a naval patrol boat purchased from the Canadian Government for $18,000. The committee's main interest in the Byington case, however, was gun running, not profiteering at rebel expense.[26]

Of larger importance was disclosure that existing laws of the United States were inadequate to prevent illegal munitions shipments. Before hearings began Robert Wohlforth reported to Raushenbush that the Chaco embargo "is a joke. . . . If you want to get anything out—just ship it, they all are doing it." Ernest A. Tupper, Chief of the Division of Foreign Trade Statistics of the Bureau of Foreign and Domestic Commerce, did not repudiate Wohlforth's charge. He told the committee that it was impossible to prevent an American manufacturer from falsely labeling his cargo and changing its announced destination after the ship was at sea. Stephen W. Hamilton, deputy collector of customs of the port of New York, complemented Tupper's testimony by explaining that customs inspectors depended upon steamship companies for notice of shipments, even those which an embargo law might prohibit. He admitted that shippers often submitted export declarations to the collector after the vessel had sailed. Nye asked Hamilton if the collector assumed that a crate labeled machinery had no relation to arms. Hamilton replied: "Absolutely, and we do not do anything about it." [27]

Merchants of death, pacifists thought, had no more respect for treaties than for national statutes, and investigators found documents which in the committee's view proved that American companies had ignored the Treaty Restoring Friendly Relations with Germany by exporting articles which the Germans intended for military use. Each instance involved aircraft equipment, mostly engines. Witnesses insisted that engines sold to Germany had been for commercial aircraft, although the German government had shown interest largely in high-powered air-cooled motors. The royal commission which investigated the British munitions industry at this time found that British firms also had exported similar engines to Germany. A British air expert, Ronald MacKinnon Wood, told the commission that Germany clearly intended such engines for military use. Supercharged engines of the type Germany was purchasing, he said, were for flying at exceptionally high altitudes, a characteristic not required for commercial aircraft. But no one in England or the United States could prove that the engines were for military aircraft, so neither government halted shipments on the ground of treaty violation.[28]

The German ambassador seconded the aircraft industry's version of the sales, and hoped the State Department would dissuade the Munitions Committee from pursuing this line of inquiry. Secretary Hull replied that he had said to the committee all he felt disposed to say on the matter of publishing materials which might offend foreign governments. The ambassador replied that he had hoped for something more than silence from Hull.[29]

German apprehensions had no foundation. The committee found no clear-cut violation of the treaty with Germany, or of any other treaty for that matter. With this failure another chunk of the merchants-of-death thesis melted away.

III

There was only one sure way to stop the merchants of death, pacifists thought. Nationalize the munitions industry. Under nationalization only government arsenals could manufacture and distribute military arms and ammunition; only the Navy's yards could construct warships. There would be no bribing of foreign officials to advance munitions sales, no economic bonanzas from the misfortunes of others, no munitions industry lobbying for large military establishment. Demise of the munitions lobby would result in a small army and navy with savings to the taxpayer. There would be a dramatic decrease in the likelihood of war (since pacifist rationale had it that when arsenals were bulging the demon of war lurked not far away).*

Nationalization would yield other good results, supporters thought. Government arsenals and shipyards, the argument went, could produce peacetime requirements of the armed forces more efficiently and economically. In government enterprise there were no $100,000-a-year executives, no expensive lobbies, no concern over dividend payments.

Private industrialists scoffed at the suggestion that nationalization was efficient or desirable. Irénée du Pont told the Muni-

---

* Apparently nationalization also would mean no sale of munitions to belligerents, since students of international law contended that a neutral government could not sell contraband to countries at war. Thus nationalization would achieve the same end as the isolationist arms embargo laws of 1935–37. But, surprisingly, hardly anyone mentioned this effect, and advocates of collective security—such as Senator Pope—urged government ownership of the munitions industry.

tions Committee that betrayal of military secrets would prove less perilous to American security than abolition of the private manufacture of armament. Government operation could be neither as efficient nor as elastic as private operation, he thought, and these qualities were mandatory if industry was to meet the exigencies of war. Referring to the World War, du Pont said: "The French made their own powder and relied on their own powder factory, and had to come to us to buy hundreds of millions of pounds. The Germans relied on their industrial people and made enough not only for their war purposes, but for Austria. That was done by private concerns. If we had not shipped powder to France and England, the possibilities are that Germany would have won the war, and we would have been taken next and been a German colony." [30]

To the surprise of some people the Veterans of Foreign War opposed nationalization. Although it favored conscription of labor and capital in wartime, the VFW advocated government supervision and regulation, not ownership, of the munitions industry in time of peace. Senator Bone responded to the VFW position by declaring: "We might as well try to regulate a Bengal tiger and make a nice private kitty out of it as to regulate the munitions manufacturers. Regulation is a sham. . . . Some of your boys were butchered in the war, and thousands of men made multimillionaires overnight, and I am surprised that you have not yet come to the point where you are willing to jump on this thing like a savage wolf and take the last degree of profit from those fellows. I hope your organization gets to the point where they do not blink at this thing. Why should we blink at socialization, when we made so many millionaires out of production during the war? They did not blink at that, and you should not blink at taking the last cent of profit from them." [31]

Nationalization had never enjoyed much popularity in the executive branch, especially in the War and Navy Departments, but leaders of the peace movement hoped the more liberal New Dealers, moved by the Nye revelations, might show interest. They hoped vainly. President Roosevelt had no more sympathy for nationalization than did Coolidge or Hoover. Nationalization would force private manufacturers to release workers and dismantle plants and machinery producing military arms. The administration thought this would reduce the capacity of industry to produce them in wartime.

There was, moreover, the argument that in event of nationalization manufacturers would lose the art of making military armament. Such a loss might prove disastrous. Private manufacturers retained the know-how by producing munitions in time of peace for the United States and foreign governments. So pressing was the need, the government thought, for keeping commercial manufacturers in practice during peace that when military stocks overflowed the War Department placed so-called educational orders with private companies. Nationalization would restrict sale of American munitions overseas. Thus the country would lose another means of perpetuating the art of producing military arms. As expressed in a memorandum by Bernard M. Baruch, sent by the State Department to Roosevelt in February, 1935 and returned without comment, munitions were not required for peace, so

the art of making them is likely to lapse and cannot be improvised in War. So long as War remains a possibility there is thus presented a major problem of national defense. The only expedient yet used is for the Governments of industrial countries at least not to discourage (and I fear almost universally to encourage) the manufacture of lethal weapons *for exportation* to belligerent countries actively preparing for War, but which have an insufficient munitions industry or none at all. Without specific evidence I still conjecture that the Nye investigation will disclose that our Government has not operated on a different policy. To put it bluntly, this is a method of providing a laboratory to test killing implements and a nucleus for a War-time munitions industry by maintaining an export market for instruments of death. Of course, it is absolutely indefensible and we could not be put in a position of excusing it.

When in 1928 Secretary of War Dwight F. Davis had invoked similar logic in a hearing, Representative Morton D. Hull (Rep.)

of Illinois had asked whether it might not become necessary, according to such reasoning, to make trouble in the world to keep American munitions makers in practice.[32] The Navy had a more subtle reason, evidence indicated, for encouraging American firms to sell munitions to a particular country—Japan. Following a conference with Captain William Baggaley of the Office of Naval Intelligence, du Pont's Washington representative, Aiken Simons, wrote in May, 1932 that the Navy Department considered it desirable for Americans to sell both munitions and munitions-producing machinery to the Japanese. The Navy reasoned that the Japanese would purchase what they wanted in any case, from Europeans if not from Americans. Naval Intelligence could better keep abreast of the nature and quantity of their purchases if the Japanese acquired their munitions in the United States.[33]

A memorandum, prepared for Secretary Hull by the Division of Western European Affairs of the State Department and sent to Roosevelt, summarized the administration view on government ownership of the munitions industry. Asserting that nationalization was not feasible at the time, the memorandum contended that government ownership would dislocate the country's economic structure, curtail or terminate the business of several hundred companies, and put the government in business to an extent unknown in the world except in the Soviet Union. Nationalization would substitute large government arsenals employing thousands of men for America's present system, which the memorandum alleged could produce according to demand. Under government ownership there would be a vested interest in continuous manufacture on a scale incommensurate with the country's needs. Countries which did not produce munitions, accustomed to purchasing arms in the United States, would have to purchase from the United States government (which, the memorandum said, would involve complications unnecessary to elaborate), make purchases in other countries, or establish factories and arsenals of their own. Government monopoly in the United States, then, would increase the arms manufactured in the world.[34]

Unity did not prevail within the Roosevelt household on the question of nationalization. Mrs. Franklin D. Roosevelt gave vocal support to the movement to nationalize the munitions industry. Speaking on "The Way to Peace" at Chicago in November, 1935, she said that "perhaps the first and most practical step that the nations of the world could take would be to buy out the munitions makers and make their business of war supplies a government business only. Then we might get somewhere on disarmament conferences, but until then we are very unlikely to accomplish anything. It would really be a good investment. Costly it might be at first, but in the end the taxpayers have to pay the bill in any case, and the bill might come down under government ownership." She warned that as long as there was chance for personal gain in the business of war supplies, "somehow or other, we will be buying them whether we make war or whether we stay at peace." [35]

Whenever nationalization became a subject of debate, one question was sure to arise: who could produce war equipment more economically, private enterprise or the government? The Munitions Committee explored this question, and while it reached no conclusion it obtained interesting evidence. Particularly arresting was an account showing the comparative cost of cartridges manufactured at the government's Frankford Arsenal Plant near Philadelphia and the plants of the Remington Arms Company, the Western Cartridge Company, the Peters Company, and the Winchester Repeating Arms Company. Prepared by the companies, the report supported arguments for government ownership!

The Chief of Ordnance of the War Department in 1928 had advised commercial manufacturers that their prices were too high, that the Army would accept no more bids on existing price schedules. Whereupon a committee representing the companies secured cost data from the four largest commercial producers of ammunition and the government plant at Frankford. Figures indicated that manufacture in the government plant cost one-third less per thousand cartridges. Witnesses from private industry challenged the conclusion that government manufacture was more economical. K. K. V. Casey of du Pont, the parent company of Remington, argued that if private companies had an equal volume of business they could manufacture cartridges at lower cost than Frankford Arsenal. Pierre S. du Pont said simply that private enterprise always was more efficient than government enterprise, a statement which prompted Senator Vandenberg to remark: "I have heretofore agreed with the general statement that you now make. That is why I am so challenged by the presentation of a formal survey by the best minds in a given industry, which leads to a directly contrary conclusion." [36]

Evidence from Navy Department files also heartened supporters of government ownership. Documents disclosed that the naval program of 1927 had provided for construction of six almost identical cruisers. Navy yards built two of the ships, the *Louisville* and the *Chicago,* for $9,331,337 and $9,635,747 respectively. Commercial builders charged the government $11,543,432 for the *Chester,* $11,689,975 for the *Northampton,* $11,596,146 for the *Houston,* and $11,569,831 for the *Augusta.* Witnesses again challenged the conclusion that such figures proved government efficiency. President Joseph W. Powell of United Dry Docks reiterated Pierre du Pont's view: "I do not think the Government can do anything without the impetus of the profit motive as well as a private company." This was too much for Senator Bone, who retorted: "It so happens that for 40 years, ever since I was a small boy, I have seen that program working with the power organizations. And my city today owns the finest power company there is, free of debt and amortized, and giving the people cheap power. I recall politicians coming in and saying 'It cannot be done,' and 'You have a white elephant and will sell it in a few years.' That plant has made so much money that they did not know what to do with it and have had to keep reducing rates." [37]

Shipbuilders had better arguments than that forwarded by Powell. They showed that ships built in navy yards had fewer items of fixed expense than commercially built vessels. Navy yards paid no taxes, an item that private yards had to figure into the cost of their ships. Private yards had to allow for penalties which the government would impose if the yards failed to deliver on schedule, if ships failed to meet speed requirements, or if they exceeded maximum tonnage or fuel consumption prescribed in contracts. Navy yards were subject to no such penalties.[38]

In the Munitions Committee's final report only four of the seven members recommended nationalization. The remaining three wanted nothing more than regulation. The majority (Nye, Clark, Bone, Pope) scoffed at control, contending that the industry would find means of evading regulation. As Nye put it in a speech: "The will of the munitions industry for profit has so totally blinded it to ordinary decency, and our committee's record reveals so clearly that the industry breeds hate, fear, and suspicion among peoples and nations to the end that there may be more profit for it, that no mere control would be sufficient." The majority said in the report that munitions magnates would not allow patriotism to interfere with duty to stockholders. Impressed by the Frankford Arsenal study and data on the 1927 cruiser program, the majority insisted that the War and Navy Departments could produce armament successfully.[39]

Although the minority (George, Vandenberg, Barbour) supported all other recommendations of the committee, it doubted the wisdom of nationalization. In stating its position, it used arguments almost identical to those of the Roosevelt administration.[40]

What conclusions did popular opinion reach regarding nationalization?

Although in their search for peace Americans of the mid-thirties accepted many pacifist ideas, few of them had interest in government ownership of the arms industry. Perhaps they sensed that nationalization would not prove the panacea predicted by the peace movement. Then unlike pacifists they could not dismiss the argument that nationalization would impair the country's military capacity. And some people disapproved of nationalization because it smacked of socialism.

This did not imply lack of support for government control of the arms trade. Polls indicated, indeed, that Americans wanted some form of regulation. Many munitions makers endorsed regulation patterned after the weak Geneva Arms Traffic Convention of 1925. A "peace poll" of the nation's college students, published in 1935, showed 91 per cent (101,702 of 111,732) for government control of the munitions industry. Early in 1936 the Council for Social Action of the Congregational and Christian Churches of America announced a poll of 200,000 Americans "from all walks of life." Of those registering an opinion, 144,030 favored government control of the arms trade, 16,847 opposed.[41]

The Munitions Committee made a mighty effort to prove that arms makers were merchants of death. Including time investigators spent in careful study of files of corporations and government departments, the committee devoted thousands of man-hours to this part of its inquiry. It found bits of evidence suggesting that munitions makers at one time or another had done about everything the committee suspected them of doing. But evidence was thin; seldom could it support general conclusions. It failed to establish existence of an international munitions conspiracy. It failed to prove that the arms industry instigated war scares, or as ordinary practice stimulated armament races by selling alternately to opposing countries. It failed to prove that munitions makers lacked patriotism or conscience. Evidence showed that the overseas munitions trade depended to an astonishing extent upon bribery, but this had slight bearing on whether the industry menaced peace. Evidence disclosed that the industry had opposed arms embargoes, but so had many other thoughtful Americans—and for sound reasons. Finally, the committee failed to prove the wisdom of nationalizing the munitions industry.

This part of the munitions inquiry attracted worldwide attention, and provided several quotable documents. Most heralded perhaps were two letters by Frank S. Jonas, an agent of the Remington Arms Company. Jonas had written in December, 1933: "The Paraguay and Bolivia fracas appears to be coming to a termination, so business from that end is probably finished.

We certainly are in one hell of a business, where a fellow has to wish for trouble so as to make a living, the only consolation being, however, that if we don't get the business someone else will. It would be a terrible state of affairs if my conscience started to bother me now." On a happier occasion (for Jonas) he had written: "The unsettled conditions in South America has [*sic*] been a great thing for me, as I sold a large order for bombs to Brazil and also a fair cartridge order. I also sold very large bomb orders for Colombia, Peru, Ecuador, Bolivia, and now have made up all my losses, and I am back on my feet. It is an ill wind that does not blow someone some good." The first of these letters inspired Helmuth Engelbrecht to write another book. He entitled it *One Hell of a Business.*[42]

The Jonas letters and a few kindred documents—the fruit of a search which had taken investigators through tons of letters and reports and memoranda—had powerful effect. They won support for the munitions investigation and assured its continuation beyond 1934. Published and republished, they obscured the committee's failure to find adequate documentation for the merchants-of-death thesis.

There were other reasons why most Americans in 1934–36 did not see the committee's failures. They had believed before the Nye investigation began that munitions makers were merchants of death. Scattered evidence supporting most particulars of the indictment bolstered such belief. There also was the committee's procedure during hearings. The committee did not take a particular article of its thesis and exhibit all documents providing support. If it had moved in this way the paucity of evidence would have become apparent. Instead, the committee—for sound practical reasons—interrogated one company or individual at a time. It exhibited all interesting documents pertaining to that company or individual. Documents usually showed that one company had done one thing, another company something else. Only a most perceptive person under such circumstances would note that on few occasions (bribery excepted) did abuses, real and alleged, reappear.

THE SHIPBUILDERS

S ENATOR Nye's committee gave separate treatment to the shipbuilding industry, for as a producer of armament that industry had peculiar characteristics. Gun and ammunition makers depended upon overseas markets for much of their prosperity. Shipbuilders constructed most of their vessels for the United States government. Such firms as the New York Shipbuilding Company had built a few vessels for foreign governments—Japan, China, Greece, and Argentina. But the foreign market for warships was small.[1]

Hence shipbuilders were not open to some of the accusations brought generally against the munitions trade. They did not bribe foreign functionaries to advance sale of warships. Nor did they increase tension among small countries.

But shipbuilders had dispatched William B. Shearer to Geneva in 1927 to forestall agreement between the United States, Great Britain, and Japan on limiting tonnage in medium-sized naval vessels. And pacifists accused shipbuilders, as they accused all armament makers, of intimate relations with departments of the Federal government and of spending money to influence Congress. The National Council for Prevention of War said that "our shipbuilders are probably our most aggressive and sinister propagandists for a policy of competitive naval building even if it brings war. They have for years been ruthless in pursuit of profits."[2]

More perceptive critics suspected shipbuilders of abuses which had slight bearing on war or peace. Most important was that the "big three" of the industry—the New York Shipbuilding Company, the Bethlehem Shipbuilding Company, and the Newport News Shipbuilding and Dry Dock Company—had come to dominate the industry. Several evils supposedly had resulted from this situation: the big three had tried to freeze out small rivals, organized elaborate lobbies, and reached agreements before submitting bids for commercial and government contracts.

I

Study of collusive bidding proved one of the munitions inquiry's more perplexing phases. From files of shipbuilding companies investigators gathered documents indicating collusion, and testimony supported this conclusion. But most of the evidence was weak, and shipbuilders countered with strong testimony in their own defense.

That the big three had been on good terms for many years and worked together on several projects lent strength to the charge of collusion. The three shipbuilding companies had conferred on business and engineering trends in the industry. They had maintained a lobby to secure passage of the Jones-White Merchant Marine Act of 1928. They had hired Shearer to "observe" the Geneva Conference. They had organized the Marine Engineering Corporation to design ships for all three firms. In view of these examples of co-operation, the Munitions Committee did not consider it improbable that the big three had sought to eliminate competition through collusive bidding. Committee liberals thought the industry would have acted out of character had it avoided collusion. Had not all big business traditionally tried to restrain competition?

Much evidence indicating collusive bidding was circumstantial. In 1928–30 the Bethlehem Shipbuilding Company had received contracts totaling $33,000,000 for Merchant Marine construction; Newport News Ship, $33,000,000; New York Ship,

$31,700,000. The committee believed that these figures indicated the big three had conspired to divide the business. President Homer L. Ferguson of Newport News explained, however, that "we had three first-class shipyards, and we were all busy. It is perfectly natural, if there is a sufficient volume of work to keep them all going, it will be distributed in a natural process." [3]

Undeterred, the Munitions Committee exhibited other circumstantial evidence, this time on big-three bidding for cruiser contracts in 1927–29. Again the business divided three ways. New York Ship and Bethlehem Ship each received a cruiser in 1927 and another in 1929. Newport News Ship received two cruisers in 1927.

There also was the matter of 1929 cost estimates vis-à-vis those of 1927. The committee showed that Newport News Ship, after realizing a return of 34 per cent on its 1927 cruisers, raised its 1929 estimate nearly a half million dollars. At the same time New York Ship lowered its 1929 estimate $777,000. Bethlehem's estimates for 1927 and 1929 were about the same. Why this fluctuation in the estimates of the New York and Newport News firms? The senators suspected that the two companies had rigged their estimates to justify bids designed to assure equal distribution and lucrative profits. Newport News bids for the 1929 cruisers (almost identical to those built in 1927), moreover, were $488,000 higher per cruiser. New York Ship, despite a lower 1929 cost estimate, raised its 1929 bid $88,000 from 1927. Bethlehem Ship, despite identical estimates, raised its 1929 bid $78,000. Thus Newport News, although earning an excellent profit from its 1927 contracts, bid itself out of business in 1929. New York and Bethlehem, increasing their 1929 bids, each received a cruiser. American taxpayers paid more for their 1929 cruisers than for those of 1927, although construction costs were no higher, perhaps lower. The Munitions Committee suspected that Bethlehem and New York had known in advance that Newport News would bid high. They could increase their 1929 bids, therefore, and still receive contracts. The committee also suspected that Newport News had drafted its high estimate in 1929 as a ruse to justify its high bid. [4]

Still, the committee could not summarily dismiss the shipbuilders' arguments. The best explanation of why estimates could be lower and bids higher on identical ships came from officials of Newport News Ship. They said that shipbuilders did not include anticipated overhead in estimates, but figured it in bids. Thus the estimated cost of labor and materials for a job in 1931 had been less than for a similar one in 1929, but because anticipated overhead was greater in 1931 the bid had been higher, despite the lower estimate.[5]

There were instances of shipbuilding firms submitting unsuccessful bids which appeared too high in comparison with cost estimates. Such instances aroused committee suspicion. The senators believed the shipbuilders had intended the disproportionately high bids to make bidding appear honest. But as usual, the shipbuilders had an explanation. They said that on occasion, because of abundance of work or expense of installing equipment for a job, they declined to submit competitive bids ("fighting bids" in their language) for contracts. Yet they submitted noncompetitive bids because they wished to be represented in all bidding. They considered it poor business to submit no bid at all.

Damaging testimony against the shipbuilders came from George B. Yard, former personnel manager and assistant to President Clinton L. Bardo of the New York Shipbuilding Company. Yard told the committee that Bardo often had consulted officials of Bethlehem Ship and Newport News Ship and that they had discussed bidding. "I think it was pretty generally understood among themselves as to what they each preferred to receive and I think there is not very much doubt that they tried to come to some such conclusion." Yard said that before bidding for the Navy's 1933 construction program Bardo, Samuel W. Wakeman of Bethlehem, and Homer Ferguson of Newport News had kept in touch. "It was pretty common knowledge around what each yard was going to get, and it turned out that that was what they did get, almost 100 percent."[6]

The Navy's building program of 1933 provided the most important charge of collusive bidding. The program was unique in that it had a dual purpose—defense and recovery. It aimed to strengthen the Navy, silencing preparedness groups which were demanding that the Navy build to the Treaty of London of 1930. Then the program aimed to combat the Depression by stimulating employment in the shipbuilding industry.

The Roosevelt administration was as interested in the relief-recovery side of the program as the defense aspect. Because the program was an antidote to the Depression, the administration considered it a public works project. The Public Works Administration appropriated $238,000,000 for its completion. Although the PWA exercised no control over the money once it went to the Navy Department, the administration intended that the Navy expend these funds in accordance with the spirit of the PWA. It determined that the work be distributed widely. It did not intend that a few shipbuilding firms win most of the contracts, even though a few might submit the lowest bids. If normal bidding did not bring proper distribution the administration planned to allocate contracts. But as matters turned out, the lowest bidders secured all twenty-one of the vessels. Apparently the natural distribution satisfied the government.

The administration had intended to keep the allocation plan secret. Presumably shipbuilders would bid in the normal manner and the government would award contracts to the lowest bidders. Such procedure, the administration hoped, would bring competitive bidding. This would result in more national defense for the money expended. It saw that knowledge of the allocation plan would move shipbuilders to submit inordinate bids.

Evidence proved, however, that the shipbuilders had known the government's intention to allocate contracts if bidding failed to bring satisfactory results. When the Navy opened the bids in July, 1933 it found them considerably higher than anticipated. The Bethlehem Shipbuilding Company bid $11,720,000 for an eight-inch gun cruiser, although seven months earlier, in December, 1932, the firm had bid $8,196,000 for an almost identical vessel. The Navy was displeased, and rumor circulated that it might reject all bids and construct the ships in navy yards. Laurence W. Wilder, formerly of the New York Shipbuilding

Company and in 1933 head of Gulf Industries, suggested to the Munitions Committee that for political reasons the administration had coerced the Navy to accept the bids as submitted. According to Wilder, a few days after the bids were opened Rear Admiral Emory S. Land, chief of the Navy's Bureau of Construction and Repair, together with two other admirals, conferred with the President at Hyde Park. A short time later the Navy made the awards on the basis of existing bids. Navy officials, as expected, denied that the administration had forced them to accept high bids against their wishes.[7]

The problem remained: why had the shipbuilders submitted what appeared to be higher bids than competition ordinarily would permit? Did each builder, figuring that allocation would assure him a portion of the work, submit high bids on his own initiative? Or did the shipbuilders, led by the big three, agree as to which companies should receive particular contracts and bid accordingly?

John P. Frey, president of the Metal Trades Department of the American Federation of Labor, told the Munitions Committee that he was sure there had been collusion among the shipbuilders before the 1933 bidding. He supported his view with interesting testimony. He said that in July, 1933, about ten days before the Navy opened bids, Laurence Wilder had boasted that he could name the lowest bidders on all contracts. Wilder wrote this information on a sheet of paper, sealed it in an envelope, and gave it to Frey, who placed it in his desk. Three days before bids were opened Frey visited the office of General Hugh S. Johnson, director of the National Recovery Administration. He testified that he told Johnson he was certain the shipbuilders had engaged in collusive bidding. He offered to unseal Wilder's envelope and show the contents, but Johnson declined the offer. Frey quoted him as saying: "That is too hot. I am not going to get mixed up in anything of that kind. I have got troubles enough of my own." The day after the Navy opened the bids newspapers published the results, and Frey was anxious to compare them with Wilder's prediction. He summoned W. A. Calvin, secretary and treasurer of his organization. "We opened the envelope,"

Frey told the committee, "and we checked them off and Mr. Wilder was accurate in every instance. He had named the lowest bidders." Calvin corroborated Frey's testimony.[8]

Intrigued, the senators were eager to probe this prediction business when the oracle himself, Laurence Wilder, appeared in the committee witness chair. Where had he obtained his information? Wilder told the committee that while it had been generally known within the industry which company would be low bidder on each ship, his information had come from Thomas M. Cornbrooks, also of Gulf Industries. Wilder did not know the source of Cornbrooks's information, but suggested it might have come from Cornbrooks's brother Ernest, operating vice-president of one of the big three, the New York Shipbuilding Company.[9]

Collusion was not something Wilder and Frey had conjured for the committee. Evidence showed that soon after the opening of bids Wilder had written Senator Park Trammell (Dem.) of Florida, chairman of the Committee on Naval Affairs, protesting the awards on the ground that they had resulted from rigged bidding. Trammell forwarded Wilder's protest to President Roosevelt and Secretary of the Navy Claude A. Swanson. Swanson replied that analysis of the bids failed to justify Wilder's charges and the government planned no action.[10]

Investigators found a letter in the files of the New York Shipbuilding Company which gave support to the view that shipbuilders had engaged in collusive bidding in 1933. The letter indicated, moreover, that officials of the Navy Department had suggested they reach agreement before bidding. Such procedure would assure wide distribution of contracts and preclude the problem of allocating work. The letter, dated June 22, 1933, was from Clinton L. Bardo, New York Ship's president, to William Flook, former chairman of the company's board of directors. Describing conversations with Navy representatives, Bardo wrote: "There was . . . expressed to us the desire that the builders themselves should get together and agree as far as we could upon what each would bid and then bid on nothing else." He then outlined the work which, according to plan, each of the big three would receive. Newport News would get contracts totaling $30,000,000; New York and Bethlehem each would receive $28,000,000. When the Munitions Committee asked if the letter could mean anything other than that the Navy had urged collusion, Flook replied: "Of course it could not." To nobody's surprise the Navy Department denied the implications of Bardo's letter, and Bardo, in a bit of doubletalk, supported the Navy's denial while insisting upon the accuracy of the letter.[11]

If Navy officers had encouraged collusive bidding for the 1933 program, they evidently had not seen the same advantages in collusion as the private shipbuilders. The Navy wanted contracts distributed throughout the industry, and assuming the accuracy of Bardo's letter, some Navy officials believed the shipbuilders could assure such distribution with greater dispatch by reaching agreement before submitting bids. This would prevent the haggling which would result from allocating work in a manner not consistent with bids. It seems incredible that Navy officials, if they encouraged collusion, failed to anticipate the probable consequences. Yet fail they apparently did, since according to Wilder's testimony the Navy was surprised and displeased by the high bids. Evidence failed to suggest a conspiracy between the Navy and the industry, as the committee suspected. Naval officers simply had acted imprudently.

During early hearings on shipbuilding witnesses from the industry denied collusion in any form in 1933. Samuel Wakeman of Bethlehem Ship told the committee that wide distribution of contracts had resulted because some yards had inherent advantages in bidding for certain types of ships. These "natural advantages" were apparent, he said. In 1933 Newport News Ship was constructing the aircraft carrier *Ranger*. Carrier construction required techniques with which only Newport News was familiar, he said. The Navy, moreover, had provided bidders with no contract plans and specifications for this type of ship. Newport News therefore had an important advantage in bidding for the carrier contract in 1933. For similar reasons, Wakeman said, New York Ship had an advantage in bidding for light cruisers, and Bethlehem for heavy cruisers. The natural advantage argument sounded plausible when advanced by Wakeman, but in the end the committee rejected it. The committee showed that prior to bidding on the *Ranger* Bethlehem Ship had constructed the carrier *Lexington* and New York Ship had built the carrier *Saratoga*. Newport News was without experience in carrier construction, but submitted the lowest bid, despite the presumed natural advantages of Bethlehem and New York. Inexperience notwithstanding, Newport News earned a 23.1 per cent profit on the *Ranger*. The committee concluded that either Bethlehem and New York had declined to compete for the *Ranger* or the natural advantage argument lacked foundation.[12]

At length the senators forced an opening in the shipbuilding industry's defense against the charge of collusion. They obtained an admission from Clinton Bardo, former president of New York Ship but in 1935 head of the National Association of Manufacturers, that the shipbuilders had reached an understanding before the 1933 bidding. He refused to concede, however, that they had decided which yards should receive each contract, as the committee suspected. The magnitude of the 1933 program, according to Bardo, precluded competitive bidding by each yard on all contracts. The shipbuilders therefore had arranged to submit competitive bids only on specific contracts. He inferred that bidding had been honest within arranged limits.[13]

So after much effort the Munitions Committee established that in one instance shipbuilders had arrived at an understanding before submitting bids. Yet the committee might have dealt more effectively with the question of collusive bidding. Although they remained unconvinced that the understanding within the industry in 1933 had been as limited as Bardo intimated, the senators failed to scrutinize his testimony carefully. If the builders had competed within prescribed categories, why were the lowest bids so unexplicably high? And if Bardo's description of the 1933 understanding was accurate, what of the ethics of limited collusion? Bardo said the complexity of the naval program in 1933 had justified such action, but the committee failed to agree or disagree. This was important. If the shipbuilders were so justified, what was to prevent bidders for future contracts from claiming immunity from conventional rules? Large programs always are complicated. If the 1933 program prevented any company from bidding in all categories, why could not the shipbuilders have explained their plight to the government and sought permission for limited collusion? Why act in secret? But why was limited collusion necessary? Why could not each company decide which contracts were most desirable and bid only for those? Bardo's testimony raised the questions, but they went unanswered.

The committee failed, moreover, to make adequate use of Laurence Wilder. He had accused the big three and their associates of collusion in 1933. But what of the years when Wilder was head of New York Shipbuilding, one of the big three? If the shipbuilders had engaged in collusive bidding in 1927–30—as the committee suspected—Wilder should have known. The committee never presented him with the question.

Evidence, on balance, hinted strongly at collusive bidding: the strange fluctuations in cost estimates and bids in the late 1920's; even distribution of contracts; demonstrable weakness of the industry's "natural advantage" argument; testimony by Yard, Frey, and Wilder; reluctant admission of limited collusion by Bardo. Yet excepting the limited collusion of 1933 which Bardo acknowledged, there was room for doubt. A letter from one shipbuilder to another discussing bidding arrangements would have sealed the issue, but there was no such letter. If shipbuilders had engaged in collusive bidding, they covered their tracks well.

II

Collusive bidding headed the committee's indictment of the shipbuilding industry, but close behind was maintenance of an efficient, well-financed lobby. In the committee's view this lobby worked feverishly to increase American naval power. Like the munitions lobby, it was a threat to peace and added to the tax burden of the people.

Lobbying by the shipbuilding industry had come to attention

of previous investigating panels. The special subcommittee of the Committee on Naval Affairs headed by Senator Samuel M. Shortridge of California had considered it briefly in 1929 while studying the activities of William B. Shearer. Shipbuilders then had denied a lobby, contending in effect that what was good for the United States was good for the industry. But the Munitions Committee, studying the problem more energetically, proved otherwise. Nye and his colleagues showed that the industry had spent large sums to influence legislation. They proved that two leaders of the industry had given perjured testimony to Senator Shortridge and his subcommittee in connection with lobbying activities.

Evidence showed that Laurence Wilder had not told the truth when he testified before the Shortridge Subcommittee that he had not lobbied for the Jones-White Merchant Marine Act of 1928. The documents compelled Wilder to admit (after his testimony had strengthened the committee's case against the industry on the question of collusive bidding) that he had headed the lobby for the Jones-White Act and that the major shipbuilders had shared the expenses. Wilder, aided by Shearer, had spent $150,000 for the measure. Senator Clark asked Wilder how much money had gone for wine and liquor. Wilder replied: "Plenty." [14]

Denials to the contrary, the shipbuilders also had lobbied for cruiser construction during the late 1920's and had sought to keep construction out of navy yards. Here the Munitions Committee found a second case of perjury. During the 1929 hearings Senator Joseph T. Robinson of Arkansas asked Clinton Bardo if his company, New York Ship, had representatives in Washington during congressional debate on the cruiser bill of 1928. Bardo admitted that the company had a man, Frank Lord, in Washington, but insisted that Lord was "not here for the purpose of mixing in with legislation." The Munitions Committee exhibited a letter by Bardo in 1928 which contradicted this testimony. Bardo had written that the main concern of his firm at the moment was defeat of the Dallinger Amendment to the cruiser bill, an amendment to assign a large part of the proposed construction to navy yards. He had said that "we are working in Washington with . . . Frank A. Lord." The committee produced another Bardo letter, this one to Lord, in which he said: "We are greatly interested in the cruiser bill and we want to make sure just as far as it is humanly possible to do so, that there will be no slip-up in disposing of the Dallinger amendment provisions of this bill when it comes before the Senate on January 3. It seems to me quite desirable that you should get in touch with Messrs. Barnes and Gauntlet, and it may be well to talk to Duff, who is a representative of the American Shipowners Association." [15]

Lobbying by shipbuilders, one must conclude, was no different than lobbying by manufacturers of guns and powder. It was open to the same criticism, the same justification. Disheartening was evidence that leaders of American industry would depart from the truth when their interest demanded. That they were offering sworn testimony to a Senate committee had failed to deter Wilder, Bardo, and those shipbuilders who had denied collusion in 1933. Such disclosures cast doubt upon all testimony by shipbuilders. They lent some support to charges pacifists were making against armament makers and Communists were making against capitalists.

Related to lobbying was the dispensation of influence in Washington, and one disclosure provided the inquiry with an arresting moment. Secretary-treasurer William Calvin of the American Federation of Labor's Metal Trades Division testified that on August 3, 1933, while the naval program was in the contractual stage, Laurence Wilder of Gulf Industries had asked him to come to a room in a Washington hotel. Wilder, confined to bed with an illness, wanted Calvin to witness negotiations for a business agreement. With one Charles H. Hyde and Wilder's secretary, Calvin was to stand outside the room and listen to a conversation. Soon a man identified as Axel B. Gravem, a Washington attorney, entered and allegedly told Wilder that for $250,000 his client could insure that the Navy Department would allocate $10,000,000 to $15,000,000 of contracts to Gulf Industries. Calvin told the committee that Gravem had referred to his client as Washington's "most influential citizen" and a "fixer." The fixer turned out to be Arthur P. Homer, a Roosevelt supporter long associated with the shipbuilding industry. Calvin later went to his office in the AF of L building and dictated a statement of what had taken place in the hotel room. He exhibited to the committee what he claimed was the statement. Wilder, his secretary Miss Judith Kitchen, and Hyde (through a deposition) supported Calvin's story.

Gravem denied proposing to fix the awards to assure a portion of the 1933 program for Gulf Industries. He told the Munitions Committee that he had become acquainted with Wilder about ten days before the August 3 meeting, talked with him for a few minutes, had not discussed business, and had not received a favorable impression of the Gulf Industries president. Still, according to his testimony he later had talked with Homer about the Gulf Industries situation. He said that Homer had agreed to help the company if it proved able to handle the business, but denied demanding $250,000. Senator Vandenberg was skeptical: "The situation is, that after having had a 5-minute conversation with Mr. Wilder 10 days before, in which there was no discussion of business whatever, you concluded that you wanted to volunteer some information to Mr. Wilder about the situation?"

Homer told the committee he had not authorized Gravem to make such a proposal as Calvin described. He admitted he had talked with Gravem and discussed the figure of $250,000 which Gulf Industries would pay if it received contracts for the 1933 program. He and Gravem had agreed to divide the money equally. But he refused to admit that he had contemplated a fix by influencing friends in the Roosevelt administration. He said he had planned merely to advise Gulf Industries on its bids.[16]

Like some other Munitions Committee melodramas, this one ended inconclusively. Evidence against Gravem and Homer seemed impressive, but the committee was uncertain of their culpability, as was the United States Attorney of the District of Columbia, to whom the committee referred the testimony for possible perjury action. The case probably was unsolvable, since

Gulf Industries had declined to employ Homer and the firm had received none of the twenty-one contracts the Navy awarded in 1933.[17]

Other complaints against the shipbuilding industry came to the attention of the committee. There were charges that the big three had "frozen out" small competitors, but evidence was inconclusive. There were charges that the industry was unfair toward labor. A shipyard worker of Gloucester, New Jersey wrote Nye that in 1932 the New York Shipbuilding Company had cut wages 15 per cent, yet received contracts upon bids which figured wages on the former scale. "At the same time Bardo claimed that 35 cents an hour was enough for any workman, but in the same breath he the big over fed scoundrel plead [*sic*] that he could not get along on $38,000 a year and the same month his pay was boosted $15,000 to the palsy [*sic*] sum of $53,000 poor Clinton. And other high saleried perasites [*sic*] had there [*sic*] pay boosted also as you already know and large amounts in bonus [*sic*] paid these same fellows at the expenses [*sic*] of human misery." Nye replied that the scope of the munitions inquiry was limited by law and did not include settling labor disputes.[18]

During study of the shipbuilding industry the committee reviewed the question of William B. Shearer's activities at the Geneva Naval Conference of 1927. Although it added nothing important to the findings of the Shortridge subcommittee of 1929–30, this phase provided the inquiry's most exciting moment. This occurred when the committee questioned Shearer about his pamphlet, *The Cloak of Benedict Arnold,* published in 1928. Shearer had called several prominent Americans unpatriotic because they did not share his big-navy views. Senator Bone asked Shearer if he still considered Newton D. Baker unpatriotic, and Shearer answered in the affirmative. Bone asked about Dr. Harry A. Garfield, son of the former President. Shearer explained that his listing of Garfield had been "a little bit of plagiarism on my part, taken from the Hearst papers." Bone told Shearer that "you ought not to admit plagiarism," to which Shearer replied: "I am a plagiarist. I am in that case."

The committee showed that Shearer had included former Attorney General George W. Wickersham among the unpatriotic. Shearer still held this view, declaring that Wickersham had been attorney for the Mistubishi interests of Japan. Bone pointed out that Shearer had included Franklin D. Roosevelt in his list.

"Hearst," Shearer said.

Retorted Bone: "Do you want to hide behind the skirts of a newspaper publisher?"

"Let me tell you Senator," Shearer replied, "I do not hide behind anything, but Hearst published an article at that time that gave me the opportunity to use it, and I took it and put it in that pamphlet. I am opposed to all foreign entanglements and to being made an adjunct of the British."

"Are you so cowardly," Bone asked a few moments later, "that you would not indict him [Roosevelt], if he required indictment, as a 'Benedict Arnold?' You told us you had lots of courage."

"I have not mentioned my courage," Shearer spoke out, "and I do not like the implication about being a coward."

"That is unfortunate," snapped Bone.

Whereupon Shearer arose from his chair and began swinging down the aisle toward Bone. Nye pounded his gavel for order and shouted to Shearer: "Go back to your seat as a witness and remain there." Shearer stopped short and returned to his chair.[19]

In its report on the shipbuilding industry the Munitions Committee concentrated upon collusive bidding and excessive profits. The committee declined to accuse shipbuilders of collusive bidding, but asserted that if no collusion had occurred there had existed sympathetic understanding among leading shipbuilders of their respective ambitions. Or, as the committee expressed it, "if there were no conversations about bidding among them, there was telepathy." [20]

In an unpublished memorandum the committee went beyond its report. The senators therein charged that no reasonable competition in bidding for naval contracts had taken place since 1927. And in 1933–34, when the government awarded contracts to private yards totaling more than $183,288,000, a sellers' market had prevailed, of which the companies took full advantage. Because of absence of competition, the committee believed, private yards had overcharged the government. The committee accused the Navy of failing to use its facilities to measure costs and efficiency of private yards. It charged that the Navy had become dependent upon private yards for certain types of vessels. It lamented failure of the executive and legislative branches of the government to define an adequate navy. It believed this failure encouraged financially interested groups to lobby in the name of patriotism.[21]

The committee urged passage of two bills then pending before Congress. The first, S. 3098, aimed to prevent collusion on government contracts by directing the Comptroller General to examine navy yard estimates and the estimates and bids of private yards before permitting the Navy to make awards. The Comptroller would analyze bids and estimates on the basis of past bids and estimates, as well as those of other shipbuilding companies and navy yards. He would recommend to the Navy whether it ought to make the awards or re-advertise. The second bill, S. 3099, sought to prevent excessive profit by private yards on Navy contracts. It provided that the Navy could pay a premium of no more than $500,000 per cruiser, $1,000,000 per aircraft carrier, or $300,000 per destroyer or submarine above cost of building such a vessel in navy yards. The bill stipulated that whenever the government assumed all or a share of the risk, as in the adjusted-price contracts of 1933 and 1934, the shipbuilders, instead of a maximum of 11.1 per cent, should receive a profit no larger than half that amount.[22]

Despite the committee's disclosures and recommendations, Congress took no steps to control the shipbuilding industry. S. 3098 and S. 3099 were not radical measures, and in light of disclosures and testimony published by the committee, deserved passage. They received no support from the administration, and S. 3098 encountered sharp opposition from Secretary of the Navy Claude Swanson, who through a representative told the Senate Committee on Naval Affairs that the bill was superfluous. Existing law, he claimed, protected the government's interest regarding shipbuilding contracts. Appealing to economy, he said that S. 3098 might eventually require the government to build all of its vessels in navy yards, thereby requiring additional appropriations to carry out the 1936 naval program. Appealing to the country's wish for security, Swanson said the Navy Department considered it essential to national defense to assure continued existence of private shipyards capable of constructing naval vessels in an emergency. Appealing to efficiency, he predicted that the measure would cause delay and confusion in shipbuilding. To reassure critics, he said the Navy was watching estimates more closely. Swanson's arguments carried the Naval Affairs Committee. The bills failed to emerge from committee and died with the Seventy-fourth Congress.[23]

The only concrete development which one might attribute in part to this phase of the inquiry was a provision in the relief appropriation measure of 1935 (Public Resolution No. 11, Seventy-fourth Congress) that "no part of the appropriation shall be expended for munitions, warships, or military or naval matériel." The provision aimed to prevent further appropriations by the Public Works Administration for national defense. It went into the bill as an amendment quietly offered by Senator Borah in March 1935—a few weeks after Munitions Committee hearings on the PWA-financed shipbuilding program of 1933. It met some opposition in the House, but was accepted without fanfare.

$$\equiv VI \equiv$$

WAR PROFITS

T H E Senate resolution authorizing the munitions inquiry directed the committee to review findings of the War Policies Commission of 1930–31. The commission had examined industrial mobilization, but had focused upon profits in wartime.[1]

These profits constituted a subject which stirred emotions in the Age of the Great Depression. For people of the United States it conjured memories of the World War. Americans—disgusted with war on other counts—recalled the extravagance of their 1917–18 mobilization. Such goings on outraged their depression-sharpened sense of economy. They also disturbed their sense of patriotism and fair play. While many Americans had enjoyed the prosperity of 1917–18, hundreds of thousands had risked their lives. If the man at the front had to display Spartan virtues, so the mid–1930 American thought, the man at home should do the same. The largest returns of 1917–18, of course, had come to industrialists and financiers, and these groups of businessmen were not in good standing in the depression-ridden mid–thirties.

Senator Nye's committee felt these popular emotions. Although their findings on manufacture and sale of munitions produced some good headlines, the committee considered that its study on war profits was more important. To be sure, the trade in arms had had large consequences. But a small number of Americans had engaged in it; only a few shared its benefits. To win support for control of the trade was therefore not difficult. Regulation of the munitions trade, moreover, seemed to present no large problems. Licensing and inspection systems and arms embargoes would suffice. But profits resulting from American involvement in a war were another matter. They presented large, more complicated, more far-reaching problems. And in the view of many people these returns or war profits—though less dramatic—were a far greater menace to peace than the munitions trade.

Two factors combined to make war profits a difficult problem. First, abnormal wartime returns in the form of dividends, bonuses, and wages—all conveniently called war profits—benefited the entire civil population. Thus feelings were mixed on the subject of ending war profits. Most Americans favored legislation to prevent profits of the magnitude reached during the World War, but to devise legislation acceptable to everyone was difficult.

Then there was the problem of removing excess profits while assuring effective operation of the country's war machine. So perplexing was this problem that many Americans believed the nation could not avoid profiteering without impairing its war effort. Most people rejected this extreme view. But the question remained: how far could the country afford to go in removing excessive wartime returns? This matter of degree was the crux of the war-profit problem.

The Munitions Committee determined to succeed where other groups, such as the War Policies Commission, had failed. It aimed to resolve the problems and push through Congress legislation to remove large profits from war. The committee considered such legislation urgent, since it shared the pacifist view that the prospect of huge returns threatened peace. Especially was such prospect a threat in time of economic crisis. The senators believed that many businessmen would welcome war—any war—as a solution to the depression. They believed that many of the unemployed likewise would find war attractive.

During study of war profits the Munitions Committee concentrated upon two areas. It examined the 1914–18 returns of companies and individuals. It also scrutinized the several plans existing in the 1930's for mobilizing industry in time of war to assure maximum production and minimum profits.

War profit removal did not remain the exclusive preserve of the Munitions Committee. The Roosevelt administration projected itself into the debate, and before the committee could complete its study Congress began to consider measures for "removing profits from and equalizing the burdens of war." For a time, in the winter and spring of 1935, this debate attracted wide attention.

I

Hardly had the committee begun to review the work of the War Policies Commission when President Roosevelt made a move which the committee suspected was to undermine the munitions investigation. At a news conference of December 12, 1934 the President leaned back at his desk with a premonitory twinkle and read off a list of people who were to meet with him at once. The list included Secretaries Cordell Hull, Henry Morgenthau, Jr., George H. Dern, Claude A. Swanson, Henry A. Wallace, and Frances Perkins; Army Chief of Staff General Douglas A. MacArthur; Assistant Secretary of the Navy Henry Latrobe; railroad co-ordinator Joseph B. Eastman; foreign trade adviser George N. Peek; Bernard M. Baruch, and General Hugh S. Johnson. Having read the names, Roosevelt looked up and gleefully remarked that he had intrigued the reporters, that the list made a puzzling combination. Then after carrying suspense almost to the breaking point he announced the mandate he had given the people on his list. Asserting that "the time has come to take the profit out of war," he explained that they would comprise a committee to draft legislation to

eliminate excessive returns in time of war. The committee
would complete its assignment before the new Congress met
in January, 1935.[2]

It was evident that Baruch and Johnson would be the main-
springs of Roosevelt's special committee (soon known as the
Baruch-Johnson Committee), and on the day of the President's announcement the two men left for Baruch's plantation
in South Carolina. They intended to return in a few weeks with
plans which Roosevelt would incorporate in a message to Congress on wartime legislation. Baruch had been identified with
similar programs for many years, and had spoken and written
on the subject. As expected, the result of the Baruch-Johnson
Committee's efforts reflected the views of Baruch; there was no
evidence that other committee members did anything other
than provide window dressing.

The Munitions Committee and its supporters reacted sharply
to appointment of the Baruch-Johnson Committee. If Congress
enacted war profit legislation, critics of the munitions inquiry
might contend that its continuation would be superfluous. Such
a view, if it received support, could prove fatal to the Munitions
Committee. The committee's funds had nearly expired, and it
was preparing to ask the Senate for another appropriation. Since
the Munitions Committee was studying the war profits question why had the President—if his motives were as pure as
driven snow—suddenly created a duplicate committee without
even consulting Nye? The Baruch-Johnson Committee could
not make such a thorough investigation as could the Munitions
Committee, which had a much larger staff.

Business circles were delighted, making no secret of a hope
that Roosevelt's move would prove the undoing of the Munitions Committee. *Business Week* exulted that Roosevelt's step
"takes the punch out of the inquisition by the two Republican
senators, Nye and Vandenberg, steals the show, saves the War
and Navy departments some embarrassment regarding their
relations with munitions makers and forestalls the Senate committee's recommendation for nationalization of the industry."
Businessmen, of course, were familiar with Baruch's position

on war profits, and knew that legislation reflecting his views would be moderate.[3]

More important was response of supporters of the Munitions Committee. Nye reported that in two weeks the committee received 150,000 messages urging continuation of its inquiry. The White House at length bowed to this pressure when on December 26, 1934 the President conferred with Nye. After the meeting the committee chairman emerged from Roosevelt's office smiling and happy. Stating that the committee had misunderstood the purpose of the Baruch-Johnson Committee, Nye told reporters that the President not only wanted the munitions investigation to continue, but expected the Munitions and Baruch-Johnson Committees to confer on a legislative program to prevent excessive war profits. Roosevelt's promise to support the Munitions Committee's request for a $50,000 appropriation to continue its work seemed to prove his sincerity.[4]

Whether Roosevelt in truth sought to undercut the munitions investigation remains a question. Some committee disclosures had embarrassed the President, and it was certain the committee would continue to probe sensitive areas without much regard for the effect upon the administration. But one can offer other explanations for his action. The American Legion's long fight for war profit removal legislation (dating back to 1920) and its current agitation for payment of the veterans' bonus provided a possible motive. One newspaper observer reasoned that Roosevelt perhaps was trying to ease Legion pressure by supporting half the Legion program. A second motive seemed less plausible. Perhaps Roosevelt had created his committee to provide employment for General Johnson, his old friend then out of a job. A third motive comes to mind. Possibly Roosevelt, an advocate of curbing excessive war profits, believed that in view of sentiment aroused by the Munitions Committee this was an ideal time to strike for legislation.[5]

Roosevelt could have achieved his purpose by working through the Munitions Committee. And if he had not planned to check the munitions investigation he could have offered assurance to Nye at the time of his announcement of the Baruch-Johnson Committee or in the days immediately following when reaction among Nye supporters was especially intense. Perhaps he bypassed the Munitions Committee because he anticipated that it would insist upon a more radical program than the administration believed advisable. Perhaps he delayed reassurance to Nye because he hoped to head off the Nye inquiry, but bowed to pressure that it continue. Perhaps he bypassed the Munitions Committee and delayed reassurance just to see what would happen. If the Baruch-Johnson Committee brought the demise of the munitions inquiry, fine; if public pressure demanded he could announce support for the inquiry's continuation. Roosevelt kept his own counsel in this matter. But whatever his motive, the President learned that the Munitions Committee had support throughout the country, that most Americans opposed ending it at this point.[6]

Meanwhile the Munitions Committee had opened hearings on war profits. (The committee had touched upon the subject earlier, but only in passing.) It easily established that during the World War many American corporations had earned exorbitant profits. This was news to no one, but the committee believed that for the record it needed explicit data on the matter. It showed that in 1917 the Savage Arms Corporation had realized a return of 60 per cent—$6,000,000 profits on an investment of $10,000,000. During the four years preceding the World War the Bethlehem Shipbuilding Company had earned an average annual profit of $6,000,000; during the four years of war it averaged $49,000,000. E. I. du Pont de Nemours and Company's business in 1916 was 1130 per cent greater than in 1913 and 1914. The regular dividend on du Pont common stock before the war had been 2½ per cent; on September 30, 1917 the company paid a dividend of 32 per cent, largest in its history. Du Pont's annual report revealed that in the early months of the war du Pont stock had sold for $125 per share; by December 31, 1918 the price had risen to $593, an increase of 374 per cent. Pierre S. du Pont told the Munitions Committee that "I doubt if any other company made such a record." [7]

Most Americans frowned on large profits during war, but they deplored no form of return more than the bonuses which key personnel in industrial firms had received during the World War. They reasoned that it was unfair for such men to receive bonuses while soldiers were fighting. As Senator Clark expressed it: "If a man is drafted . . . and is compelled to fight for the Old Flag for one dollar and a quarter a day, why should not a man engaged in the industrial end of the game—which I agree is very essential, whether he be an executive or a laboring man—also make some sacrifice for the Old Flag?" [8]

Industrial leaders defended the bonus system. Irénée du Pont said his company's bonus plan had been one of its best investments. The plan's incentive, he said, had earned more through economies than it cost. President Eugene G. Grace of Bethlehem Shipbuilding, who reputedly had received two million dollars in bonuses during the war, granted that in theory the committee was correct; in war civil workers should be as patriotic as soldiers at the front. Effort should not depend upon bonuses. But from a practical standpoint Grace believed less production would result if there were no bonus incentive. Although it galled a veteran like Clark that patriotism alone would not incite civilians to maximum support of the men enduring front-line warfare, there was merit in Grace's argument. Victory had to receive first consideration, and victory required production as well as fighting. One might have argued that it would have been a greater disservice to fighting men to abolish bonuses and deprive them of support. The lesson here perhaps was that the nature of war made it impossible to attain the noble dream of equalizing the burdens. [9]

During its study the Munitions Committee exhumed the case of the Old Hickory smokeless powder plant (near Nashville, Tennessee) which du Pont had built and operated in 1918. After the war charges circulated that du Pont had defrauded the government by padding the cost of building and operating

Old Hickory. The company's contract in this instance was of the much-criticized cost-plus type. Investigation had failed to prove du Pont guilty, but suspicion persisted. The manner in which the company maintained records at Old Hickory had prevented accounting of the operation. Documents were strewn about the premises and even stashed under office flooring. All this strengthened the view that du Pont was hiding something. The Munitions Committee studied the question, but like previous groups failed to prove fraud. Arthur Carnduff, special attorney for the Bureau of Internal Revenue, who had helped conduct an inquiry into Old Hickory in the 1920's, told the committee he was certain du Pont owed the government "at least $900,000, and possibly a great deal more." Neither he nor the committee could prove this view.[10]

Of larger interest were du Pont's legitimate profits from Old Hickory. The committee showed that du Pont had organized a new corporation, the du Pont Engineering Company, to construct and operate the plant. Capital of the new corporation was only $5,000; the original stock subscription sold for one dollar per share. On this investment, according to the committee, the du Pont Engineering Company had grossed $1,961,-000, a profit of 39,231 per cent! [11]

Headlines proclaimed this startling disclosure. Unfortunately, the du Pont response failed to receive similar prominence. Pierre du Pont, his face reddened with anger, charged that the committee's assertion amounted to an attempt to falsify the record. Insisting that the government had paid the company for its experience, du Pont compared profits in Old Hickory with returns of a physician. A physician had a small capital investment, he said, and his profits would appear exorbitant if measured against capital.[12]

The committee had based its reasoning upon investment and risk, but even in these terms its conclusion was incorrect. Capital of $5,000 in a new company was a formality to permit separate accounting; E. I. du Pont de Nemours and Company shared responsibility with du Pont Engineering Company for the Old Hickory contract. Had du Pont's risk been only $5,000 the committee would have stood on better ground in placing gross profit on the Old Hickory operation at 39,231 per cent. But the contract permitted the government to deny approval of expenditures listed as cost of construction and operation by the du Pont Engineering Company, in which case, unless the courts reversed government decisions, E. I. du Pont de Nemours and Company would have been liable.

Fortunately, the Munitions Committee saw the light. It said nothing more on the subject; during his public addresses of the time Nye refrained from assailing Old Hickory profits.

Because the war ended within a few months after Old Hickory began to operate at peak capacity, returns on the operation were not large. Had the war continued for another year du Pont's profits would have been great indeed, since the plant could produce a million pounds of powder per day. The government assumed all production costs and paid du Pont three and one-half cents per pound of powder turned out, plus half the difference between the established base price of powder and the actual cost of production when cost was less than base price. Operating at capacity, Old Hickory could earn more than $35,000 per day before taxes.[13]

A more important aspect to the Old Hickory case dealt with negotiations between the government and du Pont over construction and operation of the plant. The committee showed that the government had first sought du Pont's co-operation in the project in November, 1917, but only three months later did the company agree to terms. Lieutenant Colonel C. T. Harris, in the planning branch of the War Department during the war, told the committee that "three months were taken up in negotiations which finally led to the final agreement. There were 3 months cost in the middle of the war by these negotiations. That had a very serious effect on the military effort. Fortunately it did not have a fatal effect, but it might have had." Evidence suggested that the company, knowing it was the only American firm capable of building and operating a smokeless powder plant of such size, had delayed agreement in hope of securing better terms, although the War Industries

Board offered to pay the company one million dollars in advance if it would start construction immediately. The board promised to arbitrate additional compensation due the company if after eighteen months of negotiation government and company failed to agree. Pierre du Pont explained the company's position in a letter written in November, 1917: "we cannot assent to allowing our patriotism to interfere with our duties as trustees." This statement shocked the Munitions Committee. Senator Clark expressed committee sentiment when he said: "You take men to carry a gun and get jabbed up with bayonets without any consultation or negotiations or haggling." [14]

The committee showed that the government could have commandeered and operated this du Pont property during the war, but it seemed doubtful that the government had authority to compel du Pont personnel to operate it. And what the government needed at Old Hickory was du Pont technical ability. As Clark explained, the government had no authority "to say, 'Well, boys, it is the know-how which we want, and trains are running to Leavenworth barracks where we send men who hang back from the front-line trenches.' They had a perfect right to say, which still exists, that 'You have to haggle with us on terms,' when the Germans were about to break through." The erstwhile lieutenant colonel, Harris, agreed that "every du Pont man could have walked out and left a shell of a plant." [15]

Establishing what everybody already knew, that industrial mobilization in the World War had left much to be desired, was not the aim of the Munitions Committee. The hope of the committee was to prevent repetition of the 1917–18 experience. To this end the committee studied plans and proposals to achieve industrial mobilization without excess profits. The War Department had the most complete set of mobilization plans. In compliance with a congressional mandate the department, in co-operaton with the Navy Department, had over the past fifteen years prepared detailed plans for mobilizing the country's physical, industrial, and human resources in time of war.

The War Department's industrial mobilization plan aimed to

assure supply of war materials and prevent profiteering—in that order. The department's object was quick and complete victory should the United States become a belligerent. This demanded munitions and other supplies, and their transportation to combat areas. The department's interest in limiting profits came from belief that high wartime morale depended upon fair treatment of all elements of the population. An economic bonanza by one element, the theory went, would weaken morale of others, which might impair production. Yet in the War Department view, too much removal of profit presented equal danger. The department insisted that the country could ill afford so extreme a program that it would stifle initiative of capital and labor.

The War Department mobilization plan contained nothing radical. Several boards, presided over by civilians, would supervise industrial activities. One board would be responsible for raw materials, another for finance, another for personnel. Boards would have limited powers. They could not, for example, coerce labor. Employees could organize into associations and trade unions, and bargain through representatives of their choosing. The plan called for equal pay for equal work, and recognized the statutory work day.[16]

Unlike other mobilization proposals, price control did not figure prominently in War Department plans. The department proposed an excess-profits tax, but insisted that rates must not be so high as to impede flow of materials. Lieutenant Colonel Harris, speaking for the department, said: "I don't care what the return is. . . . My interest is in getting production." He suggested that 6 per cent would be a fair return in wartime. Such a return, moreover, would provide a sufficient spread between possible loss and profit to assure efficiency.[17]

The Munitions Committee favored the excess-profits tax (though it considered a 6 per cent return too generous). Yet it recorded testimonials from economists who contended that such a tax would present problems. Yale's P. S. Adams, former chairman of the advisory tax board of the Bureau of Internal Revenue, said that "the intricacy of the excess-profits tax is such that it is hardly an exaggeration to say that it takes more time to teach an accountant to master its mysteries than the average accountant can be retained in the service after he has attained such mastery." Arguments of this sort failed to move the committee, which continued to believe that the excess-profits tax, despite difficulties, was the best course.[18]

A more controversial question was: should the government draft capital and labor in time of war? After misgivings (it might bring fascism) peace leaders generally had accepted the view that conscription of capital and labor was necessary to equalize war's burdens. Pacifists believed, moreover, that the threat of conscription would encourage business to cast its influence against war. A majority of the Munitions Committee shared such sentiments.

The War Department was more conservative. It rejected the idea of conscripting capital and labor. Under the War Department plan mobilization would depend upon industry's willingness to co-operate; it requested no increase in government coercive power. As during the World War, the government could commandeer private property, but the owner would receive compensation. Lieutenant Colonel Harris told the committee that there was no reason to conscript industry, since the United States would lose the war anyway if industry refused to co-operate. Nye remained unconvinced. Citing violations of NRA codes which had come to committee attention, he doubted that even in time of war industry would place patriotism above profit. "If the Government has such difficulty in accomplishing cooperation in peace time, what likelihood is there that they are going to have cooperation during the stress of war, when industry does hold an extraordinary power by reason of the necessities of the Government, having access to its products?" [19]

Industrialists of course opposed conscription of capital. Eugene Grace of Bethlehem Ship, contending that there was a difference between conscripting men for military service and conscripting capital, seemed to imply that capital deserved more consideration. "It seems to me," Nye retorted, "that in time of war both groups are up against about the same classes of danger, loss of life and loss of property. Why should not they be dealt with alike?" Grace was adamant. He declared he would not expect effective production from conscripted property. It was unnecessary to add that such a calamity would lead to military defeat. Grace's argument gathered support from a memorandum by Aiken Simons of du Pont, prepared in June, 1929 after a conference with W. N. Taylor, a du Pont representative in Europe. Simons reported that "Colonel Taylor . . . spoke of the German belief that the present French law for conscription of men, women, and wealth in the next war will enable Germany, with an army not exceeding 400,000 men, to defeat and destroy France, since this law will take away all initiative and will set back the production of munitions at least 6 months." [20]

Similar opposition came from organized labor. Labor was not much concerned over the plight of capital, and probably would have had small objection to nationalization of industry in time of war. But labor leaders calculated that if government drafted capital, conscription of labor would not be far behind. Such a fate labor passionately wished to avoid. W. C. Hushing of the American Federation of Labor told the Munitions Committee that conscription would destroy organized labor and nullify the work of a hundred years. "It is slavery. And it would be one of the most unfortunate things that could happen. Men do not want to be driven. They do not want to be—certainly Americans will not submit; and while at the point of a bayonet they might give some amount of work, it would not be given in that spirit in which it was given in the last war. The results would be—well, I believe it would probably result in the loss of the war." [21]

Different sentiment came from the American Legion and the Veterans of Foreign Wars. They endorsed conscription of capital and labor, although some people doubted that the Legion meant it. Pacifist hostility notwithstanding, the Legion endorsed conscription of capital and labor at its convention late in 1934. Its judge advocate and treasurer, James A. Drain (a past national commander), reiterated this position before the Munitions Committee in 1935. James E. Van Zandt, commander of the VFW, told the committee that "we believe that human rights have a priority of claim upon property rights, gold standards, and everything else, and our idea of conscription is to take over every line of industry and go into the plants, and take over the railroads." [22]

Belief that conscription of capital would deter war moved Representative Thomas O'Malley (Dem.) of Wisconsin to draft a bill which would have put such men as Henry Ford, John D. Rockefeller, and Andrew Mellon at posts of greatest danger in event of war. From income lists provided by the Bureau of Internal Revenue, the Secretary of War would select men of greatest wealth who would serve first at the danger points. All service would be in combat areas. Only Congress could make exceptions because of age or infirmity. Only after exhaustion of the income list could the Army dispatch poor people to the front.

The New York *Times* thought the first effect of O'Malley's bill would be to "send a thrill of delight down the elderly backbones of the designated front-line men of wealth. There will be a gleam in the eyes of Henry Ford and Harvey Firestone. The wild bird will begin to sing in the heart of the senior Morgan and the du Ponts. . . . It is almost like Ponce de Leon's fountain of youth coming true. Think of it. To be recognized by law as fit for something better than sitting in an office chair and amassing millions and paying taxes! To set forth on a great adventure, *the* great adventure!" The *Times* suspected that if the bill failed to pass "the sorest disappointment will be in Wall Street and at Dearborn, Mich. Elderly eyes will dull again. Elderly pulses will sag back to their routine beat. There will be a loud sigh as elderly fingers reach for the telephone. They had been tingling to the imagined feel of the machine-gun handle." [23]

I I

Before the Munitions Committee could complete its study, war profit and industrial mobilization became a matter of congressional debate. On the first day of the Seventy-fourth Congress in January, 1935 Representative John Mc-Swain (Dem.) of South Carolina, author of many war profit resolutions in the past, introduced another measure to prevent excessive returns in wartime. In previous years introduction of such measures by McSwain, Royal Johnson, and others had been gestures to keep the question alive and retain for the sponsors the support of the American Legion; there had been no hope of passage. But times were different in 1935. Thanks largely to the munitions investigation, there was enough sentiment against war profits that such a measure had a chance of enactment.

One might describe the McSwain Bill as the fruit of the Baruch-Johnson Committee. The Baruch-Johnson group was not much of a committee, and after cursory study had reiterated the well-known views of Baruch. But this presented no problem for McSwain, since all his previous resolutions had carried the mark of Baruch.

The McSwain Bill was moderate. Its central article was a price-freezing provision which supporters believed would prevent large profits. It directed the President, upon declaration of war or an emergency arising from imminence of war, to freeze prices as of that or an earlier date. The President, however, could make adjustments upward or downward. The bill contained no provision for excess-profits taxes, although its authors expected the government to remove excess profits. The authors assumed Congress would draft such legislation at war's outbreak. The bill authorized the President to determine priority by which any manufacturer, dealer, or public servant should fill orders. Nothing resembling conscription of capital and labor appeared in McSwain's measure.[24]

Advocates of mild legislation received the McSwain Bill enthusiastically. Secretary of War Dern, the AF of L, Disabled American Veterans, Brotherhood of Locomotive Firemen and Enginemen, and the Reserve Officers Association hailed the measure in hearings before the House Military Affairs Committee. The American Legion and VFW expressed interest—the bill was a step in the right direction—but by this time they were committed to a more drastic program. Bernard Baruch and Hugh Johnson offered the most laudatory praise. Baruch told the committee that "this is a great measure, not alone to prevent war, if there be people who desire profits in war, but to make certain this country shall have the greatest war machine that we ever had, that the world has ever seen." Johnson said there were three profit incentives which could lead to war: desire for profit by munitions manufacturers; desire of business for seizure of other countries and exploitation of world markets (which Johnson believed had caused every war in modern times); and belief of depression-ridden people that war would bring recovery. Without explaining how, Johnson declared that the McSwain Bill would eliminate these incentives.[25]

Some people believed the McSwain Bill attacked the problem half-heartedly. Spokesmen for this position on Capitol Hill were Nye and Clark, who proposed legislation which would conscript capital and labor, and tax civilians to such extent that their economic return from war would approximate that of men in the armed forces. Clark on February 6, 1935 introduced seven bills to provide this sort of wartime mobilization. Passage was unlikely. He said he hoped only to stimulate discussion of such a program before an emergency arose. The most controversial of the Clark bills would have given the President control over industry in wartime, including power to fix prices and wages. It provided for draft of all male citizens above the age of eighteen, and authorized the President to conscript real and personal property. The bills, in brief, would permit socialization of the country in time of war.[26]

When committee hearings resumed on March 15, 1935 they began with consideration of a mobilization plan embodying the above Nye-Clark position. Responsibility for preparing the plan had rested with writer-economist John T. Flynn, and to him fell the task of explaining and defending the plan during hearings. But in deference to those people who advocated less drastic measures, the committee granted Bernard Baruch equal opportunity to explain and defend his position.

The Flynn plan would rely heavily upon the excess-profits tax to prevent large returns in war. Flynn, unlike Baruch and McSwain, had little faith in price-fixing. He conceded that price-fixing might merit inclusion in mobilization legislation, but believed, because of the volume of business in wartime, corporations and individuals could earn large profits although their prices might be below the lawful ceiling.[27]

Taxes would be heavy under the Flynn plan. While Baruch and McSwain would permit "normal" returns and if necessary sanction a tax scheme to remove a fixed percentage of profit considered abnormal, the Flynn plan would disallow even "normal" returns in most instances. With respect to corporations, the Flynn formula would permit an annual profit of 3 per cent of the company's real value. Nor would Flynn exempt individual incomes from heavy taxation. No person could earn more than $10,000 in a war year. On his income up to $10,000 he would pay normal (presumably, peacetime) taxes, but the government would take all earnings in excess of $10,000. This section of the plan was directed primarily against company managers, whose salaries Flynn contended went up immediately upon outbreak of war. He cited a case in which the head of a steel company had earned $17,000 annually before 1914. In the same period common laborers had earned 18½ cents an hour. By 1915, according to Flynn, following influx of war orders from Europe, the president's salary had risen to $61,000, but wages of common laborers had increased only 1½ cents an hour, from 18½ to 20.[28]

Nye questioned Flynn about the effect of such taxation upon persons accustomed to high incomes. How would they care for their families and estates on $10,000 per year? Flynn replied that this was not a matter of large concern. Anyhow, Flynn said, most individuals in that category had reserves which would sustain them through the war period.

Senator Pope asked: "It would not be a serious matter at all?"

Flynn: "It would not be a serious matter at all. It might be serious for them, but not for the Nation."

Clark: "It is not as serious as being hit by a high-explosive shell, is it?"

Flynn: "Not nearly." [29]

Flynn believed that drastic taxation would make war less likely. "I rather think that the existence of taxes like this would make war a very unpopular thing," he told the committee. "I rather think that the man who is disposed to be very sensitive, if some Japanese lieutenant fails to take his hat off in the presence of the American flag some place in Manchukuo, will not be so sensitive and will be more reasonable in his patriotism." Flynn failed to note that such an attitude might prove a double-edged sword. If taxation made war as uninviting as Flynn anticipated, might not Americans become reluctant to defend rights much worth defending? [30]

Heavy taxation would enable the United States as nearly as possible to pay for war as it fought. Flynn said that borrowing money to finance war was a great evil. The Romans, he said, "pillaged their neighbors, but we undertake to pillage our grandchildren by having our little wars and sending them the bill in the expectation that they will pay for them. Now, I might add, we are sending them another bill for the War, in a sense, by sending them a bill for the depression." [31]

Flynn believed the law should not permit corporations to defer tax payments because of disagreement with the government on the amount to be paid. A dissatisfied corporation should pay the sum demanded by the government, and submit a claim for refund. Flynn recalled how many corporations, disagreeing with the government, deferred tax payments during the World War. Most such claims were not adjusted until years later, during the 1920's when government was more sympathetic toward business. In nearly every instance the sum finally paid was less than the original government claim.

The Bureau of Internal Revenue had calculated the 1917–18 tax liability of the Phelps-Dodge Corporation at $16,378,000. The corporation argued for a liability of $6,245,000. It deferred payment. Settlement did not come until 1929, when the government required Phelps-Dodge to pay slightly more than $7,000,000.[32]

Unlike the bill which Clark had introduced the month before, the Flynn plan would not have conscripted labor. Many people who favored wartime socialization had long sympathized with labor, and sought to exempt it from drastic mobilization. Nye and Clark believed there should be no exceptions— burdens of war must fall equally. But upon reflection the senators concluded that it would be impolitic to antagonize individuals who would exempt labor, and a week before hearings resumed Raushenbush wrote Flynn of concern over the implication in the Flynn plan that the government might conscript labor. Flynn revised his formula.[33]

Conscription of management presented no comparable difficulties. Nearly all advocates of wartime socialization favored conscription of the World War's profiteers (the merchants of death, the malefactors of wealth who had triggered the depression). The Flynn plan provided that in wartime the officers of industries declared essential by the President must register for the draft. The government could induct these men into the military forces at rank not higher than colonel and at pay appropriate to that rank. They would be officers in the industrial-management forces of the Army, and could be lent to run corporations. They would be subject to military justice and could be cashiered from the Army, "a disgrace," according to Flynn, "which I think no man could very well outlive." [34]

The Flynn plan did not provide for complete socialization. The government would not take over plants. Nor would it manage private property. "The corporation shall be run as a private corporation," Flynn explained, "within the framework of the capitalistic system, and within the framework of the ownership system, and within the framework of the corporation charter." But managers would be members of the military forces, and could not accept compensation beyond their pay as military officers.[35]

Would such a system interfere with industrial efficiency? Flynn did not think so. Increased labor efficiency would nullify any loss of managerial efficiency. Labor, he explained, would cause no trouble and be more efficient if convinced that stockholders, bondholders, and managers were not enjoying large profits. Conscription of management, moreover, would act as a war deterrent. "I think all these golf-playing executives, if they knew that the moment that war was declared they were all going into the service and their salaries were going from $50,000 to $4,000, that they would be less concerned about the rape of Belgium, and they would think, perhaps, about the rape of the pay roll." [36]

Under the Flynn formula the government in wartime would close commodity exchanges and the President would fix prices of such commodities as food and coal. Flynn explained that under his system there would be no need for the speculative machinery which normally existed between producers and processors. The government also would close security exchanges. To fill the void thus created, it would establish machinery for financing industry. A company might employ private financing only with government permission.[37]

Flynn told the Munitions Committee that the government might find it necessary to commandeer property or take over industry on a large scale during war, but there was some question of constitutional authority for such action. Like other students of the problem, therefore, he advocated action which would suspend the Fifth Amendment in time of war. There should be no doubt that the government had power to confiscate capital, should capital refuse to co-operate on government terms. The government had entertained doubts on this point in 1917–18, and as a result, he said, government had surrendered to capital.[38]

Flynn conceded that his plan could not abolish wartime inflation and profits. Leaders of corporations were men with talent for and interest in making money, but he believed Americans need not endure repetition of the profiteering which had accompanied the World War. He thought his plan could succeed to that extent.[39]

The Flynn plan met mixed reaction, even in pacifist circles. Calling the plan "an honest attack on war profits," the *Christian Century* declared that Flynn had "put the proponents of stopping war by stopping war profits in a place where they must fish or cut bait." But the *Nation,* which had supported the Munitions Committee, questioned trying to equalize the burdens of war when this meant "extending the dangerous principle of conscription." Approving the drastic tax provisions of Flynn's formula, the *Nation* charged that the committee had accepted "the military fascism inherent in the War Department's conscription scheme." The *Christian Century* retorted that "perhaps the prospect of such a dictatorship will prove one effective way of insuring that the influence of American business will be exerted to keep the nation at peace." Senator Bone had similar views, and following Flynn's testimony delivered the most intemperate discourse by a committee member during hearings. Declaring that munitions manufacturers had "skinned" the government during the World War and that their patriotism depended upon profit, he proclaimed that he did not want his boy sent off to fight a war to enrich Eugene G. Grace.[40]

Business, as expected, did not take an exalted view of the Flynn plan. Businessmen reiterated the argument that drastic war profit legislation would impair American defense. As *Business Week* expressed it, such measures would "transfer the war munitions industry to foreign soil" and "provide for murderous delay in preparation in case a war is forced on this country." But the periodical predicted that war profits were doomed, that no congressman would dare vote against war profit removal measures, however dubious their merit.[41]

Bernard Baruch followed Flynn into the Munitions Committee's witness chair. He promptly endorsed Flynn's "pay-as-you-fight" proposal. But agreement between the two men about ended on that point. Price-fixing, considered of slight importance by Flynn, was basic to Baruch's plan to prevent inflation and excess profits. Baruch insisted that price ceilings were mandatory. Despite excess-profits taxes, prices would rise and real wages decline.[42]

According to the Baruch formula (an elaboration of the pending McSwain Bill), after declaring war the President would proclaim a ceiling over the nation's price structure, with prices in effect equal to those prevailing on or about the date of the declaration of war. He would establish a fair-price commission to make adjustments. The government would increase the peacetime tax rate, and subject all earnings not in excess of the peacetime average to this revised rate structure. An excess-profits tax rate (presumably much higher than the revised peacetime rate) would operate for all earnings above the peacetime average. Baruch would leave the new tax rates to the discretion of the wartime Congress, but one could assume that he did not envision taxes so severe as those in Flynn's plan. Under the Baruch formula the government would mobilize manpower by a "work-or-fight" provision, but not conscript labor. The Army and Navy would handle military matters; control of the country's economic life would remain under civil management directed by the President.[43]

Senator Bone raised a question which applied to all mobilization plans drafted in time of peace. Might not a wartime Congress succumb to pressure from business to remove profit-limiting laws? Baruch replied that he had a higher opinion of Congress than to believe it might yield to such pressure. Anyway, he said, thanks to the Munitions Committee investigation, public opinion would not tolerate repeal of war profit laws.[44]

In his appearance before the Munitions Committee Baruch reiterated oft-publicized views. He declined to attack the Flynn plan, although he did express opposition to conscription of management, a central feature of Flynn's proposal. Referring to his own formula, he said: "Under this plan . . . they [industrial management] are in control of their plants and they are responsible. If you start out to draft management, then you have got to draft labor, and then you will get into territory where you and I will have a stand-up and knock-down fight. It is not necessary. . . ." [45]

Two weeks after his appearance before the committee—on April 12, 1935—Baruch dropped his restraint. He attacked the Flynn plan. He filed a statement with the committee charging the Flynn plan would not only remove war profit, but would abolish the existing economic system. "I am not debating here whether the profit motive is right or wrong," he wrote. "I am only insisting that we recognize reality and what is here proposed. And I *am* saying that the advent of modern war and threatened national destruction, when the fate of the people, as at no other time, depends on the efficient operation at high-speed pressure, of its industrial system, is *not* the moment to select to switch from the fundamental base of our economic system to a new and wholly experimental system which was never adopted at any time in the world's history in peace or war without an immediate result of collapse and ruin." [46]

Baruch's logic, despite its merit, drew retorts from Nye, Vandenberg, and Flynn. In a radio address on April 15 Nye accused Baruch of "hedging" on the position which he had taken during Munitions Committee hearings. Baruch had urged "drastic programs" to remove profit from war, but now was attempting to make harmless any program to accomplish that end. "Now he says . . . [the Flynn plan] is too drastic, that we would be defeated in another war under such legislation because business wouldn't do its share of fighting and helping to win the war when its profits were so restricted. May Heaven preserve us! I've expected some one to say that. But Mr. Baruch, I never expected it to come from you. So American business won't produce what is needed in war if it can't have its profits! So American business will not go into a war on the same basis that the boys go in when they are called!" Vandenberg was less virulent, but charged that, while telling the committee the country should preclude postwar deflation by paying for war as it fought, Baruch had run away from the one method which could accomplish this purpose. Vandenberg was "everlastingly opposed to the collective state." But, he said, "God help capitalism if it won't defend a common national crisis without its pound of flesh." [47]

It was inaccurate to accuse Baruch of reversing his position on war profits and industrial mobilization. During his appearance before the Munitions Committee he failed to define his position as clearly as he might have, but in other speeches and writings and in testimony before the War Policies Commission and other congressional committees he had emphasized his opposition to tampering with the existing economic structure in time of war. He always had opposed conscription of capital and labor, always had contended that government must permit "normal" profit if the country were to have industrial efficiency in war. And perhaps it was a sad commentary upon American patriotism, but Baruch probably was correct in his appraisal. He doubtless was on solid ground with his view that a period of war was no time to experiment with revolutionary change in the economic system.

III

In March, 1935 there was large interest in war profit removal and industrial mobilization, spurred by appearances of Flynn and Baruch before the Munitions Committee. It was evident that the question soon would reach the floor of Congress. What kind of measure, if any, might achieve passage depended upon the administration, but at this point the administration's position was a matter of speculation. The Munitions Committee hoped Roosevelt might come down on the side of a bill modeled after the Flynn plan. In conference with committee members on March 19 the President indicated co-operation with the committee on this matter, and approved parts of the Flynn plan. During a press conference the following day Roosevelt hinted no large difference between the Baruch and Munitions Committee views on war profits. "Of course the objective is a common objective," he said, "to take the profits out of war." But a short while later, perhaps after reflection, Roosevelt began to support the McSwain Bill with its moderate Baruch-style features. By early April the administration plainly preferred no law at all to one fashioned after Flynn's plan. Raushenbush told Nye on April 16 that the most which friends of Flynn-style legislation could expect from the White House was a policy of hands off.[48]

Undeterred, the committee on April 1, 1935 issued a report that no bill which gave the President only general authority to fix prices, commandeer industry, or arrange priorities and licenses was adequate to equalize burdens and take profit out of war. The report endorsed every essential of the Flynn plan, including conscription of industrial leaders and placing them under disciplinary control of the War Department; a corporate tax scheme to limit corporations to net return of 3 per cent of their real value; an individual tax plan to confiscate earnings above $10,000 per year. Referring to a bill to incorporate these provisions, Nye told reporters that "the bill is drastic because war is a drastic thing. The tax collector who comes for one man's money is not nearly so solemn and forbidding as the draft officer who knocks at another man's door and calls for his young son." W. D. McFarlane (Dem.) of Texas introduced the Munitions Committee bill in the House on April 6. It went to the Military Affairs Committee, chairman of which was John McSwain. Introduction and referral of the measure went almost unnoticed, for House debate on the McSwain Bill was approaching a climax.[49]

Consideration of the McSwain Bill on the House floor had begun three days before. The measure met immediate but apparently not serious opposition when friends of Flynn-style legislation, such as Joseph P. Monaghan (Dem.) of Montana, Vito Marcantonio (Rep.) of New York, Marion A. Zioncheck (Dem.) of Washington, and Gardner R. Withrow (Farmer-Laborer) of Wisconsin denounced McSwain's bill as a farce. They sought to attach tax provisions similiar to those endorsed by the Munitions Committee, but their amendments went down to defeat. House approval of the McSwain Bill appeared imminent.[50]

April 6 was another day, and the House of Representatives

is a volatile body. It was the eighteenth anniversary of America's declaration of war against Germany, Army Day. Fifty thousand soldiers, sailors, and veterans paraded through the streets of Washington, and pacifists placed wreaths on statues of three members of Congress who had voted against the declaration. These proceedings had an effect on the House, and without warning it amended the McSwain Bill almost beyond recognition. Before the day ended the Munitions Committee and other supporters of drastic war profit legislation, whose cause had appeared hopeless a few hours before, stood on the verge of victory in the House. Amendments received support from impassioned oratory. Henry C. Luckey (Dem.) of Nebraska declared: "We know that wars are based on greed. Their causes are commercial; and the motive for war is gain and loot. Take the profits out of war and you remove the incentive for war." Financiers and industrialists, according to Henry Ellenbogen (Dem.) of Pennsylvania, "took the profits— to us they left the gigantic war debt; the thousands of veterans who took the blows for which these men and these corporations received the pay; the post-war inflation; the bitter memory of futile sacrifices. All that we must never have again. We shall not permit one part of a Nation to offer the lives of its young men in order that another part may secure wealth. Should war come again, we shall no longer have the youth of the land as the only ones who are being called. We should call every resource, every activity, and above all, the entire wealth, into the service of the common cause."

An amendment authorized the President to conscript material and financial resources. Another, offered by McSwain (he had insisted for three days that such amendments were out of order), provided for a 100 per cent tax on earnings considered excess-profits. The amendment failed to define excessive profits, but would remove the constitutional barrier to Senate inclusion of tax features. Another amendment authorized the President to conscript executives of industry, commerce, transportation, and communications. Another provided that pay of conscripted labor should be at prevailing unskilled wage scales. Another raised the draft age to forty-five years. Confusion was so rampant that the House adopted one amendment a few minutes after rejecting an almost identical proposal. Representative Harry Sauthoff (Progressive-Republican) of Wisconsin proposed to empower the President to draft all members of Congress who voted for war, but this amendment was ruled out of order amid laughing applause.[51]

April 9 was still another day. Most veterans and pacifists had departed, but party discipline, Democratic and Republican, remained. The House had enjoyed the heady radicalism of April 6, but the members realized the party was over; it was time to sober up. Without fanfare the House struck the conscription sections it had added to the McSwain Bill and passed it much in its original form, 367–15, 9 Democrats and 6 Republicans dissenting. The bill authorized the President, upon declaring war, to freeze prices, rents, and other compensation at the prewar level. The President could commandeer but not conscript material and financial resources, industrial organizations, and public services essential to prosecution of war. He could close stock and commodity exchanges, and license manufacturers, dealers, and public services—except publishers of newspapers, periodicals, and magazines—and make unlawful for them to operate without a license.[52]

The bill needed assent of the Senate, but Nye and his supporters determined to hold out for radical legislation. On May 3, 1935 Nye offered sweeping amendments fashioned to make the bill conform generally to the Flynn formula.

At this point the drive to enact war profit–industrial mobilization legislation lost momentum. Americans were becoming troubled over mounting tension in East Africa, and as events moved toward conflict they cast to the background the question of how to mobilize for war. The new problem was how to stay out of war. A result was legislation of the following August, the Neutrality Act of 1935. The McSwain Bill, amended to suit the Nye-Clark group, reported by the Military Affairs Committee, lost out in the shuffle. It went to the Committee on Finance and a subcommittee conducted hearings but never reported the bill back to the Senate.

The bill might have passed had it won support of the White

House, but administration hostility toward radical war profit programs remained. The administration believed the profit motive so basic to the American system that curtailment would jeopardize any war effort. It had approved the original McSwain Bill, but lacked strength in the Senate to override the Nye-Clark group. Administration spokesmen told the Senate Finance Committee's subcommittee in 1936 that passage of the McSwain Bill with the Nye amendments might be a good thing. In event of war Congress could revise the law to restore the profit incentive, and it might be useful to have the form of the bill on the books. But the administration was not so persuaded by this logic that it would work for passage of the measure, and without such support, especially in the House, the bill had no chance.[53]

What were the lessons of the debate over war profits and industrial mobilization? What, if any, were the results?

Considering lessons first, the debate demonstrated what should have been obvious, that the issue was enormously complicated. Everybody wanted to control inflation and prevent profiteering. Everybody endorsed the principle of equalizing war's burdens. But translation of principle into action was another matter. Few people agreed on what economic mobilization should involve. The debate also pointed up the improbability that the nation ever could curb profit and inflation in war. Control of the economic mechanism at such time would be almost impossible. And as Flynn pointed out, business leaders had talent for making money; they would find ways to earn large returns despite controls. Then the debate brought forth potent argument against radical change in the economic structure during war emergency. It put across the point that the purpose of war was victory; equalizing burdens was comparatively unimportant.

The war profit episode of 1934–35 also illustrated interesting points about the Roosevelt administration and the Munitions Committee. There has lingered a myth that Roosevelt was a radical of the Left who missed no opportunity to move America toward socialism. Had he been so inclined he would have thrown support to the Flynn plan with its provisions for virtual socialization of the economy in war. Instead he supported legislation fashioned after the moderate Baruch formula. Then the affair offered proof of the limited influence of the Munitions Committee. Some writers have left the impression that in munitions control, war profits, and neutrality the committee provided national leadership during the mid–thirties. Leadership assumes a following. While the committee stimulated the national desire for peace, it seldom won support for proposals. War profit removal and industrial mobilization provided one of several illustrations of this failure.

As for results—no legislation resulted. But the lessons of the debate had the effect of clearing the air. Wartime socialization had had a considerable appeal in the United States, but after the debate of 1935 it ceased to be a subject of serious discussion. When war threatened later in the decade few people thought of Flynn-style mobilization.

There was another interesting result. Information on the subject of economic mobilization brought forth by the Munitions Committee had effect in the war years of 1941–45. When Senator Harry S. Truman was preparing for his investigation of mobilization during the Second World War he examined the Munitions Committee record and from it gathered useful information and ideas on such matters as pricing policy and procurement. After the war the first Federal Price Administrator, Leon Henderson, told Stephen Raushenbush that committee material pertaining to industrial mobilization and wartime economy had helped form economic policy and brought important savings. He explained that in the First World War the government had taken the cost plus profit of the highest priced companies producing matériel and made that the price for the industry. This gave large profits to lower cost companies. In the Second World War—thanks to the studies of the Munitions Committee and other groups—the government set the going price a little above the peacetime sales price (in-

cluding profit) of the bulk of the industry, and paid induce-
ment prices to the small percentage of each industry which
had very high costs. The result was lower costs to the government and less inflation. Henderson wrote in 1962 that "undoubtedly the Nye Committee findings helped us at OPA [Office of
Price Administration] . . . I cannot put a dollar value on
them—though it was high." [54]

≡ VII ≡

RESPONSE TO
THE MUNITIONS
INQUIRY, 1934-1935

P<small>OPULAR</small> interest in the munitions investigation probably reached its peak in the autumn of 1934. It remained high through the winter and spring until—in the summer of 1935—the Ethiopian crisis and neutrality debate forced the inquiry to the background. Interest in the Munitions Committee enjoyed a brief resurgence in January, 1936, and then quickly faded.

In the period September, 1934–April, 1935 the investigation evoked a variety of responses. At home it brought serious discussion of the munitions trade and war profits. In Latin America it provoked anger when the committee published the names of Latin American officials accused of selling influence to munitions salesmen. In Great Britain a similar reaction resulted when the committee crudely implicated King George V. Yet in Latin America, England, and other countries small-scale munitions investigations followed. The inquiry, moreover, spurred efforts at Geneva to draft an effective arms-trade convention.

During this period Senator Nye symbolized the munitions inquiry, and kept himself and the inquiry in the public eye by eloquent if exaggerated speeches and statements. People began to think of Nye and the committee as one (not an uncommon occurrence in congressional investigations). At this time Nye received mostly praise, and one supporter committed sentiments to verse. Referring to Nye's activities during the Teapot Dome exposé as well as the munitions inquiry, he wrote:

> If you want a man to investigate graft
> Or to make the arms baron sigh,
> To make 'em shell out
> You have only to shout
> For Senator Gerald P. Nye.[1]

I

    In America the munitions investigation met wide approval in 1934–35. So inundated was Nye with letters of encouragement and requests for copies of speeches that he resorted to a mimeographed circular to answer his correspondence. Letters came from everywhere—Protestant and Jewish congregations, women's clubs, the Women's Christian Temperance Union, student organizations, branches of the Women's International League and other peace societies. One writer said: "When you go to investigating that Du Pont outfit I hope you can make him feel like a sick kitten with running sore eyes." After du Pont officials had testified, another correspondent urged Nye to "rub more acid on the Du Ponts. They deserve it." Typically a youth wrote: "As a potential soldier, I object to the prospect of becoming cannon fodder in 'the next war;' as a future tax-payer, I object to enriching the arms manufacturers by impoverishing my fellow Americans; and, most important, as a Christian, I object to preparing to run a bayonet through my brother from another country." People submitted drafts of bills and constitutional amendments for Nye's consideration. Some offered tips on munitions industry malfeasance. Former Secretary of State Frank B. Kellogg wrote that "I am in entire sympathy with the investigation of the activities of munitions manufacturers, their propaganda and influence in stirring up war." In a letter to Raushenbush, Woodrow Wilson's biographer Ray Stannard Baker said that "I have been delighted when I have seen notices of the fine work that you have been doing." The San Francisco *Examiner*, a Hearst paper, declared that "war lost its glamor twenty years ago when the dashing cavalry charge was replaced by trench warfare. And if any luster was left, it is being rubbed off in the Senate munitions investigation." The *Nation* said that committee disclosures had sufficed "to make thinking men and women the country over determined to bring a stop to the business of trading in death." [2]

Especial support for the inquiry came from churches. President A. W. Beaven of the Federal Council of Churches wrote (and sent a copy to President Roosevelt) that "a wave of moral indignation is sweeping through the churches against what appears to be a conscienceless and unscrupulous attitude taken by armament and munitions makers who are willing, apparently, to jeopardize the peace of the world for the sake of private gain." He reported that Northern Baptist churches were studying the investments of their boards and societies, to make sure they did not receive income from munitions industries. The General Assembly of the Presbyterian Church, U.S.A., requested that its boards scrutinize their investments on the ground that the munitions industry knew no patriotism and promoted sale of arms to citizens and governments of all nations "so that we continually hear of the slaughter of nationals by means of arms made in their own country, and by which their fellow-citizens have profited." The World Peace Commission of the Methodist Episcopal Church, South, condemned business interests which "endeavor to stir up strife among races and hatred among nations that they may profit by the sale of arms and munitions and other instruments of war." The Disciples of Christ recommended nationalization of the arms industry. The General Conference of the Colored Methodist Church and the General Assembly of the United Presbyterian Church urged strict control of the industry.[3]

Peace societies, as one would expect, responded to the munitions inquiry, and exploited its findings. The National Council for Prevention of War published a pamphlet entitled *Now It Can Be Proved,* which cited testimony taken by the committee as evidence that munitions makers were blocking disarmament and other programs of peace. On the back page appeared an advertisement urging local societies to stage a drama entitled *Repeat Hearing*, arranged by the research staff of the NCPW. Priced at 10 cents per copy or $1.00 for twelve, *Repeat Hearing* contained directions for staging, and was based on committee hearings. With the opening of the munitions hearings in September, 1934 the Women's International League dispatched a "Flying Squadron" (four young lady pacifists) on a campaign through the country. Led by Miss Elizabeth Wheeler, daughter of Senator Burton K. Wheeler of Montana, the group publicized disclosures of the Munitions Committee. It hoped to concentrate opinion upon congressional candidates before the elections of 1934.[4]

Support for the munitions investigation came from odd quarters. The *Wall Street Journal* defended the committee's work, and said the inquiry must continue, despite complaints from foreign sources. Attacking the international arms trade, the same newspaper argued: "It is a vicious system which both admits and tempts men to the commercial development of bad blood among neighboring peoples." The Chicago *Journal of Commerce* was "convinced that history has shown that the activities of munitions makers in time of peace are an important cause of war." Lammot du Pont responded to the munitions inquiry by advocating elimination of abnormal earnings in wartime; he also urged the government to regulate export of munitions.[5]

The White House co-operated, despite diplomatic embarrassment resulting from some committee disclosures. Regretting that foreign governments had reacted sharply to publication of some documents, Secretary Hull wrote that he was "in entire sympathy with the purpose of the Committee." The administration announced, moreover, that it did not encourage export of munitions, and advised diplomatic and consular officers in troubled countries not to seek trade opportunities for munitions exporters. In countries where normal conditions prevailed, officers could give information and advice only when reputable concerns wished to purchase explosives for industrial use. The administration also announced that it would not dispose of surplus armament to foreign governments or persons who might transfer it to foreign governments. Because of previous commitments the administration exempted Latin American republics from this last directive, although it hoped to discourage sale of surplus arms to them as well.[6]

From overseas came support for the investigation. Dorothy Detzer, in Geneva when hearings began, later recalled—perhaps with some overstatement—that "the corridors of the League of Nations buzzed with discussion of the Senate hearings, and proposals for similar investigations were quickly advocated in various parliaments." The well-known pacifist Philip Noel-Baker wrote Nye that "I am sure you are having messages from many quarters in Europe telling you what a magnificent success your enquiry into the Munitions Industry is having on this side of the water. . . . It is extremely interesting to see how those who two months ago were vigorously supporting the system of private manufacture are today entirely silent." The Rt. Hon. Christopher Addison, M.P., who had been Minister of Munitions in 1916–18, wrote that "the Senate Arms Inquiry has done more good than any investigation of anything during the last 10 years." The London *Daily Herald* said that "the world owes a great debt to the Americans for the determination with which they have swept aside the sectional pressure of the arms firms and rings." [7]

Of course there were dissenters. The Chicago *Tribune* feared that the inquiry would impair America's war potential, and accused Nye of securing "free publicity and its political profits through an . . . inquisition marked by gross prejudice and unfairness." The *Tribune* complained that British arms were "selling like hot cakes" the world over, and declared that increased British munitions sales had helped bring an economic upturn in Britain. The New York *Daily Worker* attacked the committee on ground that it was too deferential in treatment of the munitions industry. The communist newspaper naturally found propaganda material in the inquiry. It saw evidence that Roosevelt was pursuing a militaristic policy which would lead to war and fascism. *Collier's Weekly* called the early hearings a "shocking example of political irresponsibility." * Although the country needed an arms inquiry, it charged, the "worst chapters of yellow journalism reveal no more frivolous attempt to exploit great names." [8]

In the summer of 1935 Raushenbush came under attack by Senator L. J. Dickinson (Rep.) of Iowa who charged that the investigator's career had been tinged by association with communists and socialists. He cited an article on government control of business written for *Socialism in Our Times* and a sympathetic review of a communist drama written for the *Daily Worker*. "I wonder," Dickinson concluded, "if they [the committee] could not have found a man who is an American pure and simple and who believes in American fundamentals?" Senators Nye, Clark, Vandenberg, and George sprang to Raushenbush's defense. Nye and Clark suggested that Dickinson's attack had been part of a scheme to discredit the investigation. More moving were the statements of Vandenberg and George. George, who had questioned Rausenbush's fitness before his appointment, said that he had found Raushenbush honest and competent. Vandenberg told the Senate that "in my own rather critical and somewhat conservative judgment respecting this man, I can assent without reservation that he has done a superb and conscientious and effective piece of work which is completely beyond any possibility of legitimate criticism." One of Raushenbush's subordinates, Lawrence Brown, wrote his chief: "How does it feel to be such a big red menace? Undermine our institutions, will you? What have you done with all the information that you secretly found and didn't give the Committee? Any chance of a split on that?" [9]

One observer had a different criticism. In a letter to Nye he asked: "Why say 'munitions makers'—with munitions in the

* A few days after the *Collier's* article appeared Senator Bone wrote Raushenbush: "Collier's don't like your old munitions investigation. . . . Trust Collier's to be in the vanguard of reaction." Investigator Robert Wohlforth saw no humor in the article. Writing to Raushenbush, he said: "What a rap they took at you! It was the lousiest yellow journalism I've seen in quite a while. Why don't we find out who owns that rag? Maybe they'd show up on some of these stockholder's lists."

plural? We do not say shoes makers, though shoes are always plural. We do not say cows testing associations, nor ships builders. So many *s*'s are awkward. Even if the second word is singular, it is bad to have the modifier plural. We do not say oats meal, but oatmeal, despite the fact that oats by itself always is given the plural form. . . . If the committee would give orders to have it always printed 'munition makers,' with munition singular, general usage by the public would follow." [10]

There was, again, a marked public interest in the investigation. Critics, of the adverse sort, were few. Most of the letters and editorials were deadly serious in approving the work of the committee.

Sometimes there was a comic note. While Senator Bone, who had warned parents that their sons might have to go away to battle, was working through a pile of papers a magazine clipping with an attached letter fluttered to the floor. From a youngster in the West, the letter read: "I am sending an ad about a Vickers machine gun. The gun weighs about 33 pounds. It would make a fine war relic. . . . Please try to get it for me. It would look swell on my dresser." The letter was signed Homer T. Bone, Jr.[11]

II

The early munitions hearings, as mentioned, met some sharp responses in Latin America and Great Britain, and created trouble for the State Department.

Much of the difficulty in Latin America stemmed from the committee's practice of entering into the record the names of government and military officials accused of accepting bribes from armament representatives. One letter published by the committee named Colonel Rodriguez Familiar, a friend and protégé of the president of Mexico, as an officer who had promoted sale of Curtiss-Wright equipment to the Mexican government. Governments in Mexico, Argentina, Peru, Bolivia, and Chile lodged protests with the State Department and demanded apologies, charging the committee with insufficient evidence. Inasmuch as evidence consisted of letters by company officials and salesmen who contended that only through bribery could they secure business, this was true. The committee exhibited no letters by Latin Americans who had sold influence, no canceled checks to prove bribes. Disclosures did offend people in Latin America. But the governments doubtless feigned a good bit of the indignation. Not many Latin Americans took the view of *La Prensa* of Buenos Aires that no reputation had suffered serious damage by statements before the committee and that the committee had helped eliminate a factor for war. Few agreed with C. Bauer Avilés of *Neustro Diario* of Guatemala that "even though we are inclined to contradict indignantly the sad [disclosures of the committee], . . . honestly we can but confess with sorrow that those words contain a great deal of truth. . . . It is absolutely impossible to deny that bribery in Latin America came to constitute a very essential factor for the realization of any kind of business in which for any reason the public administration had to be consulted." [12]

Diplomats and businessmen of the United States nevertheless took alarm. Louis G. Dreyfus, Jr., chargé d'affaires in Lima, reported that "it may take years to efface the very unfavorable impression which these details have produced on local public opinion. It is believed that the investigation has resulted in creating a psychological background which will result in inestimable damage to future relations between Peru and the United States." Robert M. Scotten, counselor of embassy in Santiago, wrote that "there is no incident in Chilean-American relations which has arisen during the last few years likely to cause more ill-feeling in Chile and to undo the very fine atmosphere created as a result of our efforts in the Montevideo Conference." Businessmen feared that Latin Americans would take reprisals against United States business, and indeed, certain countries, notably Brazil and Argentina, threatened to if the Munitions Committee continued to publicize influence peddling in Latin America and if Washington failed to apologize. Chile did more than threaten. It canceled a $300,000 contract for American aviation equipment. In reply to an invitation to

The Philadelphia *Inquirer*

THE FAMILY SKELETON

155

visit American aircraft factories to inspect latest developments, the chief of the Chilean Air Force wrote: "I regret not accepting your invitation. I do not desire that my name appear capriciously exposed to suspicion as has happened with regard to officials of South American Republics during the development of the present investigation by the American Senate." The president of Tri-American Aviation wired Nye from Santiago: "Cannot believe it was desire of your committee to offend government here or to harm American firms engaged in honest and legitimate business. . . . Am certain can rely upon your spirit of fairness to both American firms and the Chilean government to correct the unfortunate impression created here." [13]

Protests did not deter the committee. When officials of a munitions company requested the committee to withhold names of foreign officials whom testimony and exhibits might incriminate, Bone declared: "Here is the sale of machine-guns, dynamite, poison gas, and shrapnel all over the world, and the war 15 years away, where 10,000,000 were shot to death, and do you want us to refrain from mentioning names?" The senator tried to mollify Latin Americans by telling them that the Munitions Committee took no pleasure in revealing that North American companies had corrupted Latin American officials. The committee had spared no American or European company whose records indicated misconduct. Explaining that criticism of a few leaders did not imply the Latin American people, he said: "To show that officials of a company have used weak men is not an indictment of a people, any more than an exposé of the racketeering of an Al Capone is an indictment of the people of Chicago." [14]

Meanwhile the Munitions Committee added to State Department difficulties by offending the British. On the fourth day of hearings the room had become so quiet that the buzzing of a few flies was audible when Senator Pope introduced a cable dated January 20, 1932 in which Florjan Ziemba, Polish agent for the Driggs Ordnance and Engineering Company, charged that King George V had pressed the Polish ambassador in London to try to prevent sale of Driggs weapons to Poland, presumably to enable British companies to secure the business. Louis Driggs, the company president, told the committee that at the time of the King's intercession the Prince of Wales was seeking to create a climate for sale of British munitions in the Argentine. Driggs did not believe the royal family held stock in British armament firms, but hoped to improve business in depression-weary Britain.[15]

The New York *Times* reported gasps of amazement from the dozen or so spectators in the hearing room, but this reaction was mild compared with the one in Great Britain. London newspapers expressed indignation that anyone during a public inquiry would mention the King. An official protest followed. The Acting Secretary of State for Foreign Affairs, Sir Robert Vansittart, called on Ambassador Robert W. Bingham and expressed astonishment that a committee of the Senate would take seriously and admit into evidence an accusation by "an irresponsible armament tout in Warsaw." He said the British would not soon forget their indignation, and described resentment over Washington's failure to offer a spontaneous expression of regret. The Polish embassy in London substantiated the British denial that the King had interfered in Polish munitions transactions. In Washington Senator Pope received a summons to the White House. Roosevelt requested that the committee show more discretion.[16]

As with allegations regarding Latin American officials, the committee's evidence in this instance was secondhand. One man, and a munitions salesman at that, had accused the King. Was it not probable that the salesman had blamed the King for his own failure? Even Anglophobes were disinclined to make an issue of Ziemba's communication, and belatedly the committee recognized the weakness of its position. Nye wrote Hull that "the Committee deeply regrets that a false impression may have been created, and that statements made by manufacturers' agents abroad, although believed by them, may be unfounded as far as those high personages are concerned, and the Committee regrets that the opinions of these agents seem to have been construed as necessarily reflecting the opinion of the Committee." The same day Hull spent nearly two hours in conference with the committee, during which he emphasized the embarrassment from publicity about heads and officials of other governments. Apparently the committee's attitude and Nye's letter satisfied the secretary. Of the letter Hull said that it "well illustrates both the righteous nature of the investigation of the munitions situation, and some of the manifold difficulties that must be dealt with by the Committee." No immediate improvement in Latin American relations followed publication of Nye's letter, but from London came a report that his explanation had appeased the British.[17]

A few weeks later in a speech to the Ottawa Canadien [sic] Club, Nye blamed munitions makers for bringing King George's name into the hearings. He explained that an armament salesman in Poland, needing an alibi for his failure, had told his superiors that he was competing against the King. Said Nye: "I am clearly of the opinion that these merchants of death, these merchants of war machines, took great pleasure in dragging the name of King George into the Senate investigation and magnifying it so that it assumed disproportionate importance." Nye seemed to forget that Pope, not a witness from the arms industry, had introduced the Ziemba cable—over the objection of Louis Driggs.[18]

Despite national indignation, the incident stirred interest for an investigation of Britain's armament industry. Ever since April, 1934 when the Senate adopted the Nye-Vandenberg Resolution to investigate American munitions makers, a movement had existed in England for a similar inquiry. The National Government dominated by Conservatives had shown no interest, but the hearings in Washington had weakened government resistance. On the first day the committee had exhibited evidence involving Vickers-Armstrong, and then came news of the Ziemba cable. Liberals in Parliament stepped up agitation for a British investigation. In Parliament on November 8, 1934 Foreign Secretary Sir John Simon attacked the American arms investigation, and declared the British would never tolerate such an inquiry. But Sir John had misgauged British opinion.

The Labour leader, Clement Attlee, expressed the view of many Britons when he said that the American investigation had "lifted a little bit of the very ragged veil that concealed the activities of the war profiteers." Such reaction, combined with a socialist victory in some British municipal elections, forced the government to reverse its stand. Sir John received the assignment of announcing on November 22, 1934 that the government would investigate the manufacture and sale of munitions. According to his announcement, the British study aimed to determine the merits of nationalization of the arms industry. Most Britishers, however, already seemed persuaded of the desirability of nationalization. The League of Nations Union had circulated a "peace ballot" among the electorate, and 40 per cent of the people had returned ballots. On the question of abolishing profit from manufacture of armament, i.e., nationalization, 10,417,329 voted yes; 775,415 voted no; 351,345 abstained; 15,078 voted doubtful.[19]

A royal commission conducted the British investigation beginning in March, 1935. Considering the government's opposition to the inquiry and open distaste for nationalization, Americans assumed that the commission would not expose the British arms industry. Philip Noel-Baker earlier had expressed concern that a government-sponsored investigation would "turn out to be a farce; or rather it would be worse than a farce, for it would give the appearance of impartiality, but would merely serve to whitewash British firms and show that they have not been guilty of the monstrous misconduct of the Americans!" But the royal commission, composed of persons outside the government, did not prove reactionary. When a Labourite demanded a Labour representative he received rebuke from Prime Minister Ramsay MacDonald who said the government had selected a commission whose members were uncommitted on questions under consideration.[20]

Yet the commission worked under handicaps, the largest of which were lack of authority to place witnesses under oath, or subpoena evidence, or obtain expert counsel. Harold Laski reported from London in February, 1936 that "with no power

to call for documents and no experts to cross-examine witnesses, a session of the commission is a quiet and genial in-
terchange of views from which the essential background is
wanting." The commission declined Nye's offer of documents
bearing upon British firms which the Munitions Committee
had gathered. The British inquiry on balance was a poor
counterpart of the Senate investigation, and indeed amounted
to little.[21]

Other countries responded to the work of the Munitions
Committee by conducting investigations and enacting legislation. Chile, Peru, Brazil, and Argentina held inquiries mainly
to prove their officials had not sold out to munitions salesmen.
Only in Argentina, thanks to a veteran socialist senator, Mario
Bravo, did the effort to whitewash the accused persons fail.
The Argentine inquiry established the culpability of several
individuals. But the government declined to take action. In
Europe the French premier issued a decree in September, 1935
regulating export of arms from France and Algeria. Companies
shipping munitions had to secure a license and answer questions about the origin and destination of the arms. At The
Hague the Dutch government secured power to embargo shipments "to further international cooperation in the interest of
Peace, or to protect the matters of vital importance to the
State in times of extraordinary international tension." In Sweden, home of the Bofors works, the Riksdag in April, 1935
enacted an arms control bill. A compromise measure, it accepted the government's proposal for licensing companies engaged in manufacture of arms, but granted companies a delay
of thirty months before applying for government license.[22]

III

During all this time the Geneva Disarmament
Conference was trying to deal with reduction of arms. When
the munitions inquiry began in 1934 the disarmament conference—meeting since February, 1932—had virtually expired,
although private negotiations and special committees carried

on work. In the summer and autumn of 1934 the delegates, hoping to profit from popular response to the Nye investigation, concentrated upon control of the munitions trade. Their aim was an agreement which would prove more effective than the Geneva Arms Traffic Convention of 1925.

The chief American delegate to the disarmament conference, Norman H. Davis, in May, 1934 said that the United States would co-operate to suppress the arms traffic and negotiate a treaty on the problem. He declared that "those who have a sordid financial interest in fomenting international suspicion and discord, which in turn increases the demand for what they have to sell, must be put in a position in which they do not have the power or the incentive to do much evil." The Geneva representative of the National Council for Prevention of War wrote back that Davis' address had received much attention in the corridors, and she predicted that the American attitude would have large influence upon the conference because "the psychological effect of the American position is always immediately felt." She urged pacifists in America to encourage the administration to retain the initiative at Geneva.[23]

The American delegation on June 14, 1934 presented a proposal for controlling the international munitions trade, and on July 2 the Special Committee on the Manufacture of and Trade in Arms accepted the principle of the American draft and submitted it to governments represented at the conference. The plan did not envision suppression of private manufacture, but that signatory governments would regulate arms trade in their own countries. It provided for publicity on manufacture and export, control of state as well as private manufacture, and control over increases and replacement of arms and arms-producing equipment. No company or individual could manufacture or export munitions without a license or visa. No firm or individual would receive a general license, and licenses would not be permanent. Each factory, state or private, could manufacture only those types of armament for which it had license. Control via publicity was central to the plan, so it provided that production, exports, imports, and orders for manufacture would receive publicity. Each firm would report to its government, which in turn would convey information to the Permanent Disarmament Commission. Besides publishing this information, the commission would check the reports against quantitative and qualitative limitations provided in the General Disarmament Convention. The commission could make continuous and automatic inspection of factories manufacturing war material, as well as armament used by signatories. To prevent interference with administration of manufacturing concerns, processes, and trade secrets, the plan permitted exceptions to these inspection provisions. The United States suggested such exceptions to allow individual competition, but believed they would not interfere with inspection efficiency. Supporters of the plan admitted that bootlegging of armament would be possible, but not probable if penalties were severe and governments acted honestly.[24]

Mild enthusiasm greeted the American draft convention at Geneva. A Polish delegate pointed out that for the first time the Subcommittee on Manufacture of Arms had accepted unanimously a text for arms trade control; and a French delegate hopefully proclaimed that the period of floundering was over— the draft marked a route which led to a general convention. The National Council for Prevention of War correspondent wrote that the proposed convention resolved problems which had impeded arms trade control during the past ten years. In her view the two basic questions had pertained to government vis-à-vis private manufacture and producing vis-à-vis non-producing countries. The "present plan," she thought, "provides for equality of treatment in the first case by the assumption of national responsibility for all manufacture and trade and, in the second case, by providing complete publicity even for orders in advance, including orders placed with a State, and for supervision by an international authority." Yet knowledge that the Special Committee on Manufacture of and Trade in Arms comprised only nineteen delegations, not including Germany or Italy, tempered enthusiasm. Japan, moreover, submitted a general reservation, and the Soviet Union never had sat with the committee. Acceptance of the American draft involved only seventeen states.[25]

It was clear by November, 1934 that no general disarmament convention would come out of Geneva, but some delegates hoped for agreement on some aspects of disarmament. Upon suggestion by the president of the conference, Arthur Henderson, the Bureau of the Conference decided to concentrate on protocols dealing with categories of the problem. Most prominent was supervision of the trade in arms by international agreement. This policy appealed to the United States, and on November 13, 1934 Secretary Hull announced that his government was negotiating for a convention to control the munitions trade. The American minister to Switzerland, Hugh Wilson, submitted to the Bureau a revised draft of articles which the United States had presented earlier. The Bureau referred this draft to the Special Committee which would meet in January, 1935. Meanwhile it circulated the draft among the governments for criticism and suggestions.[26]

The American plan prompted considerable conversation at Geneva through the winter of 1934–35, but in the United States the War and Navy departments had misgivings. The War Department objected to supervision and control of munitions manufactured by a state for its own use, and also to the provision permitting committees of signatory governments to inspect any installation. The department preferred examination of witnesses and documents in the capitals of contracting parties. President Roosevelt, vacationing at Warm Springs, retorted in a letter to Hull: "I see no reason why you should not tell the War Department that supervision and inspection must be all inclusive, including all plants in all nations. That is my policy. . . . I entirely approve of the draft and am glad that you have authorized Mr. Wilson to present it to the Bureau." [27]

The Committee on the Manufacture of and Trade in Arms settled down to work on the American draft treaty early in 1935, but at this time the crisis developed between Italy and Ethiopia, and Hitler renounced disarmament. These events caused the European democracies to drag their feet on arms control. In truth, the convention never had a chance. Arms control required assent by all major powers. Italy and Germany and Japan were not interested.

If it is impossible to measure precisely the response to such an event as the munitions inquiry, the indices available to the historian—newspapers, periodicals, letters, legislation—show that the effect of Nye's committee was considerable. During its early stages the investigation each day received front-page attention of such newspapers as the New York *Times*. Editorial comment appeared in most newspapers and periodicals, at home and abroad. It stimulated inquiries in other countries.

But for all the effort, for all the interest, what did the Munitions Committee have to show? It failed to persuade world leaders to restrict the international munitions trade. During this period the trade increased; more arms were manufactured and sold during these months than at any time since the World War. A few countries, the United States included (as the next chapter shows), adopted legislation to regulate armament makers, but it had slight effect. The committee focused upon bribery in the arms business, but it is doubtful that the practice declined. The committee brought attention to munitions lobbying. But the government took no action. The committee established collusion in the shipbuilding industry, but Congress adopted no corrective measures. The committee focused attention upon profiteering during the World War, but failed to secure legislation to eliminate excessive returns for Americans in time of war. For a time the investigation discouraged the Army from increasing its budget requests; but in May, 1936, three months after the end of the inquiry, Congress allotted the War Department more funds than requested by the administration.[28]

The Munitions Committee, in conclusion, made a spirited attack upon problems—actual and presumed—pertinent to the arms trade and war profits. It received much enthusiastic support. But essentially the situation remained unchanged.

≡ VIII ≡

THE MUNITIONS
COMMITTEE AND
NEUTRALITY, 1935

Late in April the Munitions Committee conducted its final hearing for the year 1935. By then Americans had begun to lose interest in the complicated business of removing profit from war, finding concern with another issue which, equally complicated, seemed more urgent.

A dangerous situation existed in the Far East, of course, but more ominous were the rumblings in Adolf Hitler's Germany and Benito Mussolini's Italy. German expansion under Hitler had begun the previous January when the people of the Saar Basin, after a vigorous Nazi campaign, voted for union with Germany. Hitler on March 16, 1935 then jolted Europe by renouncing the disarmament clauses of the Treaty of Versailles. Meanwhile a clash of Italian and Ethiopian troops at Ualual on the Ethiopian-Somaliland frontier in December, 1934 had given Mussolini an excuse to devour Ethiopia. Bent on conquest as well as vengeance for the defeat Ethiopia had administered Italy at Adua in 1896, the Italians refused a peaceful solution. Through the summer and early autumn of 1935, despite efforts of the League, the Italo-Ethiopian situation drifted from bad to worse. At length, on October 3, 1935 the Duce's troops crossed Ethiopia's borders.

These events increased the uneasiness which people everywhere felt for the future. Less than seventeen years before they had seen the end of history's most expensive war. They wondered if fascist salutes, torchlight rallies, and aggression against a small neighbor foreshadowed a repetition of the catastrophe of 1914–18.

Americans responded by re-examining their country's role in world affairs. They debated neutrality, and Congress in August, 1935 enacted a temporary neutrality law which proved unsatisfactory. There was further debate.

I

Questionings over neutrality were not new, and most of the proposals and arguments of 1935 had appeared before. In the latter 1920's some students of international affairs, in America and abroad, had concluded that it was anomalous for signatories of the Kellogg Pact to permit countries using war as an instrument of policy (i.e., international outlaws) to purchase munitions from other nations. According to Judge Thorvald Boye of Norway's Supreme Court, "a State which begins a war in disregard of the Kellogg-Briand Pact has thereby committed an infraction of the law not only in respect of its adversary, but against all the other contracting States. The pact-breaking State should be considered as having committed a delinquency against humanity, and it should not by its violation of law be entitled to the rights of a belligerent." Professor James T. Shotwell of Columbia University had expressed this view as early as 1926, saying that shipping arms to opposing belligerents was helping both the criminal and the victim.[1]

From such thinking came a movement to remove, insofar as the United States was concerned, the presumed anomaly between the Kellogg Pact and traditional neutrality. Supporters sought legislation authorizing the President or Congress to impose arms embargoes against pact violators. Among the first individuals to introduce such a measure in Congress was Representative Theodore E. Burton (Rep.) of Ohio, who in 1927 advanced the standard argument that a violator of the proposed Kellogg Pact would be guilty of an offense against the family of nations. Burton told reporters that "there would be hesitancy in waging war if the United States, with the facilities for furnishing arms and munitions, should establish a policy of refusal to aid an offending nation." To use a phrase of the day, Burton thought his resolution would put teeth in an antiwar pact.[2]

Some Americans found Burton's logic persuasive, but his resolution received no support from the Coolidge administration. Amended to apply to all belligerents, victims and aggressors (compromising its basic principle), the resolution inspired its critics. Secretary of War Dwight F. Davis raised a question which would reappear during the neutrality debate of 1935–36 when he told the Foreign Affairs Committee that the Burton Resolution would impair national defense, for manufacturers would not devise plans for war production if there were no possibility of exporting arms to belligerents. This prompted Representative Cyrenus Cole (Rep.) of Iowa to ask: "Should we keep our factories in practice by permitting them to send those munitions abroad to kill other people with whom we have no controversies at all? Would it not be better if we financed our factories outright instead of permitting them to finance themselves by exporting arms to assist those carrying on war against people with whom we have no grievances?" Davis persisted, and anticipating future arguments against nationalization of the munitions industry he testified that the alternative to private manufacture was government arsenals constructed at a cost of millions of dollars. He also contended that Burton's resolution would compel nonarmament-producing countries to erect plants, since they could no longer purchase arms from American companies if they became belligerents. This would bring a vast increase in the world's armament.[3]

Davis identified another problem which would perplex individuals wishing to embargo arms shipments to belligerents during the 1930's. How does one define implements of war?

He reminded the committee that most peaceful articles were essential to the conduct of war. Would an embargo achieve its purpose if limited to arms? [4]

From this question came other problems which would puzzle Americans in 1935–36. If Congress legislated in belief that embargoes of "vital materials" were necessary to discourage belligerents and preserve American neutrality, what would happen to American commerce during hostilities? Then what criteria would distinguish essential and nonessential materials? According to Davis (and the experience of the World War), nearly everything was contraband. Did "nearly everything" include foodstuffs and medicines? Was it humane to withhold such commodities from civilian populations in belligerent countries?

During debate on the Burton Resolution, Charles H. Herty, adviser to the Chemical Foundation, presented an argument which would become standard for those individuals who opposed unilateral embargoes. In absence of co-operation by all industrial countries, an embargo by one country could do little to advance peace. He argued that the American chemical industry would be a victim of unfair treatment and suffer reverses if forced to embargo chemicals capable of military use while foreign competitors were free to trade at will. He ignored the propriety of providing an aggressor or treaty-breaker with matériel for subduing his victim.[5]

If the Burton Resolution never came to a vote, proponents of embargoes continued to introduce similar measures. Most publicized was a joint resolution offered by Senator Arthur Capper (Rep.) of Kansas in February, 1929. It provided that it would be unlawful for Americans to export munitions or other articles of military use to any country violating the Kellogg Pact. Interest in the resolution doubtless surprised Capper. It dominated the first two pages of the New York *Times* on February 11, 1929, and nearly every newspaper of consequence commented editorially. The New York *Evening Post* anticipated an argument which opponents of punitive embargoes would invoke many times in the 1930's. How could one be sure which belligerent was the pact-violator—the aggressor? "If any one thing ever was clearer to the mind of the United States in 1914 than that Germany was the aggressor in the war, we do not know it. Yet look what the historians are making of that theory now." [6]

Europeans hailed the Capper Resolution, although Sir Eric Drummond, Secretary General of the League of Nations, explained that it was a delicate internal matter for the United States to decide. Americans, he thought, might consider an expression of League opinion an intrusion. But other European officials were less restrained in private remarks. They thought the resolution would ally the United States with League efforts to punish nations disrupting peace. The Capper Resolution, they reasoned, would commit the United States to an embargo against any Kellogg Pact violator. The pact-violator probably would be a violator of the League Covenant, obliging League members to impose sanctions. Thus, assuming no problem in naming the aggressor, the United States and the League would stand committed to similar action. [7]

More important was the attitude of the White House and the leadership in Congress. Although Secretary of State Kellogg showed some mild interest in Capper's resolution, the administration opposed it. Nor was much support apparent in Congress. Senator Borah, chairman of the Foreign Relations Committee, expressed a view—which members of Congress would repeat many times in the future—when he described sanctions, economic or otherwise, as dangerous. "An economic blockade is in itself an act of war and usually after one is put in operation, shooting begins on the following morning." He said the President would dare invoke the measure only against smaller countries, and it would be hazardous to invest the President with such authority. Treaties, he thought, rested upon the good faith of signatories, not coercion. The Capper resolution went the way of the Burton Resolution. [8]

The early 1930's saw attempts to achieve embargo legislation. After the Mukden Incident in September, 1931 Secretary of State Stimson toyed with the idea of a punitive embargo against Japan, but President Hoover argued that sanctions led to war. Hoover's position had changed somewhat by January, 1933, however, when with Latin America in mind he recommended legislation "conferring upon the President authority in his discretion to limit or forbid shipment of arms for military purposes in cases where special undertakings of cooperation can be secured with the principal arms-manufacturing nations." The proposal found support, and the Foreign Relations Committee prepared a measure, the Borah Resolution (Borah, like Hoover, had changed his position). President-elect Roosevelt, although declining comment, said he favored embargoes on arms shipments, particularly to aggressor nations.[9]

For a time the Borah Resolution's chance appeared good. The Democratic House probably would go along, and on January 19, 1933 the Senate approved, only to return the measure to committee. During hearings before the House Foreign Affairs Committee the resolution met old shibboleths: it would not advance peace, would involve the United States in war, jeopardize national defense, handicap business. The arguments seemed formidable, and the committee amended the resolution to allow the President to act only in disputes or wars in the Western Hemisphere. He could not act against Japan, as some members of Congress suspected was his aim.[10]

Sam D. McReynolds (Dem.) of Tennessee, chairman of the Foreign Affairs Committee, reported the amended resolution on February 15, 1933, but it never came to a vote in the House. In the Senate Hiram Bingham (Rep.) of Connecticut forestalled the measure, contending (as would other individuals in future debate) that had such a law existed in 1914–15 the Allies would have lost the World War.[11]

Proponents of the Borah Resolution did not despair. A new President was about to enter the White House, and his support was assured. Less than two weeks after Roosevelt's inauguration McReynolds introduced a measure almost identical to the original Borah Resolution.

Despite the new administration's strength, the McReynolds Resolution met sharp opposition. In a hearing before the Foreign Affairs Committee it received criticism from two international lawyers. Edward A. Harriman of George Washington University said that "a nation's interference with the ordinary trade in arms is an act which might constitute a breach of neutrality, even though it was extended to both belligerents, if the practical circumstances were such that the effect was to aid one belligerent at the expense of another." Edwin M. Borchard of Yale contended that the resolution afforded the President the opportunity to choose an aggressor and in union with other powers "strangle that nation in the name of peace." He said the term aggressor was a cloudy conception, and that it was almost impossible to name the aggressor during a conflict. "I regard neutrality as the greatest gift that God has put in the hands of the American people. By putting two oceans on each side of us, we were given the opportunity to survive, an opportunity and assurance that most foreign nations do not have. Neutrality has been regarded as the last and highest achievement of international law, but now, forsooth, the very principle of neutrality is challenged and we are invited to take part in all foreign troubles, thus creating universal turmoil. This opportunity to keep out of foreign troubles, to keep out of other people's quarrels, is a precious one." [12]

The Foreign Affairs Committee reported the resolution without amendment, and on April 13 and 14, 1933 the House debated it. Leading the opposition was Hamilton Fish, Jr., (Rep.) of New York, who saw the measure as a step toward the League. He declared that "we will prove to you before we conclude this debate that this is not the entrance into the League of Nations through the back door or through the trap door, but through the front door." Other opponents argued again that the resolution gave too much power to the President. Harold McGugin (Rep.) of Kansas cited the earlier Roosevelt as the type of President in whose hands discretion would be dangerous. "In many respects I revere the great Theodore Roosevelt. However, if he were living and were President, I think by temperament it would be exceedingly difficult for him to refrain from taking sides in any war that might spring up some place in the world. I doubt if he could refrain from using the power vested in the President by this bill to send munitions to the country whose side he was taking in the conflict. Unquestionably that would lead to war." James J. Wadsworth (Rep.) of New York anticipated the situation in 1935–36 when Italo-Americans resented an embargo against the belligerents in East Africa. Americans, he said, were not an homogeneous people, and an embargo against any country was certain to offend part of the population.[13]

Friends of the legislation, like Charles West (Dem.) of Ohio, contended that the President's control of foreign policy and military forces gave him opportunity to lead the nation into dangerous situations. West also cited Woodrow Wilson's speech of 1916 that the United States would find it impossible to stay out of future wars because war was reaching such a scale that the position of neutrals sooner or later would become intolerable.[14]

Whether because of such argument or Democratic discipline, the McReynolds Resolution passed the House on April 17, 1933 by a vote of 253–109, but it already had run into trouble in the Senate Foreign Relations Committee. At length Hiram Johnson (Rep.) of California persuaded the committee to amend the resolution to make the embargo apply to all belligerents, victims and aggressors. The Johnson amendment made the measure unacceptable to the administration. Although the President during this famous period of the Hundred Days was going from strength to strength in domestic affairs, he met here his first rebuff in foreign affairs. The neutrality question stood unresolved.

Discussion continued, much of it centering on the possibility of nonintercourse with belligerents. Arms embargoes against all belligerents or against aggressors only had occupied attention in the recent past, but harking back to the era of Thomas Jefferson and James Madison some students wondered if cutting off all trade might not be a good way to discourage belligerents and keep America out of war.

In New York in January, 1934 the Council on Foreign Relations considered this question in some detail. It believed the United States could remain out of conflicts which involved no major sea power. In any war in the Atlantic-European area which did not involve England, the United States and England (whose interests in trade would be similar) without serious risk could force respect for traditional rules of neutrality. But in any Atlantic war involving England or (to a lesser extent) Pacific war involving Japan, the United States would find traditional neutrality difficult. The experience of 1914–17 might repeat itself. The only means of assuring peace was nonintercourse with belligerents and possibly their neighbors. But such a policy would so affect agricultural and industrial interests that Congress would never adopt it. Since nonintercourse was out of the question, Congress might take such steps as restricting activities of American nationals in time of war (e.g., traveling on belligerent ships) and limiting activities of belligerents in American ports.[15]

Other students of foreign affairs ignored the difficulties of nonintercourse. Professor Thomas Jefferson Wertenbaker of Princeton said that "when our president issues his proclamation of military and naval neutrality, he would do well to add to it a declaration of economic neutrality." Lothrop Stoddard, the author of several books on world affairs, saw a curious economic advantage in nonintercourse. In a letter to Secretary Hull late in 1934 he commented on what he called the delusion of war trade. Some Americans, he wrote, believed the United States would profit from trade with belligerents during another major war, and that sharply-controlled war trade would spell sacrifices. Stoddard insisted that another war would leave all belligerents bankrupt; goods sold on long-term credit or money lent for bond issues would be lost. Americans would come out poorer for such transactions.[16]

The State Department had not forgotten the neutrality question. Early in 1934 it began to re-examine neutrality and neutral rights in hope of drafting legislation which would prove effective and acceptable to Congress. Receiving ideas from many sources, the department gave most thought to a lengthy memorandum submitted in August, 1934 by Charles Beecher Warren, a well-known international lawyer and former ambassador to Japan and Mexico.

Warren recommended a variety of measures to strengthen American neutrality. His proposals were isolationist, and departed from previous stands of the Roosevelt administration. There should be an embargo on arms shipments to all belligerents upon outbreak of war. Arms shipments to other neutrals should not exceed prewar levels. The government should prevent belligerent armed merchantmen and submarines from using American ports and aircraft from entering or landing on American territory. It should prevent Americans from traveling on belligerent ships. Warren's most striking proposal was for limited intercourse with belligerents. All trade with belligerents should not exceed the prewar average.[17]

On the basis of its studies in the year 1934 the State Department drafted several proposals for legislation but declined to press them. Late in the year and early in 1935 the department and presumably the administration seemed uncertain. It wavered in its faith in discretionary measures, and for a time seemed to flirt with isolation.

II

When Senator Nye and his colleagues on the Munitions Committee began their investigation they had no thought of becoming involved in a debate over neutrality. Yet it was inevitable perhaps that study of the arms trade, followed by recommendations on regulation, would move the committee in that direction. In April, 1934 when the Senate adopted the Nye-Vandenberg Resolution for investigating the munitions industry and war profits, neutrality was receiving scant attention. Failure of the Borah and McReynolds resolutions the year before had illustrated the difficulty of changing statutes on neutrality. There was no indication that such difficulty might disappear. Then in 1934 neutrality did not seem urgent. The Far East was momentarily tranquil, and the Chaco problem presented no threat to the United States.

When international affairs took a turn for the worse in 1935 the senators began to take interest in neutrality. Yet the committee contemplated no action on the subject until urged by President Roosevelt during a conference at the White House in March, 1935. Roosevelt's proposal took the committee by surprise. Why he made it is not clear. Probably he made it on impulse—suggesting that his ideas on neutrality at this point were not well defined. The committee attacked the problem immediately, and when Joseph C. Green of the State Department suggested to Stephen Raushenbush on March 27 that the committee delay until the President returned from vacation, Raushenbush said the senators had become so interested in neutrality and so anxious to draft legislation that he doubted they would agree. Two days later Nye and Raushenbush told Green that the committee was near agreement on legislation to withdraw government protection from American ships and citizens entering war zones or visiting belligerent countries.[18]

Meanwhile the Senate Foreign Relations Committee had resented what seemed an administration attempt to remove neutrality from its jurisdiction to that of the special Munitions Committee. According to Chairman Key Pittman of Nevada, the Nye-Vandenberg Resolution authorized no study or report on neutrality, although, of course, individual members of the investigating committee could introduce neutrality legislation. The Munitions Committee deferred to the Foreign Relations Committee, Nye expressing the wish that his committee could rid itself of neutrality. The committee, he added, had not considered action on the question until the "President laid it on our doorstep." The committee insisted, however, that its mandate was broad enough to justify neutrality legislation, although Vandenberg had said earlier that removing war profits was the only aspect of neutrality which the committee considered in its jurisdiction. On April 9, 1935 Nye and Clark introduced legislation pertaining to loans and passports in wartime, but Raushenbush explained to Green that these were not committee measures.[19]

The first Nye-Clark Bill, S. J. Res. 99, prohibited loans by American nationals or the United States government to belligerent governments or their nationals. Such legislation aimed to prevent repetition of the World War experience in which one set of belligerents secured large sums in the United States. As Nye said, "if Morgans and other bankers must get into another war, let them do it by enlisting in the Foreign Legion." [20]

The second Nye-Clark Bill, S. J. Res. 100, denied passports to Americans trying to enter war zones. If an American suffered injury or death in a war zone there would be no diplomatic action as after the *Lusitania* sinking in 1915.

A short time later Nye and Clark introduced S. J. Res. 120, providing for a mandatory arms embargo. It directed the President to embargo arms to all belligerents; he also was to proclaim an embargo when arms shipments might involve the United States in international complications or contribute to armed conflict. Advocates of national isolation believed such legislation would prevent sinking of American vessels carrying munitions to belligerent ports, and thus make involvement in foreign conflicts less likely. The measure also would advance peace by halting arms shipments to belligerents which lacked facilities for producing arms.

Inasmuch as Nye and Clark later demanded embargoes of "vital materials" as well as munitions, it is interesting that they did not advocate such sweeping measures in the spring and summer of 1935. Nye said in May that "it is virtually impossible . . . to impose a mandatory embargo on all war material because of the practical difficulties of defining articles which have a commercial use as well as a use in war time." A few months later he did not think these difficulties so large.[21]

As was his wont, Nye began a speaking campaign in behalf of the Nye-Clark Resolutions. Before an audience at Carnegie Hall he declared: "Did the American people know [in 1917–18] that they were fighting to save the skins of the bankers who had coaxed the people into loaning 2 billion dollars to the Allies? No! They all thought that they were fighting for national honor, for democracy, for the end of war!" The United States, he said, had been forced "to get into the war because American bankers had advanced $2,000,000,000 worth of credits which would have been worthless if we had not gotten into the war." He did not support his charges with Munitions Committee evidence—the committee had not yet studied neutrality in detail—but he said in a radio speech that "the investigation has given birth to a strong conviction that it is of utmost importance that America lose no time in strengthening its provision of neutrality to prevail if and when other nations go to war." [22]

It is doubtful that Nye's eloquence was responsible, but the Nye-Clark Resolutions met a friendly response in the Senate Foreign Relations Committee. On May 13, 1935 the committee reported S. J. Res. 99 and 100, and no obstacle appeared in the way of 120.

Apparent or not, there was an obstacle, the administration. Late in June, 1935, Joseph Green advised Chairman Pittman that the State Department opposed all three Nye-Clark measures. Especially did it object to S. J. Res. 120, the arms embargo resolution. Green reported that the provision requiring the President to proclaim embargoes against all belligerents contravened the policy of the administration. The administration, in brief, no longer was toying with isolation. It again was endorsing the principle of the Borah and McReynolds resolutions of 1933, that the President should have wide discretion in foreign affairs. Norman Davis expressed the administration view when he wrote that "to accept the Johnson [amendment to the McReynolds] resolution as a principle and thus to deprive the President of any discretionary power would be a blunder of the first magnitude." Such a position would destroy America's moral influence in world affairs and make countries like Great Britain wary of trying to co-operate with the United States in, for example, the Far East. Finally, the United States would be unable to halt aggression or discourage violation of treaties to which it was party.[23]

From the State Department's Economic Adviser came other arguments against the three resolutions. The provision forbidding extension of credit for belligerent purchases of contraband meant that American exporters would have to scrutinize credit orders from all over the world. Tracing trade through other neutral countries would give rise to doubtful cases and affect trade with neutrals. Then other countries might adopt similar loan-credit legislation, increasing American difficulties in securing materials if the United States became involved in war. American gold reserves could carry the country through an emergency, but the Economic Adviser believed that nine billion dollars in reserves were not inexhaustible if expenses approached the level of the World War.[24]

Such argument proved effective, and after a conference of several hours Davis extracted a promise from Pittman that he would stop the legislation. Pittman then courted the fury of Nye and Clark by prevailing upon the Foreign Relations Committee to recall S. J. Res. 99 and 100 and postpone action on 120.[25]

There appeared meanwhile another measure which would bear upon the neutrality question, the National Munitions Bill. Designed to control the munitions trade, the bill came from findings and publicity of the Munitions Committee. Senator Pope introduced and managed the measure (S. 2998) in behalf of the committee, although it was more accurately described as an administration measure. Joseph Green had drafted it, and the committee had only mild interest. Nye agreed to promote it after prompting by Roosevelt and Hull, but served notice that he favored nationalization of the munitions industry, not regulation; the administration was to understand that committee support of the bill did not preclude proposals for nationalization.[26]

The bill provided for a National Munitions Control Board composed of the Secretaries of State, Treasury, War, Navy, and Commerce. The board would license firms and individuals dealing in munitions, and keep statistics on the country's armament business. Patterned after the Geneva Arms Traffic Convention of 1925, it hoped to counter evils which the Munitions Committee had found in the arms trade. Elimination of evil could come only through publicity, since the bill did not authorize the government to refuse an arms dealer a license unless the President had embargoed munitions to the purchasing country.

All persons or companies dealing in munitions would register with the Secretary of State, and list munitions which they ordinarily exported, imported, or manufactured for export. Application for a license would contain a list of items in the proposed shipment. The bill prohibited the government from purchasing war materials from any person or corporation not registered, and from arranging sale of munitions to any foreign government.

The administration had several reasons for promoting the National Munitions Bill. One of them was intelligence. The measure would provide the executive branch with information on all arms exports, important since (as Green told the Foreign Affairs Committee) the munitions trade was "not commerce pure and simple; it is commerce, with a very definite political character." Machinery in the bill, moreover, would enable the State Department to administer restrictions already in effect. In testimony Green cited violations of the Chaco embargo to illustrate what was wrong with existing machinery. Then Green pointed out that Congress might wish more restrictions on the arms trade at some future date (he was thinking of a neutrality act which included an arms embargo), but in absence of this or similar legislation it would have no precise information on which to base regulatory measures. Green did not say so, but the White House probably saw the measure as a means of quieting people who wanted arms regulation. The administration by this time had slight reason to fear nationalization of the industry, but sentiment for control was considerable.[27]

The administration denied that the bill had any reference to neutrality. The measure nonetheless became involved in the general neutrality debate in that its provisions went into the Neutrality Act of 1935. Unlike other parts of the act, however, these provisions evoked no controversy. Munitions manufacturers and their congressional friends did not object, perhaps thankful that despite the Nye disclosures there was no serious restriction upon the arms trade. That peace leaders refrained from criticizing the provisions is more surprising. If nationalization was unobtainable, they hoped for stringent regulation of the arms business. Perhaps they believed that these provisions, while not perfect, at least looked in the direction of arms control.[28]

If the National Munitions Bill generated no controversy, such was not the case with other bills and resolutions bearing upon neutrality. As the Italo-Ethiopian situation went from bad to worse, the controversy mounted. Isolationists insisted upon mandatory legislation on the model of the Nye-Clark Resolutions—legislation requiring the President to act indiscriminately against all belligerents upon outbreak of war. The administration proposed a far different type of measure. It would give the President authority to react to foreign conflict in several ways. He could punish aggressors, co-operate with other powers to stop war, or do nothing. He could embargo arms to all or selected belligerents. He could prevent—at his discretion and discriminately—American ships from carrying arms to belligerents, belligerents from using American ports, submarines from entering United States waters, financial transactions between Americans and belligerents, travel by Americans on belligerent ships.[29]

At this point one should avoid the conclusion that Roosevelt and Hull, despite advocacy of discretionary measures, were internationalists in the 1950–60 sense. They were moving in that direction, but not yet committed to collective security, not committed to the proposition that a threat to liberty in one part of the world constituted a threat to the United States. As various pronouncements (such as the State of the Union address of 1936) reveal, Roosevelt felt some of the traditional American contempt for the Old World. He preferred to remain free of the Old World's seemingly endless conflicts. But in 1935 he wanted to retain the executive's traditional freedom of action in foreign affairs, and continued to seek—as in 1933—authority to act with other powers should such a course seem desirable. Still, if Congress had given him the authority he sought, it is probable that he would have shown much caution in exercising it in the years 1935–38.

In the neutrality debate of 1935 all the arguments which had appeared during discussion of the Burton, Capper, Borah, and McReynolds resolutions circulated with new vigor. Representatives of nearly every pressure group in the country had descended on the capital, and defying the summer heat worked overtime to persuade members of Congress to their views. Especially active were peace leaders, and although most peace organizations conceded that peace could best come through international co-operation (most of them favored American membership in the World Court and the League of Nations), they supported the Nye-Clark Resolutions or their counterparts. President Ivan Lee Holt of the Federal Council of Churches expressed the prevailing pacifist view when he wrote that pending creation of a world system of security the United States should withhold aid from all belligerents. Or as William T. Stone expressed it: "In the past I have sympathized with the State Dept's position: i.e. if the League powers really were willing to enforce the Covenant vigorously against an aggressor, then it would be both wise and expedient for the U.S. to shape its policies so as to support the League. This thesis has very little substance today. In the Manchurian controversy, and now in the Ethiopian conflict, the Great Powers have shown clearly enough that they don't intend to use sanctions of any kind against an aggressor unless they happen to coincide with their immediate national interests." Proponents of discretionary legislation also were active, although isolation was running strong in and out of Congress. Still, on their side was the President.[30]

Once more the Foreign Relations Committee proved the obstacle to administration plans. Seeking to persuade the members to the administration position, Hull and Assistant Secretary of State R. Walton Moore conferred with the committee early in July, 1935. There was no apparent change in the committee's stand, but the administration was not discouraged. It was confident of support of Chairman Pittman, who only recently had shown his influence by persuading the committee to reconsider the Nye-Clark Resolutions. But on August 19 Pittman wrote Roosevelt that all except three members of the committee still opposed granting the President authority to embargo arms to an aggressor. If the administration insisted, he would introduce a discretionary measure, but he added that he felt obliged to express his view that the resolution would receive support of neither the Foreign Relations Committee nor a majority of the Senate. Pittman told assistant presidential secretary Stephen Early: "I tell you, Steve, the President is riding for a fall if he insists on designating the aggressor in accordance with the wishes of the League of Nations. . . . I will introduce it [a discretionary bill] on behalf of the Administration without comment, but he will be licked as sure as hell." [31]

The administration was reluctant to accept defeat, and the result was an attempted compromise, a temporary measure which would give the President discretion with respect to Italy and Ethiopia only. The law would expire thirty days after Congress reconvened in January, 1936. This proposal, dispatched to Pittman on August 19, met no response.[32]

Although administration hopes had expired, the neutrality question was moving toward a climax. In the middle of August, 1935, despite nationwide interest, it had appeared that Congress, hurrying toward adjournment, would enact no neutrality legislation. On August 19, however, dispatches from Paris disclosed that the three-power negotiations aimed at averting war in East Africa had collapsed and hostilities were imminent. Gloom settled over Washington. Isolationists saw possible American involvement, and determined that Congress should not delay neutrality legislation. Thus Senators Nye, Bone, Clark, and Long on August 20 halted the rush toward adjournment for the eighth time in the session by advising the Senate that they would filibuster against adjournment unless Congress acted. Vandenberg presented a dispassionate analysis of the views of the so-called neutrality bloc. He said that in 1914–17 the absence of neutrality legislation had deprived the United States of any chance to direct its destiny, made American involvement in the World War inevitable. To avoid repetition he

thought neutrality legislation essential. Bone presented the
neutrality bloc's position more graphically:

> Everyone has come to recognize that the Great War was utter
> social insanity, and was a crazy war, and we had no business in it
> at all. Oh yes; we heard a great deal of talk about freedom of the
> seas. Whose seas? The seas upon which were being shipped muni-
> tions of war which served only to enrich a comparatively small
> group of men, and whose enrichment cost this country a stag-
> gering price, the enrichment of this group brought down upon
> our heads the terrible economic problems with which we wrestle
> right here today and we find it wellnigh impossible to solve some
> of them. Freedom of the seas! Out with such nonsense. For the
> sake of this fantastic theory that could at best serve the few and
> not the many, thousands have died, and our hospitals are filled
> with insane boys who had a right, under God's providence, to
> live their lives in peace. What a distortion! [33]

Faced with a filibuster, the Foreign Relations Committee
reported S. J. Res. 173, the Pittman Resolution, basically a combination of S. J. Res. 120 (the Nye-Clark arms embargo) and
S. 2998 (the National Munitions Bill). There was no floor fight,
and the measure passed on August 21, 1935. It prohibited export of munitions to belligerents after the President declared
existence of war, authorized the President to proclaim that
Americans could travel on ships of belligerent countries only
at their own risk, established the National Munitions Control
Board to license exporters and importers of munitions, and
restricted use of American ports by belligerent submarines.
Despite hints by Chairman McReynolds that it might withhold
approval from a mandatory measure, the Foreign Affairs Committee with consent of the White House reported an amended
version of the Pittman Resolution. The amendment did not
alter the character of the resolution, but made it temporary—
stating it would expire on February 29, 1936. The amended
resolution swept through the House without roll call on August
23. The Senate agreed to the amendment on August 24 by vote
of 77–2, and on August 31, 1935 the resolution received the
President's signature. In such manner "the same Congress which

voted almost unlimited discretion to the President in domestic matters took from the President practically all discretion in foreign affairs." [34]

The administration, of course, could have defeated the Neutrality Act, but the rising tide of isolation and pacifism had proved irresistible. Americans realized that war was imminent, and feared the United States might be drawn in. Then the session of Congress had been long and the summer hot. The result was large pressure on the administration to yield to the isolationists.

Signing the act, Roosevelt indicated displeasure at Congress' work. He approved the measure, he said, because "it was intended as an expression of the fixed desire of the Government and the people of the United States to avoid any action which might involve us in war." But no Congress or executive could foresee the future: "History is filled with unforeseeable situations that call for some flexibility of action. It is conceivable that situations may arise in which the wholly inflexible provisions of Section I of this Act might have exactly the opposite effect from that which was intended. In other words, the inflexible provisions might drag us into war instead of keeping us out." [35]

Hull expressed displeasure in stronger terms. In a letter to the President two days earlier he had said the mandatory arms embargo provision of the act invaded the constitutional and traditional power of the executive to conduct foreign relations. He called the act an attempt to impose upon the executive branch a fixed and inflexible line of conduct, depriving it of much discretion in negotiating with foreign powers in circumstances in which American interest might demand discretion. The act would deprive the United States of influence in promoting peace, and he was not thinking exclusively of discriminatory or punitive embargoes: "The question of our attitude toward collective action against an aggressor is only one of the many aspects of a much larger question." Hull failed to acknowledge that the act might have been less satisfactory. At least it was temporary. [36]

Strangely, few people anticipated one result. The general view was that Ethiopia would wish to purchase munitions abroad. Ethiopia, therefore, would suffer most from the embargo. Isolationists believed this was unfortunate but necessary, since peace for the United States must endure at all cost. Others shared the lament of Senator Tom Connally (Dem.) of Texas that the act was "a form of declaration which announces that the United States will take the side of the strong and the powerful against the weak, the unprepared, and the defenseless." In truth, Ethiopia lacked means to purchase arms in quantity. The embargo would affect only the aggressor, Italy.[37]

There was another source of some consolation to the administration. The embargo would not go into effect until the President proclaimed existence of war. In cases where adversaries formally declared war he could hardly refuse to invoke the embargo. But in the 1930's there was a tendency to conduct war without formal declaration, and in such cases he might withhold his proclamation. There had been no declaration of war between China and Japan during Japanese occupation of Manchuria in 1931–33. In the Italo-Ethiopian conflict neither side declared war. It is conceivable that Roosevelt might have refused to proclaim the existence of war had he thought Ethiopia would suffer most from the embargo.

The Neutrality Act of 1935 was not a complete victory for the so-called neutrality bloc, since it contained no provision prohibiting Americans from extending loans and credits to belligerent governments or their nationals. Pittman explained that loans and credits presented too involved a problem to pass on at that time, so the Foreign Relations Committee had ignored it. Probably the Nye-Clark-Bone-Vandenberg-Long group considered that opponents of mandatory neutrality might defeat the entire resolution if they delayed passage to fight for loan-credit clauses. Then there was small chance that the United States could become financially involved in the East African conflict. Italy could not borrow from the United States because the Johnson Act prohibited defaulters on World War debts from further indebtedness. Ethiopia, a primitive country, was such a poor risk that Americans were not apt to make loans to that unhappy kingdom.[38]

Foreign reaction to the neutrality law was mixed. The New York *Times* reported that the British were displeased, not because of the measure's effect in East Africa, but because of the potential effect on Great Britain. Because of their supremacy on the sea the British could keep American munitions from their enemies while assuring shipment to themselves. Traditional policy, therefore, was more to their liking. The French view was more realistic. Frenchmen reasoned that Congress would repeal the law if it worked against belligerents favored by the United States. History would prove their estimate correct. From Ethiopia came a report that the act had disturbed Emperor Haile Selassie.[39]

III

On October 3, 1935, following East Africa's rainy season, Mussolini's troops invaded Ethiopia. Shortly after 11:00 P.M. on October 5, President Roosevelt proclaimed the "simple and indisputed fact that Italian and Ethiopian armed forces are engaged in combat, thus creating a state of war within the intent and meaning of the joint resolution." The embargo provision of the Neutrality Act went into effect. Articles embargoed included only those used exclusively in military operations, except airplanes, engines, propellers, air screws, fuselages, hulls, tail and undercarriage units. Roosevelt also announced that "I desire it to be understood that any of our people who voluntarily engage in transactions of any character with either of the belligerents do so at their own risk." He had no statutory authority for this step, but acted in pursuance of the executive function of deciding whether through the State Department he would present claims of American citizens against foreign nations.[40]

The presidential proclamation brought immediate protest from firms and individuals exporting arms to Italy. Some businessmen contended that the situation in East Africa did not warrant action; others criticized the President for proclaiming war in absence of a formal declaration by the participants and in advance of findings by other governments. Governor J. M. Futrell of Arkansas said: "I question the action of preventing our citizens from profiting by sales to those who are fighting. Business conditions in our nation could be better, and why shouldn't we profit by the conflict . . . ?" Such protests gave credence to the merchants-of-death argument. Nye declared that "the shippers' insatiable appetite for business and profits out of the blood of other nations would lead 138,000,000 people into a war that is none of our business." Charles B. Warren wrote that the President's policy was based on the principle that the right of the nation to keep out of war was greater than the right of a citizen to engage in trade which might implicate the nation in war. He quoted Professor James B. Scott as saying: "The President has recognized that insistence upon the so-called neutral right to make profit from other peoples' wars, results in other peoples' wars becoming our wars." [41]

The embargo stopped munitions shipments to the belligerents, but exports to Italy of articles not defined as implements of war mounted, especially after the League of Nations began to arrange for sanctions against Italy. Threatened with loss of European bases of supply, Italy looked to the United States for cotton, oil, and scrap metal. The Neutrality Act had failed. It had not removed the occasion for violation of American rights. It was not thwarting hostilities in East Africa.

Isolationists of the Nye-Clark-Bone type increased their demand for expansion of the embargo list to include all trade except perhaps food.* They believed modern warfare "so complex that it spreads its tentacles out over a nation and draws nourishment from its every activity." Before 1935 ended it was

---

* Isolationists fell into several categories. Some isolationists wanted the United States to refrain from foreign entanglements, but did not wish an end to profitable overseas trade through embargoes, arms or otherwise. Others had no objection to arms embargoes, but wanted no interference with trade in other articles. Such isolationists as Nye and Clark favored nonentanglement, arms embargoes, and sharp restrictions on trade with belligerents in all types of commodities.

clear that they would try to replace the neutrality law of the previous August with one embracing their views. They would be in a strong position, for in January, 1936 the Munitions Committee would conduct hearings on American policy during 1914–17 and the effect of commerce with the Allies. For several months committee investigators had scoured files of leading financial houses and the State Department for evidence that war prosperity had "monetized" Americans and taken them on an unneutral path. Isolationists of the neutrality bloc expected the committee to construct a case which would persuade the country of the wisdom of their position.[42]

The administration also was preparing for the coming debate, but was not content to wait for Congress to reassemble. Roosevelt and Hull proclaimed a "moral embargo." In a series of pronouncements in October and November, 1935 they announced that the government disapproved abnormal commerce with belligerents in articles not on the embargo list. "Normal" trade in such commodities was acceptable, but they said abnormal trade was inconsistent with the neutrality law. Hull went a step further on November 15, condemning all trade with belligerents in materials capable of conversion to military use (oil, copper, trucks, tractors, scrap metal): "This class of trade is directly contrary to the policy of this Government as announced in official statements of the President and Secretary of State, as it is also contrary to the general spirit of the recent neutrality act." [43]

It is interesting that Roosevelt was willing to impose a moral embargo while the country was trying to recover from the depression. Roosevelt—whose New Deal administration often found no detail which might promote recovery too small to consider—was willing to take this step although no large group was requesting it, important elements in the country were sure to denounce it, and which—if effective—would impede recovery.

The moral embargo met a mixed response in the United States. Senator Nye telegraphed congratulations to Hull. The *Christian Science Monitor* thought the moral embargo would reduce danger of American entanglement and aid peace efforts of the League. It asked: "Do those who want isolation at any price except the sacrifice of war trade really want neutrality for peace or for profit?" The New York *Times* called the move "peace-loving and marked by a strong sense of our international duty." The *New Republic* and *Christian Century* endorsed the step, but warned that the aim of the administration was "a system which would leave it to the discretion of the President to decide when the United States should be neutral, and toward whom, and how much." The *Nation* wanted to go beyond the moral embargo and take action against Italy as a violator of the Kellogg Pact. The *Wall Street Journal,* on the other hand, assailed the view that abnormal trade with belligerents contravened the spirit of the Neutrality Act, and the head of the New York State Chamber of Commerce wrote Roosevelt that "we are against our being drawn into a war, and approve safeguards applied by our government, but not such extension of them as will hamper Americans *not* exporting war munitions, and trading at our own risk." The New York *Sun* said that if successful the moral embargo "would have American citizens pay in loss of normally legitimate trade for results which could but aggrandize the business of those countries which have most to gain from a defeat of Italian expansion." *Business Week* attacked Roosevelt, Hull, Frances Perkins, Harold Ickes, "and a whole string of other officials" for a policy of favoritism against Italy. The same periodical reported a poll of executives in manufacturing, banking, and exporting which revealed solid opposition to the moral embargo. Businessmen believed it would achieve nothing without support of other industrial countries. International lawyers Edwin M. Borchard and John Bassett Moore thought the administration was taking the "road to war." The Rev. Charles E. Coughlin declared that the United States was "preparing once more to become the catspaws for saving the international bankers of the British Empire." [44]

Despite the moral embargo, exports to Italy increased. Figures by the Department of Commerce in December, 1935 showed that in the preceding month shipments to Italy and Italian Africa in "sinews of war"—cotton, oil, metal, tractors, automotive parts—had risen considerably. Exports to Italian Africa of these materials in November, 1934 had been at $17,971; in November, 1935, $583,735. Later figures revealed exports to Italy and Italian Africa in 1935 had totaled $77,005,897, compared with $64,853,882 in 1934.[45]

In such manner did the program of the isolationists —people who believed it possible to legislate the United States out of war—triumph in the summer and autumn of 1935. The triumph, of course, would be transitory, for the problem of staying out of war was larger than isolationists believed. What about a war affecting American interests? And might not Woodrow Wilson have been correct that nineteenth century isolation no longer was possible? Still, isolationist writers were busily at work demonstrating (and the Munitions Committee was about to supply proof) that the United States had no business becoming involved in the World War, that an Allied victory there had been no more preferable than a German victory. They were showing that if the United States had isolated itself in 1914–17 it could have avoided the war and its associated calamities— war-debt default and the Great Depression. There was in truth a sort of logical case in favor of isolation that in the international uncertainties of the mid-thirties was difficult to confute. The President, who saw more clearly, moved as best he could, and at the beginning of 1936 when Congress would write a more lasting piece of neutrality legislation he hoped for a result more to his liking than the makeshift measure of 1935.

IX

NEUTRALITY AND
MORGAN, 1936

The beginning of the year 1936 gave evidence of no *annus mirabilis,* for the world was sorely troubled by Italy's adventure in East Africa. The Italians had achieved little in Ethiopia, however. They had taken Adua and Makale, but the capital of Addis Ababa lay three hundred difficult miles to the south. The invasion in truth had ground to a halt, and in early January, 1936 a counterthrust by Haile Selassie's troops forced the Italians to withdraw as much as sixty miles. Mussolini in Rome spoke of "indispensable pauses." In Geneva the League of Nations was trying to arrange for oil sanctions against Italy. The original sanctions program, adopted in November, 1935, had provided an arms and financial embargo but omitted oil. League officials calculated that an oil embargo might stop the Italian military machine. But sanctions could not restrain Italy without American co-operation.[1]

In Washington on January 3, 1936 President Roosevelt delivered his annual message on the State of the Union. He referred to his inaugural of March, 1933 which had contained one paragraph on foreign affairs. If he were to deliver a similar address now, he said, events would compel him to devote the greater part to world affairs. "Since the summer of that same year of 1933," he continued, "the temper and the purposes of the rulers of many of the great populations in Europe and Asia

191

have not pointed the way either to peace or to good will among men. Not only have peace and good will among men grown more remote in those areas of the earth during this period, but a point has been reached where the people of the Americas must take cognizance of growing ill will, of marked trends toward aggression, of increasing armaments, of shortening tempers —a situation which has in it many of the elements that lead to the tragedy of general war." The President spoke of neutrality. The United States had declined "to encourage the prosecution of war by permitting belligerents to obtain arms, ammunition, or implements of war from the United States." Reiterating the moral embargo principle, he said that "we seek to discourage the use by belligerent nations of any and all American products calculated to facilitate the prosecution of war in quantities over and above our normal exports to them in time of peace." He hoped that Congress and the executive would carry those policies forward. His words sounded isolationist, and the isolationists were pleased.[2]

On the same day Chairman McReynolds of the House Foreign Affairs Committee and Chairman Pittman of the Senate Foreign Relations Committee introduced the Pittman-McReynolds Bill which incorporated the administration view on neutrality. Unlike the administration's ill-fated measure of 1935, it did not permit presidential discretion in applying arms embargoes; the United States would continue to embargo arms to all belligerents, unless Congress with the President's approval decided otherwise. There were other concessions to isolationists. The bill prohibited loans and credits (although the President could except credits for customary current business), and forbade American ships to carry arms to belligerents. Americans could not travel on belligerent ships and belligerent submarines could not enter American waters. The President could negotiate modifications of existing commercial treaties which might conflict with the embargo, or—if this were impossible— terminate them. The bill incorporated those features of the Neutrality Act of 1935 providing for the National Munitions Control Board.

There was another provision—sure to arouse controversy—which the administration considered basic. Outwardly it appeared similar to the moral embargo. It prohibited shipment from the United States to belligerent countries of nonmilitary commodities, except food and medical supplies, in amounts exceeding "normal commerce." The President would have no discretion to apply this provision against selected belligerents. But the measure left authority with the President to determine the "normal" exchange of goods beyond which exports would be prohibited. Presumably he would choose a typical peacetime period and use export statistics for that period as a standard, yet the bill gave him discretion in choosing the typical period.[3]

The administration had drafted an isolationist-appearing bill which in practice would give the President considerable control over shipment of nonmilitary commodities to belligerents. The administration had come to understand that control over these shipments was as important as over munitions shipments, and under the bill the President might manipulate export quotas to the advantage of belligerents favored by the administration. It was not expedient to admit as much, of course. Through Senator Pittman the White House explained that in such a complex situation as war there should be no fixed rules but flexibility in determining normal exports. The bill stated, moreover, that the President would proclaim an embargo "upon the outbreak or during the progress of any war." The language gave the President discretion to decide when, if at all, an embargo would go into effect.[4]

Businessmen and Italian-Americans, as expected, reacted unfavorably to the Pittman-McReynolds Bill. But isolationists, such as Nye and Clark, were initially cordial. Especially did they sympathize with provisions limiting commerce in nonmilitary commodities to amounts "normally" carried between the United States and belligerents.[5]

Had the administration bill with its concessions to isolation and its limited discretionary features won support from the Nye-Clark neutrality bloc? The answer was no. Nye and Clark had strong reservations about the Pittman-McReynolds Bill, and they offered their own neutrality measure. The Nye-Clark Bill appeared similar to the administration bill, but avoided giving the President discretionary authority. Where the Pittman-McReynolds language called for embargoes "upon the outbreak or during the progress of any war," the Nye-Clark Bill made it mandatory that the President proclaim an embargo upon the outbreak of war. The Nye-Clark Bill, moreover, withheld from the President discretion to determine normal quotas of commerce in nonmilitary commodities between the United States and belligerents. He must establish quotas based upon the five years preceding war. Then the Nye-Clark Bill provided that goods shipped to belligerents went at risk of a foreign government or national, whereas under the administration bill those Americans profiting from shipments to belligerents might assume risks.[6]

Two measures had appeared, one from administration advocates of flexible policy, the other from extreme isolationists. There were other positions. Moderate isolationists wanted to continue the mandatory arms embargo of 1935, and of course some people wanted no neutrality legislation at all. Debate probably would be brief; the Neutrality Act of 1935 would expire on February 29, 1936.

By this time the Munitions Committee again was preparing for action. The topic to be aired was World War financing and 1914–17 neutrality—a timely study.

I

The committee did not hastily elect to probe neutrality to lend support to the Nye-Clark bloc's position in the 1936 debate. Early in its inquiry it determined to examine the era of 1914–17 and assess the munitions trade's responsibility for America's involvement in the World War. During the winter of 1934–35, before anyone had contemplated a national neutrality debate, committee investigators under direction of Josephine Burns had begun to gather evidence from the State

Department and elsewhere. In April, 1935 Miss Burns prepared a memorandum on findings to that point. It contained nothing of consequence that scholars of history had not published. But the committee expected new evidence in the files of financial houses which had dealt with the Allies in 1914–17. Access to these records did not come until August 19, 1935, less than two weeks before adjournment of Congress. It took time to scrutinize these materials. There thus was little opportunity to conduct hearings before the winter of 1935–36. (And there was no opportunity to delay beyond that time. Committee funds had nearly expired, and it was then or never.)

Nye and Clark, of course, hoped that testimony and documents brought forth at the hearings of January–February, 1936 would support their isolationist neutrality bill. Stephen Raushenbush had written in August, 1935 that "there is going to be very considerable significance to our banking hearings inasmuch as the Neutrality legislation will be in process of being debated again at that time."[7]

When hearings resumed on January 7, the high-ceilinged, marble-pillared Senate caucus room filled to capacity. The scene was informal, almost unruly. Departing from senatorial practice of placing a single witness before the inquisitors, the Munitions Committee, as throughout the inquiry, permitted J. P. Morgan and his partners, Thomas W. Lamont and George Whitney, to huddle at a table. Behind this front line was a corps of accountants, clerks, publicists, and messengers to assist the three masters of finance. The Morgan partners also employed new tactics. Instead of shying away from reporters and eluding interviews, as during the Pecora inquiry two years before, they came prepared, even anxious, to submit their case to the public. Whenever the committee exhibited a document a Morgan subordinate would extract a sheaf of copies from a brief case and distribute them to the forty reporters seated at two long flanking tables. J. P. Morgan offered an interview and posed patiently for photographers. Perhaps such tactics influenced the committee, for Nye and his colleagues treated the financiers deferentially.[8]

As for Woodrow Wilson's neutrality policy, only Senators Pope and George, neither of whom was participating in the inquiry at this point, defended the late President. The committee majority believed Wilson had invoked a double standard with the belligerents, and had permitted practices which virtually assured involvement in the war.

A special inquiry soon dominated the hearings. In the period 1914–17 Wilson had approved large private loans to belligerent governments. He had allowed abnormal commerce in munitions and nonmilitary materials to mushroom. All this had large interest for the Munitions Committee majority in 1936.

Committee investigators displayed interesting documents. They showed that less than two weeks after the war began, on August 10, 1914, Secretary of State William Jennings Bryan had forwarded a memorandum to Wilson stating that "money is the worst of all contrabands because it commands everything else." The committee majority had been saying the same thing for months. The memorandum continued: "The powerful financial interests which would be connected with these loans would be tempted to use their influence through the newspapers to support the interests of the Governments to which they had loaned because the value of the security would be directly affected by the result of the war. We would thus find our newspapers violently arrayed on one side or the other, each paper supporting a financial group and pecuniary interest. All of this influence would make it all the more difficult for us to maintain neutrality as our action on various questions that would arise would affect one side or the other, and powerful financial interests would be thrown into the balance." Wilson in August, 1914 had agreed with Bryan, that American financiers should not extend loans or credits to belligerent powers, and Bryan had advised J. P. Morgan and Company of this policy on August 15, 1914. Morgan disapproved and already had communicated about a possible loan to the French government. Still, the firm co-operated and made no loans to belligerents at that time.[9]

Wilson on August 19, 1914 had issued his famous plea for Americans to be neutral in thought as well as action, but the

Morgan company could not maintain a neutral attitude toward the belligerents because "we found it quite impossible to be impartial as between right and wrong." The partners also told the Munitions Committee in 1936 of their realization that "if the Germans should obtain a quick and easy victory the freedom of the rest of the world would be lost." Thus they had "agreed that we should do all that was lawfully in our power to help the Allies win the war as soon as possible." [10]

The committee had no evidence that Wall Street bankers had pressed the Wilson administration to alter its loan policy, but it did show that on October 23, 1914 the counselor of the State Department, Robert Lansing, had prepared a memorandum after conversation with the President in which he wrote that Wilson had no objection to bank credits in the United States for warring governments. Lansing had persuaded the President that there was a difference between loans and credits. When Morgan learned of Wilson's revised position the firm offered credits to the Allies. J. P. Morgan admitted to the Munitions Committee that there was no essential difference between loans and credits, only a technical difference. [11]

Despite this change, Bryan on January 15, 1915 had written Chairman William J. Stone of the Foreign Relations Committee that the administration's loan policy remained unaltered. He then defended the policy which Wilson had compromised. Had Bryan sought to deceive the Senate? Had Wilson and Lansing revised policy without informing the Secretary of State? Deception ended at any rate on March 31, 1915 when a State Department news release disclosed that the government would not discourage credits to belligerent powers. [12]

Thanks in part to American credit, Allied purchases of munitions and other commodities proceeded at an accelerated rate. By the spring of 1915 the United States had recovered from the recession of 1914, and was enjoying its greatest prosperity in years. Department of Commerce figures which the Munitions Committee exhibited revealed startling increase in exports for the period 1915–17 over 1911–13: wheat, 683 per cent; cartridges, 8,490 per cent; barbed wire, 1,710 per cent; mules,

7,038 per cent. Probably no one realized larger profits from this trade than J. P. Morgan and Company, which helped finance 84 per cent of America's 1915–17 commerce with the Allies.[13]

Soon there came a new move in American-Allied fiscal relations. In the summer of 1915 American prosperity had appeared in jeopardy, for extension of bank credit had failed to satisfy the Allied need for dollars. The Wilson administration continued to oppose Allied bond issues. Then in August, 1915 a curious train of events led to reversal of this policy, and the gates opened to loans of all types. Up to that time the Allies had paid for purchases through the foreign exchange market. To assist them Morgan had supported the pound-sterling during the previous six and one-half months, to the tune of $154,000,000, a prop which had maintained the pound at a figure near $4.71. Then without warning or explanation Morgan withdrew support on August 14, 1915, and the rate plunged to $4.51. It appeared that only a dramatic increase in dollars available to the British would save the pound—and American prosperity. The committee showed in 1936 that the British could have supported their exchange at this point, since Morgan had offered a credit of $100,000,000 for such purpose. The British declined to act, however, and Morgan notified Secretary of the Treasury William G. McAdoo that the exchange situation was serious. Whereupon McAdoo wrote Wilson on August 21 pleading for change in government loan policy—which he called "illogical and inconsistent." McAdoo dispatched a similar letter to Lansing, by this time Secretary of State, in which he said that the exchange situation was so critical that belligerent purchases in the United States might end. He found it unnecessary to explain the effect of such a calamity on America's economy. Lansing on August 25 seconded McAdoo's appeal to Wilson. On the following day the President concurred, and in effect authorized a revision of loan-credit policy. As Lansing said two weeks later, the country was "face to face with what appears to be a critical economic situation, which can only be relieved apparently by the investment of American capital in foreign loans to be used in liquidating the enormous balance of trade in favor of the United States. Can we afford to let a declaration as to our conception of the 'true spirit of neutrality' made in the first days of the war stand in the way of our national interests which seem to be seriously threatened?" Thanks to the change of policy, American investors during the autumn of 1915 purchased Anglo-French securities amounting to $500,000,000. The pound-sterling rate increased to a fraction above $4.76, and remained there through the war. American prosperity continued.[14]

It was possible that the British and Morgan had created the crisis to force a change in American policy. If the Munitions Committee could establish Morgan's culpability it would support the argument of peace leaders that Wall Street had led the country to war in 1914–17. Extreme isolation would win new adherents. But evidence proved inconclusive. And the Morgan partners denied conspiracy. Not without some justification, the committee had only a limited confidence in testimony by business leaders. It remained unconvinced. But it drew no unwarranted conclusions, and avoided using the events of August, 1915 as a foundation for a case against Wall Street.[15]

Wilson had succumbed to economic pressure in 1915, yet the question remained: had economic intercourse with the Allied belligerents led the United States to war? The Munitions Committee majority in 1936 was sure it had. The Morgan partners were sure it had not. Thomas Lamont explained that only 400,000 out of 100,000,000 Americans had direct interest in foreign securities during the World War. Senator Vandenberg retorted: "Yes; but everybody that worked in one of these munitions plants was monetized, directly or indirectly, and all of these people whom you now say had come to a realization of the tremendously important factor that this war trade was upon our economy had a sense of monetization." [16]

The committee cited a statement by German Ambassador Count von Bernstorff just before the American declaration of war in April, 1917. Describing a conversation with Colonel Edward M. House, Bernstorff had written: "He told me at that time that, as matters had turned out, Wilson no longer had the power to compel England to adhere to the principles of international law. That the reason for this was that American commerce was so completely tied up with the interests of the Entente that it was impossible for Wilson to disturb these commercial relations without calling forth such a storm of protest on the part of the public that he would not be able to carry out his intention." A similar view had come from André Tardieu, French High Commissioner in the United States after American entry into the war, later Premier of France. In his *France and America* Tardieu in the 1920's had written that tie-ups between American financial interests and the Allies had made Allied victory essential to the United States. Ray Stannard Baker in *The Life and Letters of Woodrow Wilson* had written that by the end of 1914 the trade in war material had become so much a part of America's economic structure that the possibility of keeping out of war by the diplomacy of neutrality, "no matter how skillfully conducted, had reached the vanishing point." [17]

Still, documents indicating that economic factors had swayed Wilson, except in the exchange crisis, were lacking, although individuals in the administration had understood the financial rewards of intervention. There was a cable to the State Department from the American ambassador to Great Britain, Walter Hines Page, dated March 5, 1917, in which Page said that the Allied financial situation was so desperate that termination of purchases in the United States was imminent. This, he said, would "cause a panic in the United States." He was sure the crisis was "too great and urgent for any private agency to meet." Only assistance by the United States Government could save the situation, but this presented a problem. According to international law a neutral government might not extend aid to belligerents—or as Page said: "Unless we go to war with Germany, our Government, of course, cannot make such a direct grant of credit." He concluded that "perhaps our going to war is the only way in which our present prominent trade position can be maintained and a panic averted." Not only would prosperity continue, it would be "enlarged until the war ends, and after war Europe would continue to buy food and would buy from us also an enormous supply of those things to reequip her peace industries. We should thus reap the profit of an uninterrupted, perhaps an enlarging, trade over a number of years and we should hold their securities in payment." [18]

The Morgan partners denied in 1936 that Allied finances had been desperate early in 1917. The Munitions Committee discounted their testimony, since this view countered not only Page but Sir Cecil Spring-Rice, British ambassador in Washington, who had written Lansing on July 1, 1917 that the British financial position was "urgent and critical." [19]

One other piece of evidence added to the case of the committee, a bit of candid testimony by Morgan and Lamont, both of whom repudiated the idea that—as far as their investments were concerned—American investors felt indifferent about the outcome of the war. Whenever the Germans had scored a military victory, Lamont and Morgan told the committee, it became difficult to sell Allied securities in the United States. Whenever the Allies won a victory the Allied loans became easier. If investors thus feared for their investments it seemed unthinkable that they could be neutral in thought and action. They would press the government for a course which would contribute to Allied victory and the security of their investments. But evidence of such pressure was missing.[20]

The Munitions Committee majority criticized Wilson not only for permitting the United States to become tied economically to the Allies, but also for demanding strict accountability for German violation of neutral rights while feebly protesting or ignoring Allied transgressions. In the view of such members as Nye, Clark, and Vandenberg, conduct of this sort was inexcusable, inasmuch as Wilson could have compelled Allied respect for American rights by threatening commercial non-intercourse. Wilson had avoided even the threat of such action, they believed (as had Britain's wartime Prime Minister, David Lloyd George), because he could not risk American commerce and finance. Senator Clark concluded that Germany in desperation had resumed unrestricted submarine warfare in 1917, and "for its resumption America's complete lack of neutrality, as this record has abundantly shown, was in large part responsible." [21]

On the matter of German submarine warfare the committee exhibited documents which seemed to doubt the sincerity of Wilson's and Lansing's policy—condemnation of the submarine as barbaric and unjustifiable. In a letter from Lansing to Wilson in January, 1916, Lansing had agreed with the German contention that if the Allies insisted upon arming merchant ships the rules of war should not require submarines to surface before attacking. "If some merchant vessels carry arms and others do not, how can a submarine determine this fact without exposing itself to great risk of being sunk? Unless the Entente Allies positively agree not to arm any of their merchant vessels and notify the Central Powers to that effect, is there not strong reason why a submarine should not warn a vessel before launching an attack?" In vague reply Wilson appeared to agree, yet the President had continued to protest German submarine methods, and in the end German refusal to heed his protests took the United States into the conflict.[22]

II

The committee majority, led by Nye, Clark, and Vandenberg, criticized the wartime President's failure to press the Allies to revoke their secret treaties dividing the spoils should they win the war. There was general belief that Wilson had not learned of these treaties until the Paris Peace Conference, and therefore had assumed in 1914–18 that the Allies were waging a crusade for freedom, democracy, and justice. The Munitions Committee believed Wilson had known of the treaties. It exhibited a cable from Walter Hines Page to the State Department, May 8, 1915, in which Page reported "from reliable sources" that the Allies had negotiated secret treaties. On January 22, 1917 the ambassador to Italy, Thomas Nelson Page, wrote Lansing about the Allied secret agreements. To the committee majority in 1936 it seemed inconceivable that Lansing had not forwarded such information to the President. Support for the committee view came from Charles Seymour's

Intimate Papers of Colonel House, published in 1926–28. Seymour had written that "Colonel House knew of the secret
treaties. He had told the President of the Treaty of London
before Italy entered the war, and [British Foreign Secretary
Sir Edward] Grey had told him of the demands of Rumania, so
he must have guessed the terms upon which she entered the
war." Nye added that the committee had learned from "the
highest possible sources" that Wilson and Lansing knew of the
secret treaties long before the peace conference. In a memorandum to Lansing of May 18, 1917—which the State Department had refused to clear for publication by the committee—
Arthur Balfour (Grey's successor as British Foreign Secretary)
had outlined Allied pledges for revising the map of Europe.
In hearings before the Foreign Relations Committee in 1919,
however, Wilson and Lansing had denied knowledge of the
secret treaties until after the war. This discrepancy between
documents and testimony inspired Nye to make what friends of
the munitions investigation considered the most unfortunate
utterance of the inquiry—a statement destined to terminate the
Munitions Committee and its study. He said evidence had
shown that "both the President and Secretary Lansing falsified
concerning this matter." [23]

Wilsonians rose in wrath. Such men as Newton D. Baker,
Wilson's Secretary of War; Josephus Daniels, his Secretary of
the Navy; and Joseph P. Tumulty, his personal secretary, rallied
to the defense. On the day following Nye's assertion, January
16, 1936, Tom Connally declared on the Senate floor: "I do not
care how the charges were made; they are infamous. Some
checker-playing, beer-drinking, back room of some low house
is the only place fit for the kind of language which the Senator
from North Dakota, the chairman of the committee, this Senator who is going to lead us out toward peace, puts into the
Record about a dead man, a great man, a good man, a man who
when alive had the courage to meet his enemies face to face and
eye to eye." Senator Clark, who had gone to the chamber when
told that Connally was about to attack Nye and the committee,
interrupted the Texan and suggested that he would be better

informed about his subject had he followed the munitions investigation instead of spending time opposing oil sanctions before the Foreign Relations Committee. Undeterred, Connally concluded: "Woodrow Wilson's body sleeps out yonder in the great cathedral, but his spirit stands today among the great figures of history . . . [and] some of us who loved him, some of us who honored him, are unwilling to stand mute in the presence of his traducers and those who would heap ignominy upon his memory." [24]

Later that afternoon the committee's interrogation of Morgan witnesses was proceeding smoothly when just before four o'clock Senator Pope, conspicuously absent from hearings the preceding week, entered the room and took a seat at the table. Raushenbush was debating Morgan and Lamont about the Allied loan situation in 1916. Pope waited fifteen minutes before receiving recognition from Nye. Whereupon the Idaho Democrat explained that he had collaborated with Senator George (the committee's most inactive member) in preparing the statement he was about to read. As Pope proceeded J. P. Morgan leaned far over the table, pipe smoke rolling up to the ceiling. The room became quiet and tense.

Pope and George stated that for years they had believed a thorough exposé of the armament trade necessary for the peace of the United States and the world, and as a result believed that most of the munitions inquiry was of value to the American people. "It appears now, however, that the investigation has degenerated into an attack upon our wartime President, Woodrow Wilson, and his Secretary of State, Robert Lansing." The two senators resented "any effort to impugn the motives of Woodrow Wilson and to discredit his great character." Concluding that there was need for a true munitions investigation and remedial legislation, they promised that when the committee reformed they would accord it support.

This revolt visibly distressed Nye, but he regained composure and made an impressive defense. He pointed out that neither George nor Pope had appeared during recent hearings, and that their information (as acknowledged in their statement) had come from secondhand sources. As for whether Wilson had told the truth in 1919, he said that such inquiry would be useless if it failed to handle evidence without prejudice, regardless of how distasteful some individuals might find it. Nye said that he, a Republican, had supported Wilson in the election of 1916, and still had faith in Wilson's determination to keep the United States out of the World War. Vandenberg was equally forceful. After voicing respect for Wilson and the witnesses before the committee, he said it was not the committee's function to persecute anybody, that "Congress, the President, the members of the Cabinet, could not be in possession of all the knowledge that we have today respecting the interlocking factors. These gentlemen [the Morgan partners] who have done us the honor of testifying here for nearly 2 weeks could not have known all the interlocking factors that were involved in the situation 21 years ago. It seems to me that our problem objectively is to see what we can do to profit by mistakes that are disclosed, and to benefit by the errors. . . ." [25]

Next day Nye from the Senate floor reiterated his view that Wilson and Lansing had lied to the Foreign Relations Committee, and entered supporting documents into the *Record*. He denounced the "gutter English" which his opponents were using to discredit the inquiry. His defense failed to silence the committee critics, and a few moments later Carter Glass of Virginia directed at Nye one of the bitterest personal attacks heard in the Senate in modern times. Before Glass's speech a quorum call brought senators into the chamber. A large delegation of House Democrats appeared, the galleries filled with spectators. Every seat on the Democratic side was occupied when Glass began his reply to Nye's "shocking assault" upon Wilson. Fully using his noted vocabulary, and pounding his desk until blood came to his knuckles, Glass in a voice shaking with emotion and rasping with anger cried: "Oh, the miserable demagogy, the miserable and mendacious suggestion, that the house of Morgan altered the neutrality course of Woodrow Wilson." After admitting that he had voted funds for the munitions inquiry, he promised he would never vote another dollar to a committee

"any one of whose members is so insensible to every consideration of decency as to stand on the Senate floor and bitterly assail
two dead men who are honored by this entire Nation." He concluded: "Now, Mr. President, lest I should infringe those rules
which I always obey, perhaps I should better desist, because
what I feel like saying here or anywhere else to the man who
thus insults the memory of Woodrow Wilson is something
which may not be spoken here, or printed in the newspapers, or
uttered by a gentleman." Applause broke from the Democratic
side, although one commentator reported it unclear whether
Glass, a long-time friend of financial interests, had been "more
wroth for Morgan alive or Wilson dead." Connally then drew
laughter by ridiculing Nye's defense, but failed to show that
dishonesty had moved Nye in his statements about Wilson and
Lansing, or to confute evidence with which Nye supported his
view. Glass spoke again, and read into the *Record* the names of
deceased individuals mentioned during recent munitions hearings with the implication that these men, incapable of defending themselves, had come under attack (not true in most
instances): "This, Mr. President, is the solemn list of the
honored dead whom the Munitions Committee would gladly
disinter and reveal to the amused gaze of a coarse and common
headline-reading public!" [26]

The following day Clark offered a long defense of Nye in
which he described as beside the point the complaint that the
committee had studied actions of dead men. He said that "any
man taking part in public affairs of great moment, going to influence the policy of a great nation in time of great stress, must
know when he is doing so that he is making history and that his
words, his letters, and his acts are the fair subject for investigation by his fellow countrymen or by anybody else in the
world at a later time in the ascertainment of historic facts in
connection with the events with which he was connected." The
Daily Worker carried a banner: "The Bloody Knuckles of Senator Glass Are Used to Shield the Bloody Hands of the House
of Morgan and Wilson." The same newspaper contended: "Not
the reputation of Woodrow Wilson is what concerns the Glasses
and the Connallys, but protection of the blood profiteering of

the House of Morgan and concealment of the web of secret diplomacy and intrigue woven by the Wilson administration to further the interests of America's War Racketeer No. 1." In a private letter to a constituent Senator Norris conceded that Nye's remark had offended Wilson admirers. He regretted that Nye had made it, but declined to question its accuracy. He believed the committee should "by all means" complete its investigation; he cautioned supporters of the inquiry to restrain themselves, and by no remark "excite the prejudices and animosities which might arise and stop the work at this point." [27]

Clark, Norris, and other friends of the investigation were too late. Admirers of Wilson, preparedness advocates, business spokesmen, opponents of isolation, and individuals who thought the investigation had outlived its usefulness were calling for its end. Spokesmen for business and preparedness agreed with the Chicago *Tribune,* no admirer of Wilson, that Nye had received from Glass what "he has richly deserved on other counts." The *Tribune* seized this opportunity to charge that collectivists were operating inside the committee to promote socialism in America. In the *Tribune* lexicon "Simon" Raushenbush was a Marxist; Robert Wohlforth, Lawrence Brown, Josephine Burns were socialists; Nye was a collectivist. The newspaper did not mention Alger Hiss.[28]

Stopping the inquiry presented no problem, since committee funds had almost expired. In his speech of January 17, 1936 Glass, speaking for the Democrats, had made clear that the committee could expect no more money. Nye and his colleagues had planned other studies, but it appeared the committee would have to abandon them. Father Coughlin declared that his National Union for Social Justice would supply money if the Senate refused, but Nye declined funds from outside sources. Instead Nye accepted defeat of long-range plans and requested an appropriation of $7,369 to complete investigations in progress, and publish a report. On January 30, 1936 the Senate voted this amount, while stipulating that the committee make its final report with recommendations during the current Senate session.[29]

Interrogation of the Morgan partners ended on February 5,

1936. J. P. Morgan, his briar pipe billowing smoke and his face beaming good-naturedly, shook hands with Nye, and said: "I have had a fine time; I would not have missed this investigation for the world." Nye and other committee members said they had proved nothing to the discredit of Morgan and his banking house in more than two weeks of investigation of the company's wartime operations. During the next two weeks the committee completed several studies scheduled earlier. Then at four o'clock on the afternoon of February 20 Chairman Nye let fall his gavel and adjourned the munitions hearings for the last time.[30]

How did Nye react toward those individuals who had scuttled his inquiry?

Instead of bitterness toward such men as Pope, George, Glass, and Connally, Nye was willing to forgive and forget. As Pope said many years later, "Nye was a good scout." Nye remained one of Pope's better friends in the Senate, and when Pope sought confirmation to the Tennessee Valley Authority board in 1938 he received Nye's support. As for Glass, whose oratorical assault went beyond fair play, Nye recalled the episode twenty-two years later. He laughed and said Glass had been a fine old gentleman "whose god [Wilson] had been attacked, and by golly, that was more than he could take." [31]

In its report the committee stated "most definitely" that its study of American neutrality during the World War was in no way a criticism of the "sincere devotion" of Woodrow Wilson to peace. "President Wilson was personally impelled by the highest motives and the most profound convictions as to the justice of the cause of our country and was devoted to peace. He was caught up in a situation created largely by the profit-making interests in the United States, and such interests spread to nearly everybody in the country. It seemed necessary to the prosperity of our people that their markets in Europe remain unimpaired."

On other points the committee was not so generous toward Wilson and 1914–17 neutrality. It criticized Wilson's failure to inform Congress and the country on the change in loan-credit policy in the autumn of 1914. The committee concluded from the World War experience that loans to belligerents worked against neutrality, that they were certain to influence the position of individuals holding them. Loans were particularly dangerous when used to convert a neutral country into an arsenal for the belligerent controlling the seas. When this happened the arsenal became an object of military strategy for the other belligerent. The result—as in 1914–17—was war. The report contended that when banking houses had interest in munitions companies belligerents had power of securing financial support through favors to the companies. This was criticism of Morgan and Company's interest in other firms doing business with the Allies during the war. The committee found no evidence that the Allies had exploited the situation to secure greater support from Morgan, or that Morgan had wanted to curtail support of the Allies only to be prevented by effects upon affiliated firms. But the committee saw danger in such a situation.

The committee reported that wartime inflation, such as the United States had experienced in 1914–17, was almost impossible to check, and affected foreign policy. It believed America's failure to force its largest customers to respect its rights as a neutral in 1914–17 proved this assertion. Although the committee declined to accuse the British and Morgan of provoking the exchange crisis of 1915, it opposed belligerents or bankers securing a position, as in 1915, when sudden lack of support of foreign exchange could move the administration to reverse policy.

The committee made three recommendations. First, Congress should retain the loan-credit provisions of the Neutrality Act of 1936 (enacted by the time the committee report appeared). These provisions forbade loans or credits to belligerents, except American republics engaged in war with non-American states. Congress should strengthen these provisions to prevent extension of large credits to belligerents in the form of bank acceptances, and prevent neutrals from selling long-term securities for belligerents. Second, Congress should consider limiting export to belligerents of commodities other than medicines and hospital supplies to the amount sent to such countries in peacetime. Third, Congress should consider a definition of armed merchantmen. Pending international agreement, the committee recommended that the United States during any war in which it was a neutral should refuse clearance to armed merchantmen carrying passengers, and regard American citizens serving on such vessels as enlisted in the armed forces of nations under whose flags the ships sailed.[32]

These recommendations appear isolationist, and it is perhaps surprising that Senators George and Pope (especially Pope, one of the Senate champions of the League of Nations and collective security) failed to dissent. Closer study of the recommendations, however, indicates little inconsistency with their position. The first recommendation was a logical extension of the loan-credit provision of the Neutrality Act of 1936, already approved by the President. The third dealt with a problem facing all neutrals, and advocates of collective security had to consider that American interests might require neutrality in some future conflict. The second recommendation was most isolationist in appearance, but Pope and George probably realized it was not unlike the administration's 1936 neutrality proposal. A law patterned after the recommendation could be a mandatory measure similar to the Nye-Clark Bill of 1936. On the other hand, Congress might grant Presidential discretion in proclaiming the embargo and choosing the "typical peacetime period" for quotas of nonmilitary commodities shipped to belligerents. Such a measure would permit some flexibility in meeting the problem of foreign war.

III

While the Munitions Committee was scrutinizing Wilsonian neutrality, the Foreign Relations Committee and Foreign Affairs Committee were considering measures to replace the temporary Neutrality Act of 1935 upon its expiration on February 29, 1936. Discussion centered on the administration measure, the Pittman-McReynolds Bill. There was little doubt that Congress at least would renew the act of 1935. The question was whether it would enact a more inclusive law. Since the administration had more strength than the group supporting the Nye-Clark Bill, its measure received greater attention. As in 1935, the administration could count on the Foreign Affairs Committee, and was confident of passage of the Pittman-McReynolds Bill in the House. The Senate remained an obstacle, although the administration had support of Chairman Pittman of the Foreign Relations Committee. Pittman in truth had no more enthusiasm for administration plans in 1936 than in 1935, but supported the administration out of loyalty. At heart he was an isolationist.

Administration strategy was to obscure discretionary features of the Pittman-McReynolds Bill. Such a course might win support of the Nye-Clark neutrality bloc, since the Pittman-McReynolds and Nye-Clark Bills outwardly were similar. Reverse strategy moved the Nye-Clark group. Also noting the similarities, the bloc hoped to persuade the administration to support the Nye-Clark Bill. Neither group was deceived; both saw the wide differences in the two measures. Occupying the middle position were those individuals who wanted to renew the 1935 law. The administration preferred that to the position of Nye and Clark, whereas the Nye-Clark group considered discretionary neutrality no neutrality at all, and favored the 1935 law to the Pittman-McReynolds Bill.

There was a way out of the impasse between the administration and the neutrality bloc, as the National Peace Conference —a conference of peace societies—demonstrated. The group suggested a law which would withhold supplies from both sides at the outside of war, but if world opinion later condemned one side as the aggressor, as a violator of peace pacts, Congress could allow the President to revoke the embargo in favor of the adjudged victim. The *Christian Science Monitor* said "this proposal would limit the President's power sufficiently to keep America neutral just as long as neutrality were at all consistent with the Kellogg Pact." The proposal failed to generate much interest.[33]

Opponents attacked the Pittman-McReynolds Bill on five counts. They charged that it abandoned the nation's rights under freedom of the seas, gave the President power to be unneutral at his discretion, would result in serious economic reverses, aimed to support the League's sanctions, and was unfair to the East African belligerents for it would constitute change of policy during war.

As for freedom of the seas, the Pittman-McReynolds Bill had embargo provisions, and any legislation having such provisions received scorn from individuals dedicated to the freedom of seas principle. Some people considered any concession a national humiliation. Professor Edwin M. Borchard of Yale said that "no belligerent has the right to say to all the rest of the world, 'We have now lost our heads and have gone to war; therefore, the rest of you countries keep off the seas. This is our private domain.'" John Bassett Moore insisted that the United States had not become involved in the World War because of German violation of freedom of the seas, but because "of our undertaking to guarantee the safety of belligerent merchantmen and our taking the position that armed belligerent merchantmen were to be considered as peaceful vessels." [34]

Green H. Hackworth, legal adviser to the State Department, countered that freedom of the seas had two aspects, one in peace, another in war. During peace the seas were common highways open to every country. But in war all countries recognized that belligerents might circumvent freedom of the seas to prevent contraband from going to the enemy. Hackworth failed to move to the conclusion that in modern war the definition of contraband had become virtually all-inclusive. Hence debate on the question was superfluous. As Lothrop Stoddard said a few days later: "It seems to me, gentlemen, that all this talk about freedom of the seas is flogging a dead horse, because every attempt to enforce our so-called neutral rights, those rights which crystallize around the phrase, 'the freedom of the seas,' refers to noncontraband of war. The old distinction between contraband and noncontraband no longer exists. It was blown sky-high by the late war and practically any belligerent can write his own ticket and put anything that they [*sic*] please on the contraband list." [35]

A better argument against the administration bill was that it would enable the President to be neutral or unneutral. Despite efforts to obscure this aspect, it was there, and in the administration's view it was the heart of the bill. The administration, in a word, as in 1935, wanted flexibility. It wanted authority to join other powers—if that seemed desirable—to punish violators of peace. The Roosevelt-Hull position was enlightened, but in 1935–36 most Americans wanted peace for America at almost any price.* They had slight interest in maintaining the world's freedom at risk of war for the United States. As Charles A. Beard was saying: "We tried once to right European wrongs, to make the world safe for democracy. Even in the rosiest view the experiment was not a great success. Mandatory neutrality may be no better, for aught anyone actually knows. But we nearly burnt our house down with one experiment; so it seems not wholly irrational to try another line." Few Americans agreed with the *Commonweal* that "really too bad would be an approach to the problem through the doctrine that everything is rosy in all the Americas and the rest of the world be d——d." [36]

Opposition came from people who argued that the administration's broad embargo plan would interfere with American trade. Observers in New York reported exporters adamantly opposed the Pittman-McReynolds Bill. To attack the bill openly, however, would raise accusation of opposing the measure for business reasons. Walter Lippmann wrote that a total embargo in a general war would prove economically disastrous, and assure a war party in the United States: "If anyone thinks that unemployment, unsalable surpluses, financial disorders in the United States and a series of insults abroad will make the American people like their neutrality, he is mightily deceiving himself. If, as many think, excessive prosperity made us war-

---

* The Council for Social Action of the Congregational and Christian Churches of America in January, 1936 published results of a poll representing a cross section of the American population. When asked if they favored national isolation through strict neutrality, 83,682 people answered yes, 54,786 no. New York *Times*, January 13, 1936.

minded in 1917, they may be certain that misery and humiliation will make us even more war-minded." Professor Borchard said that "I think you are undertaking here to cripple the trade of the United States. Why should we take our trade off the sea voluntarily and without revocation, just on the hypothesis that it is going to get us into trouble? . . . All we shall do is to throw that trade into the hands of our competitors." [37]

Critics of the administration position carried the economic argument farther. The Chicago *Tribune* believed that if the United States became a belligerent it would need large overseas purchases, but if the United States enacted a sweeping embargo law other countries might do likewise. This could hurt an American war effort. Asserting that Congress should interrogate military experts as well as professors of international law, Walter Lippmann cited Brooks Emeny's *Strategy of Raw Materials:* the United States was self-sufficient in the "great essentials" (food, power, iron, machinery, coal, chemicals, petroleum), but of nineteen "critical raw materials" there were twelve which the United States had to import from one-half to all of its supplies (rubber, manganese, nickel, chromite, tungsten, antimony, tin).[38]

Opponents of the Pittman-McReynolds Bill suspected that the administration wanted to co-operate with the League of Nations. While evidence is lacking, it is probable it did hope to co-operate insofar as the measure permitted. In the van of individuals attacking the bill on this ground was the veteran League-baiter from California, Senator Hiram Johnson. Johnson argued that the measure virtually would enable the United States to join the League. Hull sought to quell such fears by insisting that the United States was proceeding on its "own separate, independent course, without collaboration or consultation directly, indirectly, remotely, or speculatively with anybody anywhere abroad." The fear remained.[39]

Among people believing that the administration intended to co-operate with the League were some of the country's Italian-Americans. The usual charge was that the British dominated the League and were waiting for the United States to enact the

Pittman-McReynolds Bill before dictating that the League proceed with oil sanctions. One Italian-American stated: "Let not Italy's little colonial adventure throw dust in our eyes. England's friends seek a commitment by us here and now ensuring our position in tomorrow's war against the only possible enemy she can have, namely, Germany." [40]

There also was the charge that the Pittman-McReynolds Bill violated neutrality by altering policy during a conflict. According to time-honored rule, no belligerent had cause to protest a neutral government's policy if in effect on or before the outbreak of hostilities, and if applied indiscriminately to belligerents. That a policy was almost certain to have unequal effect upon the belligerents was beside the point. As Secretary Lansing said during the World War, "if one belligerent has by good fortune a superiority in the matter of geographical location or of military or naval power, the rules of neutral conduct cannot be varied so as to favor the less fortunate combatant." Change of rules would be unneutral. [41]

Some critics concentrated upon details of the Pittman-McReynolds Bill. Senator Borah, supported by Connally, attacked that section decreeing that even normal trade with belligerents would be at risk of individuals conducting it. By permitting normal trade, he argued, the government would declare such trade legitimate; that trade should receive the same protection that government gave other legitimate trade. Assistant Secretary of State Moore countered by saying of the exporter engaged in normal trade with belligerents: "He is engaged in business that he has a right to engage in under our laws, but he realizes that there are great dangers in that business in some cases that we can conceive of, and we say to him in that instance: 'If you care to pursue your business, which is a profitable business to you, you do so at your own risk.' " [42]

There was fear that any law which imposed an embargo, arms or otherwise, would nullify the Monroe Doctrine, since it would prevent the United States from furnishing help to Latin American nations should they come under non-American attack. The Monroe Doctrine, however, said that the United States would intervene, with force if necessary, to protect Western Hemisphere countries. Even a mandatory law would not prevent such intervention, although it would seem anomalous to intervene in behalf of a country which could not receive help via shipment of munitions and abnormal quantities of nonmilitary commodities. Administration spokesmen could have replied (but did not, since they were seeking to obscure the discretionary features of the Pittman-McReynolds Bill) that the President could avoid acknowledging existence of war between an American state and its non-American enemy, in which case the embargo would not go into effect.

During the neutrality hearings Nye and Representative Maury Maverick (sponsor of the House version of the Nye-Clark Bill) explained their mandatory, all-inclusive measure. They hoped that Munitions Committee hearings would win support for their neutrality proposals, and believed the committee had proved that only the measure they proposed could have prevented American involvement in the World War.

Nye startled his interrogators when he acknowledged that under the Nye-Clark Bill foodstuffs, like any other nonmilitary commodity, would be subject to the bill's "normal trade" provision. Despite acquiescence in the British "starvation blockade" of Germany during the World War, Americans had considered it inhumane to deprive noncombatants of food and medical supplies. Hiram Johnson declared that Nye and Clark would withhold abnormal quantities of food from starving populations in the same manner that they would withhold oil. Explaining that under the Nye-Clark Bill the President could determine whether any commodity, including wheat, was essential in the conduct of war, Nye said it was worthwhile to restrict food shipments if it would end war. The North Dakota Progressive, whose political support came from agrarian interests and who had spent much time in the Senate working for farmers, asserted that Congress should ignore any hardship which these provisions might bring the farmer. "If we are going to argue that this is going to be a hardship upon the farmer, we ought to remember that the provisions of the bill work a possible hardship upon every industry . . . and I do not believe that the farmers of this country are in any better position to object to a restriction of their increased trade in time of war than the ordinary gun maker or powder maker or industrialist is." [43]

Despite Munitions Committee disclosures, Nye, Clark, Maverick, and their supporters worked in vain. Most isolationists had no more sympathy for such sweeping (and unprofitable) isolation as the Nye-Clark Bill provided than for the ideas of Roosevelt and Hull. And as indicated earlier, the administration considered extension of the Neutrality Act of 1935 a lesser evil than the Nye-Clark Bill. Since the Nye-Clark group could not get its measure through Congress without support from either the administration or moderate isolationists, it was evident that their plans would go for naught.

Although the administration had more strength than the Nye-Clark bloc, its position was much the same. It needed support from people who had aligned themselves with other positions. When it became clear that the Pittman-McReynolds Bill would not receive the necessary support in its existing form, the administration made concessions. Most important was deletion of part of the controversial section four, which implied that the United States might co-operate in collective ventures to halt foreign war. But critics knew that removal of this passage failed to alter the character of the bill. The President would have discretionary authority which he might use in collective peace efforts. The concession was unimportant, and did not silence opposition to the measure.

By mid-February, with expiration of the Neutrality Act of 1935 drawing near, it was clear that the administration could not pass the Pittman-McReynolds Bill. It gave up the fight, and endorsed extending the existing neutrality law until May 1, 1937. Added to the measure was an embargo on loans and credits to belligerents and exemption in favor of American republics engaged in war with non-American states. The amendments aimed to appease people who feared that the act of 1935 had nullified the Monroe Doctrine, and to prevent

Americans from becoming financially interested in foreign belligerents. The Munitions Committee's investigation of American financial houses and the Allies during the World War helped produce the latter amendment. In the administration view such a measure would work to the disadvantage of Mussolini's Italy, and satisfy the clamor that Americans have a law to keep them out of war.

Nye and his followers vainly sought an amendment changing the act's expiration date from May 1, 1937 to April 30, 1936. This would have forced action on neutrality again during the current session of Congress. Meantime the Nye group hoped to secure support for legislation along lines of the defunct Nye-Clark Bill. Rumor circulated that the neutrality bloc might filibuster against the compromise measure, but there is no evidence it considered such a maneuver. Probably Nye and his supporters knew the administration and moderate isolationists preferred no neutrality legislation to the Nye-Clark Bill and were not apt to change their minds. And the neutrality bloc considered renewal of the amended 1935 act better than nothing; they were unwilling to jeopardize that much isolation for a useless struggle in behalf of the Nye-Clark Bill.

Nearly everyone wanted to renew the neutrality law with its two amendments by February 29. Because of the rule that enactment of new neutrality programs during a war was unneutral, many individuals feared that if Congress permitted the 1935 law to lapse only to renew it later, the East African belligerents might accuse the United States of an unneutral act. But late in February, 1936 the House and Senate approved the compromise, and on February 29, despite protest by such advocates of collective security as Oswald Garrison Villard who criticized the President for abandoning the fight, Roosevelt affixed his signature to the Neutrality Act of 1936. One might say the President also was affixing his signature, however reluctantly, to the death certificate of the sanctions program of the League of Nations.[44]

Upon signing the act Roosevelt reiterated the moral embargo.

Americans, he said, should restrict export of nonmilitary materials to belligerents to amounts normally exported in peacetime. The President conceded that the "high moral duty" which he urged upon Americans had not been the subject of legislation. Nevertheless, he said, large shipments to belligerents of nonmilitary materials, bringing profits not possible during peace, would assist the conduct of war—would magnify the evil which Americans were seeking to prevent. Thus he renewed his appeal of the previous autumn that Americans trade with belligerents in such a way that no one could charge them with seizing new opportunities for profit or, by changing their peacetime trade, helping war to continue.[45]

Upon conclusion of the munitions investigation, passage of the Neutrality Act of 1936, and adjournment of the Seventy-fourth Congress, interest in munitions makers, war profits, and (for the time being) neutrality abated. During the election of 1936 few speakers mentioned these subjects, although they had been important issues in the preceding two years. The so-called merchants of death quietly slipped from their place of prominence.

In large measure the national concern waned because Americans had tired of these questions which had appeared so simple but proved so complex. Interest also waned because the questions did not seem so important in 1936 as in previous years. The Munitions Committee had demonstrated that while evils existed in the arms trade, they were not so large as suspected. Then the Federal government had taken steps to eliminate the evils through the National Munitions Control Board. As for war profits, munitions hearings had revealed determination in and out of government to prevent recurrence of the profiteering of 1917–18, and while the recent attempt in Congress to pass a law had failed, there was little doubt that legislation would come in event of war. Finally, the Neutrality Act had removed the possibility of American involvement in war as a result of attacks upon American ships carrying munitions to belligerents, and thanks to the 1936 amendments there was no danger that financial interests, seeking to guard investments, would take the United States to war.

To be sure, Americans who felt secure behind the Neutrality Act had failed to grasp or accept the conclusions of the Munitions Committee. The committee believed munitions shipments and loans were not solely responsible for American involvement in the World War. The enormous trade in nonmilitary commodities, the committee thought, had been important. But perhaps it was easier to grasp the idea that munitions shipments and Wall Street had led America to war. Captains of industry and finance, after all, were not in high repute during the Great Depression.

There were other reasons why people had less interest in the committee's work by the spring of 1936. The world situation seemed less menacing. A year had passed since Hitler renounced disarmament, and he was relatively quiet. Mussolini had nearly completed his conquest of Ethiopia. The situation in Manchuria had stabilized. Then 1936 was an election year, and it was evident that the depression, the New Deal, and the Liberty League were the campaign issues.

There seemed no need, therefore, to meditate further upon the thorny questions explored by Senator Nye and his committee. In such atmosphere the munitions investigation, which had reached its climax with the sensational inquiry into Wilsonian neutrality and the House of Morgan, expired.

It ended on a note of failure. It had failed to convince Americans of the desirability of total isolation, failed to win passage of the Nye-Clark neutrality bill, failed to parry the attacks of its detractors. Its single success was the loan-credit amendment to the Neutrality Act—no small accomplishment perhaps, but one that fell far short of the committee majority's ambition.

All that remained was the prosaic task of preparing a report which few people would read.

THE MUNITIONS INQUIRY
IN RETROSPECT

I N the years following the inquiry the Munitions Committee became an object of much criticism. People who at first praised it later concluded that Senator Nye's search for merchants of death had been a deplorable episode in American history, that it had helped steer the United States to an isolationist course, shown undue interest in newspaper publicity, treated business unfairly, intimidated witnesses, and generally given aid and comfort to enemies of the American system. Historians have charged that the committee did not conduct "a restrained inquiry but rather a ruthless investigation," gave impetus to "the thesis that American entry into the [World] war was the work of wicked Wall Street bankers, aided and abetted by sinister arms barons," and aroused the public "over the wrong things, and this state of mind contributed powerfully to the passage of the heads-in-the-sands neutrality legislation of the 1930's." In his memoirs former Secretary of State Cordell Hull wrote that "the Nye Committee aroused an isolationist sentiment that was to tie the hands of the Administration just at the very time when our hands should have been free to place the weight of our influence in the scales where it would count." President Harry S. Truman has said that "the Nye Committee, which was backed by isolationists and 'America Firsters,' was pure demagoguery in the guise of a congressional investigating committee." The country's first Secretary of Defense, James V. Forrestal, wrote in his diary in 1947 that "the Nye Committee . . . was staffed by Communist attorneys and . . . had much to do with the curtailment of our own armaments industry in the period 1936 to 1939." [1]

As chairman, and the person who gave his name to the committee, Gerald Nye has received most of the criticism—just as he received most of the plaudits in the years 1934–36. Of course it was unfair to give him either principal credit or blame for the inquiry. The munitions investigation never was a one-man performance. The committee took no important step without majority (usually unanimous) approval, and every member signed the final report, although Senators Vandenberg, Barbour, and George opposed the majority recommendation on nationalization of the munitions industry. Raushenbush and the investigative staff determined most of the questions raised in hearings, and in interrogation of witnesses Clark, Vandenberg, and Raushenbush did much more than Nye.

A view has persisted that Nye and his committee were hostile toward business. Nye was a Progressive who had spoken out against large corporations. And did not the investigation provide propaganda for the Communist and Nazi parties (which now could "prove" the rottenness of America's system)? There is no evidence to support this view. When one recalls that a conservative of the stature of Arthur Vandenberg was a guiding spirit of the inquiry, such a view is transparently naive. The committee found wrongs in the armament trade— munitions salesmen had bribed foreign officials, companies had violated embargoes, and builders of warships had engaged in collusive bidding. But the committee never implied that wrongs evident in manufacture and sale of armament extended to American business generally.

Part of the claim that the committee was antibusiness rests upon the fact that Alger Hiss—later involved in a celebrated lawsuit in which a witness accused him of communism—was a member of the committee staff. Presumably all communists in the 1930's were active in tearing down the American system. In truth Hiss was no large figure in the investigation, just a bright, personable lawyer who recently had joined government employ.

During the years 1934–36 few spokesmen for business publicly criticized the munitions investigation. In the early stages many businessmen, as well as the *Wall Street Journal* and the Chicago *Journal of Commerce,* applauded the work of the committee.

As for handling witnesses, the Munitions Committee usually was careful. There were no personal attacks, nothing to compare with the famous imbroglio between Senator Joseph R. McCarthy and Brigadier General Ralph Zwicker in 1954—when McCarthy accused Zwicker of being ignorant, a disgrace to the uniform, unfit to be an officer, and a shield for communists. Such men as Charles W. Deeds of Pratt and Whitney, William S. Carpenter of du Pont, George Whitney of J. P. Morgan, and William Flook of the New York Shipbuilding Company later were generous in appraisal of committee conduct. In a letter to the author (written in the present-day climate of opinion hostile to the munitions investigation, when it would be credible to claim intimidation) Flook said simply that "my treatment by the Committee was entirely courteous and unobjectionable." During interrogation of J. P. Morgan and his partners the *Wall Street Journal* stated that "on the whole, the committee has not been too flagrantly unfair to any of them, the senatorial point of view being what it is." Witnesses brought counsel and evidence into the hearing room, entered into the record statements and documents even remotely relevant to the inquiry, and defended themselves at any length. Men representing such firms as du Pont and Morgan frequently received deference as pillars of American business. It is interesting that only one witness from the business world, Clinton L. Bardo, former president of the New York Shipbuilding Company and in 1934–35 head of the National Association of Manufacturers, publicly denounced committee methods.[2]

The view that the committee intimidated witnesses and drew unwarranted conclusions probably has come from Nye's speeches during this period. Because of the volume of documents and testimony taken by the committee (so Raushenbush not long ago pointed out to the author), casual students have read the chairman's speeches and concluded that they indicated the approach of the committee. In a speech before the National Education Association at Denver on July 4, 1935—after suggesting that the "next war" be called a "war to make the world safe for Du Pontcracy"—Nye said of munitions makers: "These racketeers go out over this world and build up the hates, fears, and suspicions that build wars, that drive people into war, and then getting them there, they keep them there as long as they can." Committee evidence could not sustain such reckless statements, and Nye himself, years later, said that most of the men who had testified before his committee were honorable gentlemen.[3]

The Nye of the speakers' platform, however, was not the Nye of the hearing room. In a memorandum to the author the du Pont public relations department stated: "The Senator did not carry his platform eloquence over into the hearing room, at least during du Pont's appearance. By comparison, his conduct of the hearing was restrained." In the hearing room Nye spoke infrequently. He sometimes interjected questions or opinions or made statements, but seldom cross-examined. On occasion he indicated that the committee must defer judgment until all evidence was in. During a dispute between Raushenbush and Thomas W. Lamont over the cause of American entry into the World War he remarked that there should be "a little agreement here that before we undertake, as members of the committee, spokesmen for the committee, or as witnesses, to declare whether or not it was the submarine which got us into the war, or industry and business and banking, that we will take the record of the documents on the subject into consideration, and then after that record has been completed, we can all have our say as to what the real cause was."[4]

The senator was a man who had a marked sensitivity to his

lack of advanced formal education. And, despite exaggerated platform statements, he felt a deep sense of responsibility regarding his chairmanship of the committee. These sentiments restrained him in the hearing room. But before a radio microphone—or better yet, on the speakers' platform face-to-face with a throng of admiring people—his restraints departed. Nye delighted in the limelight, and he strove to remain there in 1934–36 by proclaiming the pacifist gospel about the munitions industry. Although he believed the gospel, he must have known that the inquiry over which he was presiding seldom proved these heady notions about merchants of death.

The criticism that the Munitions Committee had more interest in headlines than information appeared early. *Collier's* made the charge a month after hearings began. Whitney H. Shepardson and William O. Scroggs, writing for the Council on Foreign Relation's annual *The United States in World Affairs* for 1936, opined that the committee had suffered loss of public esteem because of "Senator Nye's apparent desire to see Senator Nye's name on the front page of newspapers." Perhaps there was some truth in this, for the committee did seek newspaper attention. Its members were political leaders who needed publicity, and they also believed that headlines pointing up evils in the munitions trade would advance the cause of peace. Then, as chapter iii shows, Nye hoped that early hearings would attract enough support to ensure appropriations to continue the inquiry. In October, 1934 Raushenbush wrote Nye that "it occurred to me . . . to try to keep the main points of the investigation before the editors of the country and I sat down and summarized 21 points, hoping that the editors . . . would be interested." John T. Flynn of the committee's advisory council wrote Raushenbush in February, 1935: "The papers seem to be blossoming out a little more freely. The Hauptmann horror will be out of the papers I suppose in a week and it will be good if you could have a striking revelation ready for that moment when the papers, bereft of their pet, are looking around for headlines." Still, there is no reason to believe that the Munitions Committee was more guilty of headline hunting than the average congressional investigating committee, or that publicity was its first aim. The committee exhibited hundreds of documents and spent many hours on topics of little popular interest.[5]

Critics of the committee have not criticized the journalists, who perhaps were the most active headline seekers of the munitions investigation. News stories on the inquiry emphasized intrigue and mystery. On one occasion a document which the committee exhibited without large attention became the object of a sensational Washington dispatch. The New York *Times* on September 7, 1934 carried a front-page headline that the committee had produced evidence that Germany, in violation of the Treaty of Versailles, was building U-boats in camouflaged plants in other European countries. The committee had attached no importance to the document, a letter by an agent of the Electric Boat Company in 1929, because it did not consider the author reliable. It did not exhibit the document to show that Germany might be violating treaty obligations.[6]

Some people have suspected that Nye's desire for publicity resulted from presidential ambition. Referring to the munitions inquiry, Roger Williams of the Newport News Shipbuilding and Dry Dock Company wrote in 1958: "There was Senator Nye trying for the Republican Presidency." Talk in 1934–36 had it that Nye might become a presidential or vice-presidential candidate (one reporter in 1935 said that as good a bet as any for the GOP ticket in 1936 was Vandenberg-Nye). A North Dakota correspondent in June, 1934 urged Nye-for-President clubs, and in January, 1935 a Washington reporter wrote that Nye was "frequently referred to as a potential republican candidate for the presidency." The same correspondent reported Nye taking presidential talk seriously, adding: "Who in the senate does not yearn to be President?" Nye of course would have accepted the presidential nomination in 1936. But there is no evidence he sought it or entertained hope it might fall his way. There was no serious movement among Progressives, isolationists, or pacifists; to orthodox Republicans he was anathema, and knew it.

His candidate in 1936, the candidate of Republicans of his views, was William E. Borah.[7]

One hears the statement that despite lack of evidence the committee had determined to prove that the merchants of death —in this instance Wall Street financiers—had drawn the United States into the World War to save their loans to Allied governments. In truth the committee did not proceed on the hypothesis that Wall Street had taken America to war (although some members suspected the financiers might have, and were alert for evidence of pressure by bankers on the government). The committee's attitude stood out in a news story from Washington, dated January 2, 1936: "Committee officials made it clear that they would not try to establish that the Morgan firm or any of its members had done anything wrong. They would try to show how the machinery of finance and credit, once it was allowed to function in wartime, inevitably tended to drag a creditor nation into the conflict on one side or the other." During this stage of the inquiry the committee aimed to discover whether commerce with the Allies after August, 1914 had inspired the double standard of neutrality which, the committee majority believed, the Wilson administration had applied to the European belligerents. It also sought to discover whether this commerce had invited German retaliation. On both points the committee majority believed the evidence provided affirmative answers. The majority hoped to persuade Americans that the United States should avoid economic ties with countries at war, that it should not become an arsenal for belligerents.[8]

I I

Most students of the 1930's take note of the Munitions Committee on the ground that the inquiry bore large responsibility for the neutrality laws of 1935-37. Charles A. Beard wrote in 1939 that "the Nye committee's findings spread distrust of presidential discretion in handling foreign affairs and stimulated the popular interest that culminated in the neutrality legislation of 1935." President Truman has written that "this committee made it appear that the munitions manufacturers had caused World War I, and as a result, the Neutrality Act was passed." In his *Isolationist Impulse,* published in 1957, Selig Adler emphasized the connection between the Munitions Committee report and the Neutrality Act of 1935— although the only part of the report to appear in 1935 dealt with the shipbuilding industry. Robert A. Divine in his excellent volume, *The Illusion of Neutrality,* published in 1962, saw a conflict between the Munitions Committee's ideas on the international arms trade and those of the administration, and that the revelations of the munitions inquiry did much to bring passage of the Neutrality Act. Former Secretary of State Cordell Hull (basing his view on the erroneous recollection that Vice-President Garner, upon the urging of Key Pittman, had appointed Nye chairman) seemed to think isolationist legislation a committee aim from the outset.[9]

I have some reservation about all of the above conclusions. The munitions investigation probably bore only a minor responsibility in passage of the neutrality laws.

Far deeper than the committee's activities were the American frustrations of the early 1930's over war and peace. Americans at this point in their history wished to avoid another war. And they did not think only of themselves; loose in the United States in these years was an idealistic or altruistic spirit born of the hardships and disappointments of the era following the World War; Americans had genuine interest in peace for all mankind. The word peace struck a chord in these years in the United States whenever it found its way into a speech or sermon or prayer. War and peace had become great moral questions. The literature of peace took on a theological quality. All Americans —advocates of collective security as well as isolationists—felt similar emotions about peace.

In the view of most Americans of the early 1930's the munitions trade seemed to work against peace. Without restriction upon the arms trade, people said, disarmament would be a farce. Moreover, the trade—carried on by profit-seeking merchants of death—supposedly spurred all countries, especially smaller ones, to war. It created a vested interest in war, people thought, and caused individuals who prospered by it to go to great lengths to disturb peace.

The idea behind the munitions inquiry, therefore, was to curb the munitions makers. Neutrality legislation—measures to keep the United States from getting involved in a war already in progress or about to begin—took their origin from different developments. Easily missed is the point that while isolationist neutrality legislation included arms embargoes, control of the munitions trade was not the exclusive preserve of isolationism.

When Senator Nye's munitions investigation began in 1934 there was no suggestion, publicly at least, in Congress or the administration, that the committee's purpose was isolationist neutrality legislation. Nor did news analysts and editorial writers propose such a purpose. They did not intimate that isolationist measures might result. Nye himself failed to see the investigation as a vehicle for isolationist legislation; it took much prodding by Dorothy Detzer before he even agreed to offer a resolution for an arms inquiry. When Nye's resolution to investigate the munitions industry went to the Foreign Relations Committee in February, 1934 the isolationist chairman, Key Pittman, refused to consider it, maneuvering it instead to the unfriendly Military Affairs Committee. Senator James P. Pope of Idaho had large enthusiasm for the investigation during its first year, and took an important part in proceedings. He was the Senate's outspoken advocate of collective security. In her book *Appointment on the Hill* Dorothy Detzer recalled Cordell Hull's sympathy for the resolution to investigate, and letters and memoranda by Hull in 1934–35 (his memoirs notwithstanding) demonstrated support for the inquiry. Hull was no isolationist. The *Wall Street Journal* was not an isolationist organ; the *Nation* was one of the country's more eloquent sounding boards for collective security; both these papers supported the investigation. There was, moreover, no conflict between the Munitions Committee and the administration in 1934–35 over whether munitions control should be national or international. Roosevelt's support of arms trade control at the Geneva Disarmament Conference in 1934 received no criticism or opposition from Nye. Nye supported international control of the arms trade, and tried to show that sinister armament makers had defeated previous attempts at such control.

The munitions investigation had a broad base of support in its first year because at that point it concentrated upon the alleged wrongs of the arms business and the question of economic mobilization in wartime. Was there an international munitions ring? Had the arms trade created trouble in South America, the Caribbean, Middle East, China? Had the trade perpetuated wars and revolutions? Had salesmen corrupted foreign functionaries? Had arms manufacturers sabotaged disarmament and other peace measures? Had builders of war vessels hoodwinked the government? Had businessmen gouged taxpayers during the World War? How could a country prevent excessive profit in war and assure productivity?

These were questions upon which the committee focused attention before August, 1935, the month in which Congress passed the first neutrality law of the 1930's.

In those months the Munitions Committee was not talking about the idea that the arms trade might invite belligerent retaliation and drag a neutral country into somebody else's war. There was occasional reference to such ideas, but these received no publicity. Hearings and pronouncements on neutrality and American entry into the World War did not take place until January, 1936—more than four months after passage of the Neutrality Act of 1935.

Nye and a majority of the committee members, of course, were isolationists. They wanted peace for the world, but especially peace for the United States. Rather early in the investigation the committee without fanfare determined to study commerce between Americans and belligerents in 1914–17. Possibly some members saw that this study might stir interest in isolationist legislation. But the committee did not show interest in the neutrality question until March and April, 1935.

It quickly dropped the subject upon objection by the Senate Foreign Relations Committee. Nye and Clark—acting as individual senators—introduced isolationist measures, and took a leading part in the neutrality debate. Debate flourished for a time, but in mid-August it appeared that Congress would pass no neutrality legislation.

Then came news that war was imminent in East Africa. This news, not Munitions Committee disclosures, spurred Congress to action.

The part of the Neutrality Act providing for the National Munitions Control Board was another matter. It did result from findings and publicity of the committee. But this provision of the Neutrality Act had come before Congress as legislation quite apart from neutrality, and been joined to the arms embargo resolution late in the neutrality debate. As a provision of the Pittman Resolution for a neutrality law it aroused slight interest.

In an intangible way, to be sure, the munitions investigation contributed to passage of isolationist legislation. The committee, having pacifist origins, stimulated interest in peace. A passion for peace—if not for the world, at least for America—brought the neutrality laws of 1935-37. Then Nye and Clark, wheel-horses of the committee, were in the van of individuals calling for legislation similar to that enacted in August, 1935. Although not acting in their capacities as members of the committee, their words had larger effect as a result of the publicity they had received from the munitions inquiry. Their words on how to preserve peace, moreover, carried an aura of authority deriving from their study of one of the factors supposedly disturbing peace.

What were the achievements of the munitions investigation? Perhaps the most notable one was debunking—inadvertently to be sure—the merchants-of-death thesis. For some twenty months the committee focused on the thesis, proving in the end that it had limited validity. Thereafter the thesis, a national distraction during a critical period, faded from the American mind. By 1938 hardly anybody bothered with merchants of death.

Another worthwhile result of the inquiry was the National Munitions Control Board. Though not the agency for rigid control sought by pacifists, the board maintained watch over the munitions industry and arms trade. And it facilitated military aid to the Allies after 1939, and helped mobilization when the United States entered a new World War in 1941.

Finally, the investigation provided information on the economy in wartime which the government found useful in 1941–1945.[10]

It would seem that on balance the credits outweigh the debits.

BIBLIOGRAPHICAL
ESSAY

THE Nye investigation receives a sentence or paragraph in most textbooks in American history, and somewhat more attention from authors treating foreign affairs in the twentieth century. But it has not been an object of thorough study and many of the statements about it have been hasty and offhand. One of the better brief accounts—despite a bias in favor of the Munitions Committee—appeared in Charles A. Beard's *America in Midpassage*, published in 1939. More recently Robert A. Divine, in *The Illusion of Neutrality* (Chicago, 1962), considered the inquiry in some detail insofar as it related to foreign affairs. Divine's analysis of the committee's part in making foreign policy is similar to that set forth in Cordell Hull's memoirs (2 vols., New York, 1948) and accepted by most historians. His attitude is generally critical. His conclusions, though sometimes at variance with mine, fall within bounds that are intellectually defensible.

There are, of course, a few special books having large importance for this study. Most notable are Helmuth C. Engelbrecht and Frank C. Hanighen's *Merchants of Death* (New York, 1934), George Seldes's *Iron, Blood and Profits* (New York and London, 1934), and Philip Noel-Baker's *Private Manufacture of Armaments* (London, 1937). These volumes, appearing in the mid-thirties, reflected a widely held view of the munitions trade and did much to stimulate the movement to control the trade.

Basic sources in the study of any congressional investigating committee are hearings and reports. When published, the Munitions Committee hearings with exhibits, filled 13,750 pages. There are forty parts. Part 40—in a single volume—is an index of hearings and exhibits. As for the recorder's transcript of hearings, it is in the Legislative Branch of the National Archives, and a spot check revealed no changes in the published hearings. The committee report, published in 1935 and 1936, comprises seven small volumes. Much of the report consists of excerpts of hearings and documents which the committee considered especially important.

Committee records also are very important. The Munitions Committee records came to the Legislative Branch of the National Archives in January, 1945 when Senator Nye, following his election defeat the previous November, cleaned out a storage cage in the old Senate Office Building. Although catalogued by the Archives, the records still have the arrangement given them by the committee. Sometimes this arrangement seems haphazard (minutes of committee meetings appear at odd places), but with patience one can locate important material. The great bulk of the records is exhibits, the most important of which the committee published during hearings. The most useful and voluminous correspondence is that of Secretary Raushenbush. Senator Nye had surprisingly little correspondence in his capacity as chairman of the committee.

Much easier to investigate, and equally important, are the records in the Foreign Affairs Branch of the National Archives. Material there is carefully arranged, and each document is numbered and briefly described in the so-called archival "purport books." To use this material the researcher must secure permission from the Office of the Historical Adviser of the Department of State and submit notes for review. The office bluepenciled none of my notes. Most of the material pertaining to the munitions inquiry is in files 811.113 Senate Investigation,

811.113 Firearms-Ammunition-Explosives-United States, and 811.04418 Offenses Against International Law. Some of these documents, of course, appear in *Foreign Relations of the United States* for 1934 and 1935.

Personal papers proved disappointing. Senator Nye's personal files yielded little. His sparse official correspondence regarding the munitions investigation is in the Archives. His personal papers include many scrapbooks bearing upon his career in the Senate, and some of these, along with odd pamphlets and broadsides, proved useful. Much of the material in the Franklin D. Roosevelt Library pertinent to the inquiry duplicates State Department papers in the National Archives. The President's personal files and the R. Walton Moore papers, however, yielded a few important letters. The papers of Norman H. Davis and George W. Norris in the Library of Congress have some interesting letters. The papers of William E. Borah, James Hamilton Lewis, Key Pittman, Thomas T. Connally, George H. Dern, Wallace Humphrey White, and Alben W. Barkley (the latter's papers are at the University of Kentucky) revealed nothing of value to this study.

Interviews and correspondence with people who had a part in the events of 1934–36 provided much background information and answers to questions raised by documents. There were interviews with Senator Nye, Senator Pope, and Stephen Raushenbush. On important issues the procedure was to address the same questions to all three men. When answers matched I accepted them.

Memoirs and published diaries had limited use. Most helpful was Dorothy Detzer's *Appointment on the Hill* (New York, 1948). The volume provided a colorful account of the origin and passage of the resolution to investigate the munitions industry. Cordell Hull's memoirs did not prove reliable on this subject, and most other references in memoirs and diaries were expressions of opinion based upon little knowledge.

The Swarthmore College Peace Collection has little correspondence of value to this study. But the files of the National

Council for Prevention of War and the Women's International League for Peace and Freedom, both at Swarthmore, have memoranda and reports providing important information.

Hearings and reports of the Naval Affairs Subcommittee of 1929–30, the War Policies Commission, the Foreign Affairs Committee, the Foreign Relations Committee, the House Military Affairs Committee, and the Senate Finance Committee were indispensable. And there also was the *Congressional Record*. Debates and statements in the *Record* mirrored attitudes and defined issues. Members of Congress, moreover, entered material, such as the 1915 and 1919 resolutions of the Women's International League, which I found in no other source. Providing helpful background information were the proceedings of the Geneva Arms Traffic Conference of 1925, the League of Nations's *Statistical Year-Book of the Trade in Arms and Ammunition* (Geneva, 1928–36), and the Council on Foreign Relations's annual *The United States in World Affairs*.

Because of its excellent coverage and splendid index, the New York *Times* was a basic source in this study. It proved an ideal supplement to committee hearings and records, and offered additional information, analysis, and in some instances graphic description of events. I consulted other newspapers for editorial opinion—the Chicago *Daily Tribune*, Chicago *Journal of Commerce, Christian Science Monitor*, Louisville *Courier-Journal*, New York *Daily Worker*, New York *Sun*, St. Louis *Post-Dispatch*, San Francisco *Examiner*, and *Wall Street Journal*.

Periodicals have similar value for a study of this type. *Business Week* has analysis reflecting a business view. *Army Ordnance* takes a similar position. Comment in the *Christian Century, Nation, New Republic*, and *World Tomorrow* indicate pacifist thinking. Other helpful articles appear in such periodicals as the *American Journal of International Law, American Magazine, American Mercury, Annals of the American Academy of Political and Social Science, Atlantic Monthly, Catholic World, Collier's Weekly, Commonweal, Congressional Digest, Current History, Foreign Affairs, Fortune* Magazine,

Forum and Century, Harper's Magazine, International Conciliation, Literary Digest, Living Age, National Republic, North American Review, Railroad Telegrapher, Saturday Evening Post, Scholastic, Scribner's Magazine, and *Women's Home Companion.*

NOTES

CHAPTER I

1 Most of the information on the history of the arms trade control
came from: summary of American arms embargo activity prepared
by the State Department, Norman H. Davis papers, Library of
Congress; summary of attempts to control arms trade, Records of
the Special Senate Committee Investigating the Munitions Industry,
1934–36, Record Group 46, Legislative Branch, National Archives
[cited hereinafter as Munitions Committee Records], Executive File,
Box 156; Eleanor Pinkham, "Summary of Earlier Proposals for the
Control of Trade in Munitions," National Council for Prevention of
War file, Swarthmore College Peace Collection; League of Nations,
*Proceedings of the Conference for the Supervision of the Interna-
tional Trade in Arms and Ammunition and in Implements of War,
Held at Geneva, May 4–June 17, 1925* (Geneva, 1925); "Arms
Manufacturers and the Public," *Foreign Affairs*, Vol. XII, No. 4
(July, 1934).
2 Report by Dorothy Detzer, executive secretary, Women's International League for Peace and Freedom, *Cong. Rec.*, 74 Cong., 1 Sess.
(Aug. 5, 1935), 12463; G. W. Norris remark, *Cong. Rec.*, 65 Cong.,
Special Sess. (April 4, 1917), 213.
3 Theodore E. Burton remark, *Proceedings of the Conference . . .
Held at Geneva*, 251.
4 New York *Times*, August 22, 1929.
5 *Ibid.*, September 7, 1929.
6 U.S. Senate, *Alleged Activities at the Geneva Conference*, Hearing
before a Subcommittee of the Committee on Naval Affairs, pursuant
to S. Res. 114 (71 Cong.), 71 Cong., 1 Sess.

7　Pamphlet quotation, *Alleged Activities at the Geneva Conference,* Appendix, 590.

8　U.S. Senate, *Munitions Industry,* Hearings before the Special Committee Investigating the Munitions Industry, pursuant to S. Res. 206 (73 Cong.), 73 Cong., 2 Sess., 74 Cong., 1 Sess., 74 Cong., 2 Sess. [cited hereinafter as Munitions Hearings] (March 15, 1935), Pt. 21, 6064.

9　New York *Times,* September 16, 1929; *Alleged Activities at the Geneva Conference,* Appendix, 655.

10　New York *Times,* June 12, 1930.

11　"The Secret International, Armament First at Work" (London, 1932); George Seldes, *Iron, Blood and Profits; An Exposure of the World-Wide Munitions Racket* (New York and London, 1934), 150; Philip Noel-Baker, *The Private Manufacture of Armaments* (London, 1937), 357.

12　Patrick J. Hurley remark, Munitions Hearings (March 13, 1935), Pt. 21, 5994.

13　*War Policies Commission,* Hearings before the commission appointed under authority of Public Resolution 98 (71 Cong.), 71 Cong., 2 Sess. (Douglas A. MacArthur remark, 355, Richard Bartholdt remark, 492–93, Bernard M. Baruch remark, 33); War Policies Commission recommendations in Munitions Hearings (March 13, 1935), Pt. 21, 5990–91.

14　R. G. Swing, "Morgan's Nerves Begin to Jump," *Nation,* Vol. CXL, (May 1, 1935), 504.

15　Resolutions on control of trade in munitions, National Council for Prevention of War file, Swarthmore College Peace Collection; others in press release by NCPW (February 19, 1934), Gerald P. Nye papers, Chevy Chase, Md.; broadside by Stop Organized Slaughter, Munitions Committee Records, General Subject File, Box 20.

16　Releases by Nofrontier News Service, June 26, October 9, 1934, Munitions Committee Records, General Subject File, Box 13; poem from undated clipping, Minneapolis *Tribune,* Nye papers.

17　H. L. Stimson letter, New York *Times,* January 11, 1933; F. B. Kellogg to Nye, May 29, 1934, Munitions Committee Records, General Subject File, Box 20; William E. Dodd and Martha Dodd, *Ambassador Dodd's Diary, 1933–1938* (New York, 1941), 167; Sir William White statement, clipping from *Evening Sun* (otherwise unidentified), April 20, 1934, Munitions Committee Records, General Subject File, Box 22.

18　"Arms Manufacturers and the Public," *loc. cit.,* 646; letter by Manley O. Hudson, New York *Times,* October 16, 1932.

19　"Arms and Men," *Fortune* Magazine, Vol. IX (March, 1934), 53–57, 113–26.

20 *Cong. Rec.*, 73 Cong., 2 Sess. (March 6, 1934), 3783.
21 Helmuth C. Engelbrecht and Frank C. Haniglen, *Merchants of Death* (New York, 1934), 9, 216–17.
22 New York *Times,* April 29, 1934.
23 Hoffman Nickerson, "Munitions Makers and Common Sense," *Army Ordnance,* Vol. XV (September–October, 1934), 71–74.
24 Interview of Nye by author, Washington, May 9, 1958.
25 Briey Basin and Fort Douamont stories and Pierre-Étienne Flandin quotation, article by Carlyle Morgan, "Patriotism or Profits," *Christian Science Monitor Weekly Magazine* (December 5, 1934); F. D. Roosevelt quotation, *Cong. Rec.*, 73 Cong., 2 Sess. (May 18, 1934), 9095; editorial positions, *Christian Science Monitor,* September 7, 1934, *Wall Street Journal,* September 8, 13, 18, 1934, Chicago *Journal of Commerce,* April 10, 1935.

CHAPTER II

1 Information on campaign for an arms inquiry: Dorothy Detzer, *Appointment on the Hill* (New York, 1948), 151–57; Dorothy Detzer to President Franklin D. Roosevelt with enclosure, May 29, 1933, Roosevelt papers, Official File 178, Munitions, 1933–40, Box 1, Franklin D. Roosevelt Library; press release by National Council for Prevention of War, February 19, 1934, Nye papers; undated report by Dorothy Detzer, *Cong. Rec.*, 74 Cong., 1 Sess. (August 5, 1935), 12464. All quotations from Detzer, *Appointment on the Hill.*
2 Biographical material in this section, *Washington Merry-Go-Round* (New York, 1931), 197–200; G. Gould Lincoln, "Nye Joins Great Probers," Washington *Sunday Star,* December 23, 1934; E. Francis Brown, "The Crusading Mr. Nye," *Current History,* Vol. XLI (February, 1935), 521–27; Beverly Smith, "Voice from the Bleachers," *American* Magazine, Vol. CXIX (May, 1935), 47, 116–18; Maxine Block (ed.), *Current Biography, Who's News and Why, 1941* (New York, 1941), 618–21; clipping from news feature entitled "Nye— Warmongers' Pet Hate," *Social Justice* (March 3, 1941), Nye papers; Nye interview (1958). Quotations in this paragraph, Smith, "Voice from the Bleachers," *loc. cit.,* 116.
3 G. H. Moses statement, *Cong. Rec.*, 71 Cong., 1 Sess. (November 8, 1929), 5332–34; Nye retort, New York *Times,* January 13, 1930; Nye's later-day views, Nye interview (1958).
4 Nye editorial, Block (ed.), *Current Biography,* 619.
5 Nye remark, Smith, "Voice from the Bleachers," *loc. cit.,* 116.
6 Nye's appearance in 1925, Brown, "The Crusading Mr. Nye," *loc. cit.,* 522; Nye remark on tariff, *Washington Merry-Go-Round,* 198.

7 Nye reference to Herbert Hoover, Brown, "The Crusading Mr. Nye," *loc. cit.*, 523; quotation on Nye support of Hoover, *Washington Merry-Go-Round*, 197.

8 Quotations on Nye's dealings with NRA, Block (ed.), *Current Biography*, 620. Nye's scrapbooks contain scores of newspaper and magazine clippings on his war against the NRA.

9 Quotation, undated biographical sketch, Nye papers.

10 "My Christian Church in the Nation," address by Nye before the international convention of the Women's Missionary Federation, Grand Rapids, Michigan, October 28, 1954, Nye papers.

11 Detzer, *Appointment on the Hill*, 157–58; *Cong. Rec.*, 73 Cong., 2 Sess. (February 8, 1934), 2153.

12 Detzer, *Appointment on the Hill*, 158–59.

13 *Ibid.*, 159. War Policies Commission treated in chapter 1, 18–20.

14 *Ibid.*, 160.

15 *Ibid.*, 160–61; undated report by Dorothy Detzer, *Cong. Rec.*, 74 Cong., 1 Sess. (August 5, 1935), 12465.

16 Detzer, *Appointment on the Hill*, 161.

17 Second interview of Nye by author, Chevy Chase, Maryland, August 23, 1960; Mrs. Dorothy Detzer Denny to author, September 26, 1960; Brooke Alexander, Assistant to the Publisher, *Fortune* Magazine, to author, September 23, 1960. "Arms and Men" treated in chapter 1, 26–29.

18 W. E. Borah speech, *Cong. Rec.*, 73 Cong., 2 Sess. (March 5, 1934), 3688–92. *Merchants of Death* treated in chapter 1, 29–30.

19 *Cong. Rec.*, 73 Cong., 2 Sess. (April 12, 1934), 6472–75, 6484–85; Detzer, *Appointment on the Hill*, 162–63.

20 *Cong. Rec.*, 73 Cong., 2 Sess. (April 12, 1934), 6485.

21 "Murder Incorporated," *New Republic*, Vol. LXXVIII (April 25, 1934), 298; A. H. Jenkins, "Nye Goes After the Munitions Makers," *Railroad Telegrapher*, Vol. LI (May, 1934), 364; John Gunther, "Slaughter for Sale," *Harper's Magazine*, Vol. CLXVII (May, 1934), 659; Johannes Steel, "World's Greatest Racket," *Nation*, Vol. CXXXVIII (June 6, 1934), 646–48.

22 Copy of radio address by Nye, Munitions Committee Records, General Subject File, Box 20; Washington *Daily News*, April 30, 1934; New York *Times*, May 1, 1934.

23 Nye to Walt Disney, Munitions Committee Records, Correspondence with the General Public File, Box 176. Disney was uninterested.

24 New York *Times*, April 29, 1934.

25 *Cong. Rec.*, 73 Cong., 2 Sess. (May 18, 1934), 9095. The Geneva Arms Traffic Convention of 1925 treated in chapter 1, pp. 7–9.

26 Roosevelt statement, *Ibid.*

27 Nye interview (1958).

28 Quotations respectively, Block (ed.), *Current Biography*, 154, and Smith, "Voice from the Bleachers," *loc. cit.*, 116. Additional information on B. C. Clark, Nye interview (1958), interview of Stephen Raushenbush by author, Washington, May 7, 1958, interview of James P. Pope by author, Knoxville, June 11, 1958.

29 Reference to A. H. Vandenberg's intelligence, Raushenbush interview.

30 Quotations, Maxine Block (ed.), *Current Biography, Who's News and Why, 1940* (New York, 1940), 821, 823.

31 Nye interview (1960).

32 Arthur M. Schlesinger, Jr., *The Age of Roosevelt, III, The Politics of Upheaval* (Boston, 1960), 123; Homer T. Bone to author, March 2, 1959.

33 Description of Bone, Smith, "Voice from the Bleachers," *loc. cit.*, 116.

34 Nye interview (1960); Pope interview.

35 New York *Times,* November 23, 1943; Raushenbush interview.

36 Nye interview (1960); Pope interview.

37 New York *Times,* April 24, 1934; Nye interview (1958); Pope interview; Bone to author, March 2, 1959.

38 Nye interview (1958); Pope interview; Raushenbush interview.

39 J. T. Flynn to Nye, May 22, 1934, Munitions Committee Records, General Subject File, Box 18; Detzer, *Appointment on the Hill,* 166–68; Nye interview (1958).

CHAPTER III

1 Raushenbush interview.

2 Raushenbush to author, August 22, 1962; Detzer, *Appointment on the Hill,* 169–70.

3 Biographical information on Raushenbush: undated biographical data sheet and unidentified radio script, Munitions Committee Records, General Subject File, Box 20; Baltimore *Sun,* June 2, 1934; Raushenbush interview; Detzer, *Appointment on the Hill,* 166; remarks by Senator L. J. Dickinson of Iowa, *Cong. Rec.,* 74 Cong., 1 Sess. (June 24, August 5, 1935), 9954–56, 12465–75.

4 Quotation, Baltimore *Sun,* June 2, 1934.

5 Whittaker Chambers's accusation, New York *Times,* June 3, 1949; J. C. Green deposition, New York *Times,* December 14, 1949, Fred J. Cook, *The Unfinished Story of Alger Hiss* (New York, 1958), 109–10; Nye opinion, Nye interview (1960).

6 Background of Hiss's employment, Raushenbush interview; Carter Glass comment, Margaret Coit, *Mr. Baruch* (Boston, 1957), 473; Bone to author, March 2, 1959.

7 Nye to Hudson, May 24, 1934, Munitions Committee Records, General Subject File, Box 17.

8 Script of world observer's broadcast, June 18, 1934, *Ibid.*, Box 14.

9 Robert Wohlforth to Raushenbush, July 18, 1934, *Ibid.*, Box 21.

10 Wohlforth to Raushenbush, July 13, September 13, 1934, *Ibid.*

11 Brown to Raushenbush, June 14, 1935, Brown to Nichols, July 17, 1935, Brown to Raushenbush, November 8, 1935, *Ibid.*, World War Financing Investigation Administrative File, Box 323; Raushenbush to Stone, July 16, 1935, *Ibid.*, Neutrality File, Box 150; Raushenbush to Bone, November 11, 1935, *Ibid.*, Administrative Files, Administrative Correspondence and Working Papers, Box 161.

12 Wohlforth to Raushenbush, August 16, September 24, 1934, *Ibid.*, General Subject File, Box 21.

13 Wohlforth to Raushenbush, November 15, 1934, *Ibid.*

14 Raushenbush to Wemple, November 10, 1934, Wemple to Raushenbush, November 15, 1934, *Ibid.*, Box 20.

15 Minutes of Munitions Committee executive meeting, June 5, 1934, *Ibid.*, Executive File, Box 157.

16 Raushenbush to Wohlforth, September 22, 1934, *Ibid.*, General Subject File, Box 21.

17 Raushenbush to Nye, December 13, 1935, *Ibid.*, Neutrality File, Box 149; Raushenbush to Bone, November 26, 1935, *Ibid.*, World War Financing Investigation Administrative File, Box 323.

18 Wohlforth to Raushenbush, August 3, 1934, *Ibid.*, General Subject File, Box 21.

19 Wohlforth to Raushenbush, August 4, July 12, 1934, *Ibid.*; J. T. Robinson remark, *Cong. Rec.*, 74 Cong., 2 Sess. (January 17, 1936), 577.

20 Nye to Cordell Hull, April 25, 1934, Hull to Nye, April 27, 1934, memorandum by Green, June 9, 1934, 811.113 Senate Investigation/ 7, 13 (citations followed by file number refer to the unpublished records of the Department of State, National Archives).

21 Green to Hull, February 7, 1935, *Ibid.*/210; Hull to Nye, February 7, 1935, Munitions Committee Records, General Subject File, Box 22. Details on Latin American and British reactions to committee disclosures treated in chapter 7 of this book.

22 Memorandum by Hull, March 14, 1935, 811.113 Senate Investigation/216.

23 Sir Ronald Lindsay to Hull, March 20, 1935, Hull to Lindsay, March 21, 1935, memorandum by Hull, March 21, 1935, Green to Hull,

March 20, 1935, *Foreign Relations of the United States Diplomatic Papers* (cited hereinafter as *FR*): 1935 (Washington, 1953), I, 364–66; minutes of committee meeting of March 22, 1935, Munitions Committee Records, Executive File, Box 157.

24 Memorandum by Hull, April 4, 1935, Lindsay to Hull, April 8, 1935, André de Laboulaye to Hull, April 9, 1935, memorandum by Phillips, April 10, 1935, *FR:* 1935, I, 367–70.

25 Memorandum by Green, April 10, 1935, 811.113 Senate Investigation/234; memorandum by William Phillips, April 18, 1935, *FR:* 1935, I, 370–71 (misprint in *FR* gives date of this document as April 13); Nye remark, New York *Times,* April 19, 1935.

26 Memorandum by Green, April 20, 1935, 811.113 Senate Investigation/252.

27 Memorandum by Green, June 3, 1935, Italian Embassy to Division of Western European Affairs, July 3, 1935, *Ibid./*266, 269.

28 Nye to Hull, August 13, 1935, Green to Hull, August 14, 19, 1935, *Ibid./*285, 288, 305; minutes of Munitions Committee meeting, April 14, 1935, Munitions Committee Records, Executive File, Box 157.

29 Memorandum by C. W. Yost, Office of Arms and Munitions Control, State Department, January 16, 1936, 811.113 Senate Investigation/384.

30 Memoranda by Green, January 18, 20, 1936, *Ibid./*385.

31 Clipping from Washington *Herald,* November 14, 1937, Hull to Lindsay, November 15, 1937, memorandum by Green, November 16, 1937, *Ibid./*414, 413B, 415.

32 Nye to Hull, January 4, 1936, Munitions Committee Records, Neutrality File, Box 152; Hull to Nye, January 30, 1936, *Ibid.,* Executive File, Box 159.

33 Brown to Raushenbush, June 14, 1935, *Ibid.,* World War Financing Investigation Administrative File, Box 323; F. W. Ashley to Nye, July 22, 1935, Nye to Ashley, July 23, 1935, *Ibid.,* Executive File, Box 157.

34 Nye to Allen Dulles, August 22, October 3, 1935, January 23, 1936, Raushenbush to Nye, January 27, 1936, *Ibid.,* Executive File, Box 157.

35 Frank A. Tichenor, "And—Roosevelt and Farley Charged 'Fraud and Collusion'!!," *Aero Digest* (October, 1936), 17–24.

36 Walter George to Nye, October 9, 1936, Clark to Nye, October 8, 1936, handwritten draft of telegram from Nye to Clark, undated (probably October 9, 1936), Munitions Committee Records, General Subject File, Box 16; Elliott Roosevelt remark, New York *Times,* October 8, 1936.

37 Nye opinion, Nye interview (1958).

CHAPTER IV

1 Memorandum by Nye, July 24, 1934, Munitions Committee Records, Executive File, Box 156; Nye interview (1958).
2 New York *Times*, July 8, August 28, 1934.
3 Nye statement, Munitions Hearings, September 4, 1934, Pt. 1, pp. 1–2.
4 Seldes, *Iron, Blood and Profits*, 13; Engelbrecht and Hanighen, *Merchants of Death*, 142–43.
5 Munitions Hearings, September 4, 5, 1934, Pt. 1, pp. 11–14, 164, 187, September 13, 1934, Pt. 5, pp. 1081–111.
6 *Ibid.*, September 13, 1934, Pt. 5, pp. 1111–14.
7 *Ibid.*, September 4, 1934, Pt. 1, pp. 35–51; New York *Times*, September 5, 1934; pamphlet by John Haynes Holmes, *The Wickedest Man Alive, Who Is He, and Why?* (New York, 1934).
8 Munitions Hearings, December 4, 1934, Pt. 9, pp. 2135–37.
9 "Death Business Again," *Nation*, Vol. CXXXIX (December 19, 1934), 699.
10 Munitions Hearings (April 3, 1935), Pt. 23, pp. 6719–23.
11 *Ibid.* (September 11, 1934), Pt. 4, p. 781.
12 *Ibid.* (February 11, 1936), Pt. 37, p. 12469.
13 *Ibid.* (September 11, 1934), Pt. 4, p. 731.
14 *Ibid.* (September 14, 1934), Pt. 5, pp. 1168–71 (December 10, 1934), Pt. 11, p. 2478.
15 Nye comment, *Ibid.* (September 12, 1934), Pt. 4, p. 830.
16 *Ibid.* (September 7, 1934), Pt. 2, pp. 475–87 (September 19, 1934), Pt. 7, pp. 1696–700.
17 *Ibid.* (September 10, 1934), Pt. 3, pp. 587–88, 660 (September 11, 1934), Pt. 4, p. 783.
18 Statement by Raushenbush, October 18, 1934, Munitions Committee Records, General Subject File, Box 14.
19 Raushenbush remark, *Ibid.;* salesman's statement, Munitions Hearings (September 7, 1934), Pt. 3, p. 560.
20 Shearer case treated in chapter 1.
21 Munitions Hearings (September 5, 1934), Pt. 1, p. 112.
22 *Ibid.* (September 5, 1934), Pt. 1, pp. 199–200 (September 4, 1934), Pt. 1, pp. 31–33.
23 *Ibid.* (September 13, 1934), Pt. 5, pp. 1111–36 (December 11, 1934), Pt. 12, pp. 2717–53.
24 *Ibid.* (December 6, 1934), Pt. 10, pp. 2317–36.
25 *Ibid* (September 21, 1934), Pt. 8, pp. 1991, 2001.
26 Byington case, *Ibid.* (February 17, 18, 19, 1936), Pt. 38, pp. 12767–3249.

27 Wohlforth to Raushenbush, July 11, 1934, Munitions Committee Records, General Subject File, Box 21; Munitions Hearings (September 21, 1934), Pt. 8, pp. 2017–36.
28 Munitions Hearings (September 17, 1934), Pt. 6, pp. 1494–515; R. M. Wood remark, New York *Times,* July 18, 1935.
29 Memorandum by Hull on conversation with Herr Hans Luther, *FR: 1934* (Washington, 1951), I, 442–43.
30 Munitions Hearings (September 13, 1934), Pt. 5, pp. 1136–42.
31 *Ibid.* (March 4, 1935), Pt. 21, pp. 6028–29.
32 Baruch memorandum returned by Roosevelt to Hull, February 23, 1935, 811.113 Firearms-Ammunition-Explosives-United States/582; Morton Hull remark, U.S. House of Representatives, *Exportation of Arms, Munitions, or Implements of War to Belligerent Nations,* Hearing before the Committee on Foreign Affairs, 70 Cong., 1 Sess., on H. J. Res. 183 (March 15, 1928), 9–10.
33 Munitions Hearings (December 11, 1934), Pt. 12, pp. 2672–74.
34 Secretary Hull to Roosevelt, March 14, 1935, *FR: 1935,* I, 318–19.
35 New York *Times,* November 2, 1935.
36 Munitions Hearings (December 19, 1934), Pt. 16, pp. 3948–73.
37 *Ibid.* (February 21, 1935), Pt. 20, p. 5586 (April 4, 1935), Pt. 23, p. 6873.
38 *Ibid.* (February 21, 1935), Pt. 20, p. 5577.
39 U.S. Senate, Special Committee Investigating the Munitions Industry, *Munitions Industry,* Senate Report 944, pursuant to S. Res. 206 (73 Cong.), 74 Cong., 1 Sess., 74 Cong., 2 Sess. (cited hereinafter as Munitions Committee Report), Pt. 3, pp. 15–16; Nye remark in New York *Times,* June 30, 1935. The majority exempted the aircraft industry from its nationalization recommendation.
40 Munitions Committee Report, Pt. 3, pp. 16–17.
41 New York *Times,* February 16, 1935, January 13, 1936.
42 Munitions Hearings (September 11, 1934), Pt. 4, p. 769 (September 19, 1934), Pt. 7, p. 1704.

CHAPTER V

1 The committee did consider the Electric Boat Company, builder of submarines, concurrently with manufacturers of guns, ammunition, and airplanes.
2 "You Must Curb Shipbuilders, Mr. President," *Peace Action,* Vol. I (June, 1934), 2.
3 Munitions Hearings (February 14, 1935), Pt. 20, pp. 5369–70.
4 *Ibid.* (February 27, 1935), Pt. 21, pp. 5853–54.
5 *Ibid.* (February 9, 1935), Pt. 20, pp. 5471–74.

6   *Ibid.* (February 11, 1935), Pt. 19, pp. 5147–52.
7   *Ibid.* (January 30, 31, 1935), Pt. 18, pp. 4773–74, 4782–83 (February 22, 1935), Pt. 21, pp. 5713–28 (April 9, 1935), Pt. 24, pp. 7121–26. Check Pt. 40, Index, for many other references to 1933 naval program.
8   *Ibid.* (January 25, 1935), Pt. 18, pp. 4691–93.
9   *Ibid.* (January 30, 1935), Pt. 18, pp. 4747–48.
10 *Ibid.*, 4759–64.
11 *Ibid.* (February 11, 1935), Pt. 19, pp. 5179–88 (April 10, 1935), Pt. 24, pp. 7114–15 (April 5, 1935), 6911–12.
12 *Ibid.* (February 28, 1935), Pt. 21, pp. 5894–96; Munitions Committee Report, Pt. 1, p. 41.
13 Munitions Hearings (April 5, 1935), Pt. 23, pp. 6912–13.
14 *Ibid.* (January 30, 1935), Pt. 18, pp. 4768–70 (January 31, 1935), Pt. 18, pp. 4786–96 (February 20, 1935), Pt. 20, pp. 5545–54.
15 *Ibid.* (February 4, 1935), Pt. 19, pp. 5027–35.
16 *Ibid.* (January 29, 1935), Pt. 18, pp. 4734–41 (January 30, 1935), pp. 4743–46 (January 31, 1935), pp. 4796–815 (February 4, 1935), Pt. 19, pp. 5001–5002 (February 15, 1935), Pt. 20, pp. 5379–83.
17 Leslie C. Garnett, U.S. Attorney, District of Columbia, to Nye, September 23, 1935, Munitions Committee Records, Executive File, Box 8.
18 Austin B. Geist to Nye, February 11, 1935, and Nye reply, February 20, 1935, *Ibid.*, General Subject File, Box 8.
19 Munitions Hearings (March 12, 1935), Pt. 21, pp. 5980–84; New York *Times,* March 13, 1935. Shearer case treated in chapter 1.
20 Munitions Committee Report, Pt. 1, p. 4.
21 Undated memorandum, Munitions Committee Records, Neutrality File, Box 150.
22 Munitions Committee Report, Pt. 1, pp. 11–12.
23 U.S. Senate, Hearings before the Committee on Naval Affairs on S. 3098, 74 Cong., 2 Sess. (January 21, 1936).

CHAPTER VI

1   The War Policies Commission treated in chapter 1.
2   *Christian Science Monitor,* December 13, 1934; New York *Times,* December 13, 1934.
3   "War Profits," *Business Week* (December 22, 1934), 22.
4   New York *Times,* December 27, 1934.
5   Views of observer, *Christian Science Monitor,* December 13, 1934.
6   In the range of manuscript collections, public documents, newspapers, periodicals, and secondary works surveyed by the author,

there is nothing establishing Roosevelt's motives in this matter. The man who might provide answers, Bernard Baruch, has declined to do so.

7 Munitions Hearings (December 13, 1934), Pt. 13, pp. 2920–27 (February 25, 1935), Pt. 21, p. 5746 (September 12, 1934), Pt. 4, pp. 1017–51.

8 *Ibid.* (February 25, 1935), Pt. 21, p. 5754.

9 *Ibid.* (December 17, 1934), Pt. 15, p. 3639 (February 25, 1935), Pt. 21, pp. 5755–57.

10 *Ibid.*, Pt. 14, Appendix, 3347–52 (December 14, 1934), Pt. 14, pp. 3257–58.

11 *Ibid.*, 3222.

12 *Ibid.*, 3222–25; New York *Times*, December 15, 1934.

13 Munitions Hearings (December 17, 1934), Pt. 15, pp. 3594–95, Pt. 14, Appendix, 3300.

14 *Ibid.* (December 14, 1934), Pt. 14, pp. 3191–210 (December 13, 1934), Pt. 13, pp. 2959–71 (December 21, 1934), Pt. 17, p. 4282.

15 *Ibid.* (December 21, 1934), Pt. 17, p. 4273.

16 *Ibid.*, 4282, 4302–23 (April 9, 1935), Pt. 24, pp. 7078–80.

17 *Ibid.* (April 9, 1935), Pt. 24, pp. 7080–85.

18 *Ibid.* (April 9, 1935), Pt. 17, pp. 4330–35.

19 *Ibid.* (December 21, 1934), Pt. 17, p. 4282 (March 15, 1935), Pt. 21, p. 6056.

20 *Ibid.* (February 25, 1935), Pt. 21, pp. 5734–38 (December 20, 1934), Pt. 17, p. 4198.

21 *Ibid.* (March 15, 1935), Pt. 21, pp. 6057–59.

22 *Ibid.* (March 14, 1935), Pt. 21, pp. 6013–50; *Peace Action,* Vol. I (September, 1934), 5, 11.

23 *Cong. Rec.*, 74 Cong., 1 Sess. (January 9, 1935), 239; New York *Times*, January 10, February 20, 1935.

24 U.S. House of Representatives, *Taking the Profit Out of War,* Hearing before the Committee on Military Affairs, 74 Cong., 1 Sess., on H.R. 3 and H.R. 5293 (January 22, 1935), 1–2.

25 *Ibid.* (January 22, 25, 26, 28, 29, 1935), 1–334.

26 Munitions Committee Report, Pt. 4, pp. 1–2.

27 Munitions Hearings (March 19, 1935), Pt. 22, pp. 6179–83.

28 *Ibid.* (March 19, 1935), Pt. 22, pp. 6179–90.

29 *Ibid.* (March 21, 1935), Pt. 22, p. 6237.

30 *Ibid.* (March 19, 1935), Pt. 22, p. 6186.

31 *Ibid.*, 6184.

32 *Ibid.* (March 21, 1935), Pt. 22, p. 6250 (March 28, 1935), Pt. 22, pp. 6339–40.

33 Raushenbush to Flynn, March 8, 1935, Munitions Committee Records, Executive File, Box 156.

34 Munitions Hearings (March 19, 1935), Pt. 22, pp. 6190–91.

35 *Ibid.*, 6191.

36 *Ibid.*, 6192–93.

37 *Ibid.*, 6194–95.

38 *Ibid.*, 6196–99.

39 *Ibid.* (March 20, 1935), Pt. 22, p. 6220.

40 "Honest Attack on War Profits," *Christian Century,* Vol. LII (April 3, 1935), 419; "Should Wealth be Conscripted," *Nation,* Vol. CXL (April 24, 1935), 469; "Taking the Profits Out of War," *Christian Century,* Vol. LII (May 1, 1935), 567; Munitions Hearings (March 19, 1935), Pt. 22, pp. 6201–204.

41 "War Profits Doomed," *Business Week* (April 13, 1935), 9–10.

42 Munitions Hearings (March 27, 1935), Pt. 22, pp. 6274–75.

43 *Ibid.*, 6267–68.

44 *Ibid.*, 6277.

45 *Ibid.*, 6281.

46 *Ibid.*, Pt. 22, Appendix, 6633–43.

47 New York *Times,* April 16, 1935; Munitions Hearings (April 16, 1935), Pt. 24, pp. 7269–70.

48 Memorandum of telephone conversation with Nye, by Joseph C. Green, March 20, 1935, 811.113 Senate Investigation/241; Press Conference #192, March 20, 1935, Press Conferences, Vol. V, 169–70, Roosevelt papers; Raushenbush to Nye, April 16, 1935, Munitions Committee Records, Executive File, Box 156.

49 Memorandum with enclosure, by Joseph C. Green, April 2, 1935, 811.113 Senate Investigation/240; Nye remark, New York *Times,* April 3, 1935.

50 *Cong. Rec.,* 74 Cong., 1 Sess. (April 3, 1935), 4953–55.

51 *Ibid.* (April 6, 1935), 5178–200; New York *Times,* April 7, 1935.

52 *Cong. Rec.,* 74 Cong., 1 Sess. (April 9, 1935), 5325–26.

53 U.S. Senate, *To Prevent Profiteering in War,* Hearing before a Subcommittee of the Committee on Finance, 74 Cong., 2 Sess. (April 3, 1936), 74.

54 Raushenbush interview; Raushenbush to author, August 22, 1962; Henderson to author, October 9, 1962. During hearings the committee, though touching upon them many times, never focused upon government procurement contracts. But in Part 4 of its report, published in June, 1936, it devoted a section to findings and views on this subject.

CHAPTER VII

1 Lincoln, "Nye Joins Great Probers," *loc. cit.*, December 23, 1934.
2 William Ragsdale, Russellville, Arkansas, to Nye, September 1, 1934, J. D. Eastburn, Tuscon, Arizona, to Nye, September 29, 1934, Donald G. Anderson, Oakland, California, to Nye, September 1, 1934, Munitions Committee Records, Correspondence with the General Public File, Boxes 175–76; Kellogg to Hull, September 7, 1934, 811.113 Senate Investigation/41; R. S. Baker to Raushenbush, September 4, 1935, Munitions Committee Records, World War Financing Investigation Administrative File, Box 323; San Francisco *Examiner*, September 18, 1934; "Death Business Again," *loc. cit.*
3 A. W. Beaven to Roosevelt with enclosure, September 29, 1934, 811.113 Senate Investigation/89; *Christian Science Monitor*, September 7, 1934.
4 Letter with enclosure, NCPW to Hull, January 7, 1935, 811.113 Senate Investigation/193; circular by WIL Campaign Director Mabel Vernon, October 27, 1934, WIL file, Swarthmore College Peace Collection.
5 *Wall Street Journal*, September 8, 13, 18, 1934; Chicago *Journal of Commerce*, April 10, 1935; New York *Times*, November 19, 1934.
6 Hull to Kellogg, September 7, 1934, State Department Information Series No. 61, 811.113 Senate Investigation/41, 204B.
7 Detzer, *Appointment on the Hill*, 168–69; Noel-Baker to Nye, September 22, 1934, Munitions Committee Records, General Subject File, Box 17; Christopher Addison, "Taking the Profit Out of War," *Christian Science Monitor Weekly Magazine* (March 13, 1935); London *Daily Herald* editorial, Ray Atherton, London, to Hull, October 1, 1934, 811.113 Senate Investigation/124.
8 Chicago *Daily Tribune*, April 2, 1935; New York *Daily Worker*, September 13, 14, 15, December 7, 1934; "Yellow Journalism in the Senate," *Collier's Weekly*, Vol. XCIV (October 27, 1934), 58. Bone to Raushenbush, October 31, 1934, Wohlforth to Raushenbush, November 9, 1934, Munitions Committee Records, General Subject File, Boxes 17, 21.
9 *Cong. Rec.*, 74 Cong., 1 Sess. (June 24, 26, August 5, 1935), 9954–56, 10131–53, 12460–75; Brown to Raushenbush, August 6, 1935, Munitions Committee Records, World War Financing Investigation Administrative Files, Box 323.
10 William C. Lee, Washington, to Nye, September 3, 1934, Munitions Committee Records, General Subject File, Box 10.

11 Undated clipping from a Tacoma, Washington newspaper, datelined Washington, D.C., January 21, 1935, Munitions Committee Records, General Subject File, Box 19.

12 Alexander W. Weddell, Buenos Aires, to Hull, September 21, 1934, Matthew E. Hanna, Guatemala, to Hull, September 12, 1934, 811.113 Senate Investigation/56, 57.

13 L. G. Dreyfus to Hull, September 14, 1934, *Ibid.*/50; R. M. Scotten to Hull, September 15, 1934, *FR:* 1934, I, 434–36; Hugh Gibson, Rio de Janeiro, to Hull, September 15, 1934, *FR:* 1934, p. 434; Henry H. Sevier, Santiago, to Hull, September 14, 1934, 811.113 Senate Investigation/33; memorandum by Legal Adviser Green H. Hackworth for Hull, September 13, 1934, 811.113 Senate Investigation/ 72½; Gibson to Hull, *FR:* 1934, I, 447–48; John K. Montgomery to Nye, September 14, 1934, Munitions Committee Records, General Subject File, Box 20.

14 Munitions Hearings (September 19, 1934), Pt. 7, pp. 1685, 1690– 91.

15 *Ibid.* (September 7, 1934), Pt. 2, pp. 495–96.

16 New York *Times,* September 8, 1934; R. W. Bingham to Hull, September 10, 1934, *FR:* 1934, I, 429–30; Pope interview.

17 Nye to Hull, September 11, 1934, press release by Hull, September 11, 1934, *FR:* 1934, I, 437–38.

18 Letter with enclosure, Warren D. Robbins, Ottawa, to Hull, November 21, 1934, 811.113 Senate Investigation/153.

19 New York *Times,* November 9, 23, 1934, June 28, 1935.

20 Noel-Baker to Manley O. Hudson, October 10, 1934, Ray Atherton, London, to Hull, February 19, 1935, Munitions Committee Records, General Subject File, Boxes 18, 22.

21 Harold Laski, "The British Arms Inquiry," *Nation,* Vol. CXLII (March 4, 1936), 272–73.

22 Theodore Marriner, Paris, to Hull, October 8, 1935, Greenville T. Emmet, The Hague, to Hull, October 7, 1935, Lawrence A. Steinhardt, Stockholm, to Hull, April 12, 13, 1935, Munitions Committee Records, General Subject File, Box 22.

23 N. H. Davis statement, *FR:* 1934, I, 79–83; Mrs. Laura P. Morgan, "As Latest U.S. and U.S.S.R. Statements Look to Geneva," *Peace Action,* Vol. I (June, 1934), 3–4.

24 Memorandum by American Delegation to General Disarmament Conference, June 14, 1934, *FR:* 1934, I, 120–21; draft of the American proposal, Munitions Committee Records, General Subject File, Box 22; Morgan, "U.S. Proposal Termed 'Revolutionary,'" *Peace Action,* Vol. I (July, 1934), 3–4.

25 Morgan, "Disarmament Committee Makes Technical Progress," *Peace Action,* Vol. I (August, 1934), 3.

26 State Department Information Series No. 66, January 30, 1935, 811.113 Senate Investigation/204B; Morgan, "Disarmament Conference Should Curb Arms Trade," *Peace Action*, Vol. I (November, 1934), 11; Hull to Roosevelt, November 22, 1934, *FR:* 1934, I, 191–92.

27 Hull to Roosevelt, November 22, 1934, Roosevelt to Hull, November 24, 1934, *FR:* 1934, I, 191–93.

28 John W. Killigrew, "The Impact of the Great Depression on the Army, 1929–1936," unpublished Ph.D dissertation, Indiana University, 1960.

CHAPTER VIII

1 Thorvald Boye, "Shall a State which Goes to War in Violation of the Kellogg-Briand Pact have a Belligerent's Rights in Respect of Neutrals?" *The American Journal of International Law*, Vol. XXIV (October, 1930), 766–70; New York *Times*, May 14, 1926.

2 Burton remark, New York *Times*, November 19, 1927.

3 U.S. House of Representatives, *Exportation of Arms, Munitions or Implements of War to Belligerent Nations*, Hearing before the Committee on Foreign Affairs, 70 Cong., 1 Sess., on H. J. Res. 183 (March 15, 19, 1928), 9, 12–13, 80.

4 *Ibid.* (March 15, 1928), 13–14.

5 *Ibid.* (March 16, 1928), 20–39.

6 Editorial response to Capper Resolution, New York *Times*, February 12, 1929, *Cong. Rec.*, 70 Cong., 2 Sess. (February 27, 1929), 4581–604.

7 New York *Times*, February 11, 12, 1929.

8 Kellogg and Borah responses, *Ibid.*, February 12, 1929.

9 *Cong. Rec.*, 72 Cong., 2 Sess. (January 10, 19, 1933), 1448, 2096 New York *Times*, January 11, 12, 1933.

10 U.S. House of Representatives, *Exportation of Arms or Munitions of War*, Hearing before the Committee on Foreign Affairs, 72 Cong., 2 Sess., on H. J. Res. 580 (February 7, 8, 10, 12, 14, 1933), 1–70.

11 *Cong. Rec.*, 72 Cong., 2 Sess. (February 8, 1933), 3589–91.

12 U.S. House of Representatives, *Exportation of Arms or Munitions of War*, Hearing before the Committee on Foreign Affairs, 73 Cong., 1 Sess., on H. J. Res. 93 (March 28, 1933).

13 *Cong. Rec.*, 73 Cong., 1 Sess. (April 13, 14, 1933), 1683–702, 1746–77.

14 *Ibid.*

15 Henry L. Stimson and Allen W. Dulles, Report on informal meeting of Council on Foreign Relations, New York, January 10, 1934,

R. Walton Moore papers, Neutrality (1934), Franklin D. Roosevelt Library.

16 Copy of article by T. J. Wertenbaker, February 5, 1935, 811.04418 Offenses Against International Law/23½; Lothrop Stoddard to Hull, December 22, 1934, *Ibid./18*.

17 C. B. Warren memorandum, *Ibid./28*.

18 Memoranda by Green, March 27, 29, 1935, 811.113 Senate Investigation/242, *FR:* 1935, I, 323–24.

19 Raushenbush to Nye, March 30, 1935, Munitions Committee Records, General Subject File, Box 20, minutes of committee meeting, April 1, 1935, Executive File, Box 157; memoranda by Green, March 30, April 10, 12, 1935, *FR:* 1935, I, 324–25, 329–30, 339–40; Pittman to Wallace S. Murray, *FR:* 1935, p. 330.

20 *Cong. Rec.,* 74 Cong., 1 Sess. (May 28, 1935), 8338–41.

21 *Ibid.*

22 Copy of Nye address entitled "Profiting from Experience," given at Carnegie Hall, May 27, 1935, Munitions Committee Records, Neutrality File, Box 149; newspaper release of Nye address over National Broadcasting Company network, June 7, 1935, Nye papers.

23 Memoranda by Green, June 28, July 9, 1935, 811.04418/55, and 811.113 Firearms-Ammunition-Explosives-United States/698; Davis to Phillips, July 18, 1935, Moore papers.

24 Memorandum by Office of the Economic Adviser, July 9, 1935, 800.51 Financial Affairs—General/1143.

25 Phillips to Hull, June 28, 1935, 811.04418/55; Josephine J. Burns to Lawrence Brown, July 11, 1935, Munitions Committee Records, World War Financing Investigation Administrative File, Box 324.

26 Memoranda by Green, May 7, 16, 25, 1935, 811.113 Senate Investigation/255, 267, Firearms-Ammunition-Explosives-United States/616; minutes of committee meeting, May 16, 1935, Munitions Committee Records, General Subject File, Box 19.

27 U.S. House of Representatives, *National Munitions Act,* Hearing before the Committee on Foreign Affairs, 74 Cong., 1 Sess., on H.R. 8788 (July 16, 1935), 7–31.

28 Memorandum by Green, June 3, 1935, and memorandum by Phillips, July 29, 1935, 811.113 Firearms-Ammunition-Explosives-United States/627, 677.

29 Administration bill, Phillips to Pittman with enclosure, July 31, 1935, *FR:* 1935, I, 345–50.

30 Grace M. Sisson and Jeannette Rankin to Roosevelt, July 26, 1935, Roosevelt papers, Official File 1561, Neutrality, 1934–39; Jeannette Rankin to Hull, July 12, 1935, I. L. Holt to Hull, July 30, 1935, and memorandum by Phillips, July 30, 1935, 811.04418/56, 68, 72;

Stone to Raushenbush, August 5, 1935, Munitions Committee Records, Neutrality File, Box 150.

31 Pittman to Roosevelt, August 19, 1935, Roosevelt papers, President's Personal Files 745 (Key Pittman), 1933–41. Pittman comment to Stephen Early recorded on this letter.

32 Roosevelt to Pittman, August 19, 1935, *Ibid.;* Roosevelt to McReynolds, August 20, 1935, *Ibid.*, 5236 (Sam D. Reynolds).

33 *Cong. Rec.*, 74 Cong., 1 Sess. (August 20, 1935), 13777–79.

34 Quotation, "Hard Task of Staying Neutral," *Collier's Weekly*, Vol. XCVI (November 23, 1935), 78.

35 State Department information release, August 31, 1935, 811.04418/83.

36 Hull to Roosevelt, August 29, 1935, Roosevelt papers, Official File 1561, Neutrality, 1934–39.

37 Tom Connally remark, *Cong. Rec.*, 74 Cong., 1 Sess. (August 24, 1935), 14432.

38 Pittman view, *Ibid.*, 13954.

39 New York *Times*, August 23, 1935.

40 *Ibid.*, October 6, 1935.

41 Business response, *Ibid.*, October 9, 1935, *Wall Street Journal*, October 10, 1935; J. M. Futrell remark, *Christian Science Monitor*, October 12, 1935; Nye remark, New York *Times*, October 12, 1935; Warren, "Safeguards to Neutrality," *Foreign Affairs*, Vol. XIV (January, 1936), 199–215.

42 Quotation, Thomas J. Wertenbaker, "Price of Neutrality," *Atlantic Monthly*, Vol. CLVII (January, 1936), 105.

43 U.S. House of Representatives, *American Neutrality Policy*, Hearing before the Committee on Foreign Affairs, 74 Cong., 2 Sess., on H. J. Res. 422, Appendix, 306.

44 Nye telegram, New York *Times*, October 17, 1935; *Christian Science Monitor*, November 9, 1935; editorial, New York *Times*, November 8, 1935; "Dress Rehearsal for Neutrality," *New Republic*, Vol. LXXXV (November 13, 1935), 4–5; "American Neutrality," *Christian Century*, Vol. LII (November 20, 1935), 1478–80; "Sanctions Under Neutrality," *Nation*, Vol. CXLI (November 13, 1935), 553; *Wall Street Journal*, November 18, 1935; Charles H. Sherrill to Roosevelt, Roosevelt papers, Official File 176, Embargoes, 1933–35; New York *Sun*, November 30, 1935; "For Honest Neutrality, Not Favoritism," *Business Week* (November 30, 1935), 40; "Plan for Neutrality," *Business Week* (December 28, 1935), 14; E. M. Borchard to R. Walton Moore, November 2, 1935, 811.04418/91$\frac{1}{2}$; John Bassett Moore to editor, New York *Sun*, December 10, 1935; C. E. Coughlin remark, New York *Times*, November 4, 1935.

45 New York *Times,* December 22, 1935; *The World Almanac and Book of Facts, 1937* (New York, 1937), 667–68.

CHAPTER IX

1 New York *Times,* January 5, 1936.
2 *Cong. Rec.,* 74 Cong., 2 Sess. (January 3, 1936), 27–30.
3 Administration bill, House, *American Neutrality Policy,* 1–6.
4 *Ibid.;* Pittman remark, New York *Times,* January 4, 1936.
5 New York *Times,* January 5, 1936.
6 U.S. Senate, *Neutrality,* Hearing before the Committee on Foreign Relations, 74 Cong., 2 Sess., on S. 3474 (January 27, 1936), 149–69.
7 Raushenbush to Calvin J. Nichols, August 23, 1935, Munitions Committee Records, General Subject File, Box 19
8 New York *Times,* January 12, 1936.
9 Munitions Hearings, January 7, 1936, Pt. 25, pp. 7482–518.
10 *Ibid.*
11 *Ibid.,* 7518–23, January 13, 1936, Pt. 27, pp. 8200–8202.
12 *Ibid.,* January 7, 1936, Pt. 25, pp. 7533–34.
13 *Ibid.,* January 9, 1936, Pt. 26, pp. 7786–89.
14 Munitions Committee Report, Pt. 6, pp. 3–4; Munitions Hearings (January 9, 1936), Pt. 26, pp. 7822–71 (January 10, 1936), Pt. 26, pp. 7882–83 (January 16, 1936), Pt. 28, pp. 8579–85.
15 Munitions Hearings (January 10, 1936), Pt. 26, p. 7894.
16 *Ibid.,* 7922
17 *Ibid.* (January 15, 1936), Pt. 28, pp. 8499–500 (January 8, 1936), Pt. 25, p. 7566 (February 4, 1936), Pt. 29, p. 9055.
18 *Ibid.* (January 15, 1936), Pt. 28, pp. 8504–505.
19 *Ibid.,* (January 16, 1936), pp. 8584–633.
20 *Ibid.* (January 9, 1936), Pt. 26, pp. 7835–43.
21 *Ibid.* (January 15, 1936), Pt. 28, pp. 8487–508.
22 *Ibid.* (January 14, 1936), Pt. 27, pp. 8274–75.
23 *Ibid.* (January 15, 1936), Pt. 28, pp. 8509–14.
24 *Cong. Rec.,* 74 Cong., 2 Sess. (January 16, 1936), 501–13.
25 Munitions Hearings (January 16, 1936), Pt. 28, 8633–37; New York *Times,* January 17, 1936.
26 *Cong. Rec.,* 74 Cong., 2 Sess. (January 17, 1936), 562–79; New York *Times,* January 18, 1936; observer's remark, Ernest S. Bates and Alan Williams, *American Hurly-Burly* (New York, 1937), 30.
27 *Cong. Rec.,* 74 Cong., 2 Sess. (January 18, 1936), 650–57; New York *Daily Worker,* January 21, 1936; Norris to Mildred L. Green, January 27, 1936, Norris papers, Library of Congress.

28 Chicago *Daily Tribune,* January 20, 21, 1936.
29 Coughlin offer, New York *Times,* January 20, 1936.
30 Morgan remark and committee response, New York *Times,* February 6, 1936.
31 Pope interview; Nye interview (1958).
32 Munitions Committee Report, Pt. 5, pp. 8–9, Pt. 6, pp. 2–7.
33 *Christian Science Monitor,* January 4, 1936.
34 House, *American Neutrality Policy,* January 9, 1936, p. 58; Senate, *Neutrality,* January 29, 1936, p. 185.
35 House, *American Neutrality Policy,* January 8, 15, 1936, pp. 38, 239.
36 Charles A. Beard, "Heat and Light on Neutrality," *New Republic,* Vol. LXXXVI (February 12, 1936), 9; "Week by Week," *Commonweal,* Vol. XXIII (January 17, 1936), 311.
37 New York *Times,* January 19, 1936; Walter Lippmann, "Today and Tomorrow," St. Louis *Post-Dispatch,* February 3, 1936; Borchard statement, Senate, *Neutrality,* January 29, 1936, p. 212.
38 Chicago *Daily Tribune,* August 23, 1935; Lippmann, "Today and Tomorrow," *loc. cit.,* February 3, 1936.
39 Hull remark, Senate, *Neutrality,* January 15, 1936, p. 67.
40 House, *American Neutrality Policy,* January 14, 1936, pp. 177–83; Senate, *Neutrality,* February 5, 1936, p. 281.
41 House, *American Neutrality Policy,* January 14, 1936, pp. 177–218; Robert Lansing remark, Julius W. Pratt, *A History of United States Foreign Policy* (New York, 1955), 469.
42 Senate, *Neutrality,* January 10, 1936, pp. 21–29.
43 *Ibid.,* January 27, 1936, pp. 149–69.
44 O. G. Villard, "Roosevelt Betrays Neutrality," *Nation,* Vol. CXLII (February 26, 1936), 239.
45 Roosevelt statement, press release, February 29, 1936, Official File 1561, Neutrality, 1934–39, Roosevelt papers.

CHAPTER X

1 Arthur S. Link, *American Epoch, A History of the United States since the 1890's* (New York, 1955), 464; Dexter Perkins, *The New Age of Franklin D. Roosevelt* (Chicago, 1960), 96; Thomas A. Bailey, *The Man in the Street, The Impact of Public Opinion on Foreign Policy* (New York, 1948), 126; *The Memoirs of Cordell Hull* (New York, 1948), I, 404; *Memoirs by Harry S. Truman,* I, *Year of Decisions* (Garden City, 1955), 190; Walter Millis (ed.), *The Forrestal Diaries* (New York, 1951), 242–43.
2 C. W. Deeds to author, December 5, 1958; W. S. Carpenter to

author, December 24, 1958; Whitney to author, December 16, 1958; William Flook to author, December 4, 1958; *Wall Street Journal,* January 23, 1936; C. L. Bardo statement, Munitions Hearings (January 24, 1935), Pt. 18, p. 4635.

3   Raushenbush interview; Nye, "The Munitions Investigation," *Journal of the National Education Association,* Vol. XXIV (September, 1935), 185–92; Nye interview (1958).

4   Memorandum by Department of Public Relations, E. I. du Pont de Nemours and Company, enclosed with letter, William S. Carpenter to author, December 24, 1958; Munitions Hearings (January 8, 1936), Pt. 26, p. 7568.

5   "Yellow Journalism in the Senate," *loc. cit.;* W. H. Shepardson and W. O. Scroggs, *The United States in World Affairs, An Account of American Foreign Relations 1936* (New York, 1937), 120; Raushenbush to Nye, October 19, 1934, Munitions Committee Records, General Subject File, Box 18, Flynn to Raushenbush, February 9, 1935, Executive File, Box 156.

6   Munitions Hearings (September 6, 1934), Pt. 1, 235–36.

7   Roger Williams to author, December 4, 1958; all quotations from clippings in Nye papers: unidentified column by Rodney Dutcher; column by Thomas L. Stokes, Washington Daily *News,* May 31, 1934; column from Valley City (North Dakota) *People's Opinion,* June 28, 1934; column by George A. Benson, Minneapolis *Journal,* January 28, 1935; column by Frederic William Wile, Washington *Star,* December 17, 1934; copy of article by Leslie Eichel, "Republicans View Nye as Possible Nominee," Brooklyn *Times-Union,* September 3, 1935.

8   New York *Times,* January 3, 1936.

9   Beard, *America in Midpassage* (New York, 1939), I, 421; *Memoirs by Harry S. Truman,* I, 189; Selig Adler, *The Isolationist Impulse, Its Twentieth Century Reaction* (New York and London, 1957), 257–58; R. A. Divine, *The Illusion of Neutrality* (Chicago, 1962), 57–117; *The Memoirs of Cordell Hull,* I, 398.

10 Murray S. Stedman, *Exporting Arms: The Federal Arms Export Administration, 1935–1945* (New York, 1947), 126–36.

INDEX

259

29; appointed to Senate, 29; wins (*1932*) election, 29; allied with Progressive-Republicans, 29–30; attitude toward New Deal, 30–31; in Teapot Dome inquiry, 31; investigates (*1930*) elections, 31; views on foreign affairs, 32; religious activity, 32 n; offers munitions inquiry resolution, 32–33; agrees to combine Nye and Vandenberg resolutions, 33–34; assails war profits, 35; speaks against arms trade and war profits, 38; seeks Walt Disney's help, 38–39; helps select Munitions Committee members, 42; named chairman of Munitions Committee, 46; believes Alger Hiss spied, 53; hopes for more funds, 56; seeks State Department support, 58–59; apologizes to Cordell Hull, 60; meets with F. D. Roosevelt, 61–62; on Balfour memorandum, 63–65; on Lansing diaries, 66–67; handling of Fokker affidavit, 67–68; assails du Pont, 72–73; on relations between United States government and munitions industry, 81; favors nationalization of munitions industry, 97; imbroglio with W. B. Shearer, 114; confers with F. D. Roosevelt, 121; on conscription of capital, 128, 129; proposes war profit legislation, 132–33; questions heavy taxes, 133; on conscription of labor, 135; assails B. M. Baruch, 139; on war profits, 141; offers McSwain Bill amendments, 143; symbolizes munitions inquiry, 147; subject of verse, 148; receives encouragement, 148–49; receives report from Philip Noel-Baker, 151; criticized, 151, 222; defends Stephen Raushenbush, 152; receives letter on term "munitions maker," 152–53; urged to avoid offending Latin Americans, 156; apologizes for implicating King George, 157–58; offers documents to royal commission, 160; introduces neutrality resolutions, 175–76; on embargo of "vital materials," 176; speaks for neutrality legislation, 176–77; supports National Munitions Bill, 178; threatens filibuster, 182; assails embargo crit-

ics, 187; lauds moral embargo, 188; reacts to Pittman-McReynolds Bill, 193–94; introduces Nye-Clark Bill, 194; defers to financiers, 195; criticizes Woodrow Wilson policy, 201–202; on Woodrow Wilson's and Robert Lansing's knowledge of secret treaties, 203; denounced by Tom Connally, 203; defends munitions inquiry, 204–205; denounces critics, 205; assailed by Carter Glass, 205–206; declines outside funds, 207; called collectivist, 207; on J. P. Morgan and Company, 208; adjourns last munitions hearing, 208; on critics of committee, 208; explains Nye-Clark Bill, 216–17; urges amendment of Neutrality Act, 218; attitude toward business, 222; reckless statements, 224; hearing room conduct, 224–25; accused of publicity seeking, 225; presidential ambition, 226–27; position on munitions control, 230; isolationism, 230–31

Nye-Clark Bill (*1936*), 195, 210, 211, 217, 218, 220; introduced, 194; provisions, 194; explained, 216–17

Nye-Clark Resolutions (*1935*), 181, 183; introduced, 175–76; promoted by Nye, 176–77; considered by Foreign Relations Committee, 177, 178; supported by isolationists and pacifists, 180, 181

Nye Committee: *See* Munitions Committee

Nye-Vandenberg Resolution (*1934*), 56, 58, 158, 174, 175; offered and adopted, 33–37

Old Hickory smokeless powder plant: investigated, 123–26

O'Malley, Thomas: sponsors bill to conscript capital, 130

Pacifists, 86, 90, 91, 97, 100, 111, 142, 143, 226, 232; attack W. B. Shearer, 12–13; on munitions combine, 78; on conscription of capital and labor, 128. *See also* Peace leaders, Peace movement, and Peace organizations